THE GRIQUA CAPTAINCY
OF PHILIPPOLIS, 1826–1861

THE GRIQUA CAPTAINCY OF PHILIPPOLIS, 1826–1861

Karel Schoeman

2002
PROTEA BOOK HOUSE
PRETORIA

The Griqua Captaincy of Philippolis, 1826–1861
Karel Schoeman

First edition, 2002, published by:
Protea Book House
PO Box 35110, Menlopark, 0102
protea@intekom.co.za

Cover design by Tienie du Plessis
Illustration: Kaptyn Adam Kok III (Philip album),
reproduced with permission from the
University of Cape Town Libraries

Typography, design & map by Tienie du Plessis
Reproduction by PrePress Images, Pretoria
Printed and bound by Interpak Books, Pietermaritzburg

ISBN 1-919825-39-8

© Text 2002 Karel Schoeman
© All rights reserved.
No part of this book may be reproduced
in any form, without prior permission in writing
from the publisher.

Foreword

Over the past few decades South African historiography has fortunately begun to recover from its previous eurocentric bias to reflect the realities of a multiracial society. Most of the various non-white groups which form part of the population of the country have begun to receive closer attention, but two have still been largely neglected: the Korana, who no longer exist as an identifiable group, and the related Griquas, who still form a largely recognisable people with a sense of their own identity. The last full-length study of the Griquas and their history was, however, *Adam Kok's Griquas* by Robert Ross, which appeared as long ago as 1976 and was moreover a relatively superficial survey of less than 200 pages, limited by the scope of the series of which it formed part.

In an attempt to help recover something of the Griqua past, I have compiled a collection of official and semi-official documents emanating from the Philippolis Captaincy, which has been published by the Van Riebeeck Society under the title *Griqua Records: the Philippolis Captaincy, 1826–1861* (1996). In order to put to use the large amount related material I have collected which could not be used in this work, as well as the knowledge of the subject I have acquired in the course of my research, I have now written what may be described as an accompanying socio-cultural and historical survey of the Captaincy, consisting mainly of précis of and quotations from contemporary non-Griqua sources.

I am aware of the fact that the account given here of the important political developments of the 1840s and 1850s is inadequate, but these are covered fully in the documents published in the companion volume, and the two books must be read together for a complete understanding of Griqua affairs.

I have not attempted any profound analysis of or comment on the data I have presented, but I trust that this work may serve as background and complement to the *Griqua Records*, and also indicate possible fields of study to the researcher, for which reason full source notes have been provided. At the same time I hope that the book may be interesting and illuminating to the general reader and serve as a reminder of the fact that during the first half of the nineteenth century the Griquas were a factor of considerable importance in South African affairs and helped to determine official policy on the Northern Frontier.

Inevitably, if unfortunately, the great majority of the accounts on which this work is based emanate from white observers, and due allowance must therefore be made for ignorance and prejudice: such texts by Griqua witnesses as have survived are mostly to be found in the companion volume. Inevitably too, given the nature of the records, much of the information available refers to the work of the missionaries at Philippolis and the affairs of the congregation there. Given the central position of the LMS in the affairs of the Captaincy during the first thirty years of its existence, however, this is not quite as unfair as it might seem.

This book was written during 1993–94, and then laid aside because of other commitments. In preparing it for publication several years later, I have not been able to undertake any meaningful revision or further research, or to note research by others which has possibly been published in the interim.

I wrote this book in English, very much against my personal inclination, because I imagined that it would find a publisher more readily in this form. None of the English-language publishers approached by me showed any interest, however, and I am most grateful to Nicol Stassen of Protea Book House for undertaking publication at a stage when I myself had long abandoned all hope in this regard. I am likewise grateful to Mark Ingle of Philippolis for his practical help and his continued interest in the work, and Mrs Hetta Hager of the Mary Moffat Museum, Griquatown, for her interest and encouragement.

11 December 2000   Karel Schoeman

Contents

Abbreviations & Notes, *8*

Introduction: The Kok dynasty and the Griquas of the Transorange (1713–1825), *9*

1. Dr Philip in the Transorange (1825), *39*
2. The early years of the Captaincy (1826–1832), *61*
3. The development of the Captaincy (1832–1843), *79*
4. The people of the Captaincy, *97*
5. Life in the Captaincy (1826–1843), *117*
6. The Government of the Captaincy: Officials, *141*
7. The Government of the Captaincy: Laws and customs, *161*
8. The Captaincy in the 1840s (1843–1851), *173*
9. The Captaincy in the 1850s (1851–1861), *201*
10. The trek to Nomansland (1861–1863), *235*

Appendix: Statement by Adam Kok II, *249*

Chronology, *251*
Endnotes, *255*
Sources, *285*
Sources of illustrations, *289*
Index, *290*

The illustrations appear between pp. 96 & 97
Map, p. 11

Abbreviations & Notes

CA—Cape Town Archives Repository
LMS—London Missionary Society
NLCT—National Library (formerly South African Library), Cape Town
Rd(s)—Rixdollar(s)
VA—Free State Archives Repository, Bloemfontein
VOC—Dutch East India Company

Note: In the text of this book, the term "Transgariep" has been used for the area between the Orange and Vaal Rivers, and "Transorange" for the territory north of the Orange in general, but more particularly for that beyond the Middle Orange, where the mission stations Griquatown and Kuruman were situated.

The following are the dates of the visits to or sojourns at Philippolis and Griquatown by the observers most frequently quoted in this book:

Atkinson, Theophilus (missionary): 1836–40
Backhouse, James (visitor): 1839
Burchell, William (visitor, Griquatown): 1811
Campbell, John (visitor, Griquatown): 1813, 1820
Freeman, John (visitor): 1849
Gebel, August (visitor): 1834
Kolbe, G.A. (missionary): 1831–37
Melvill, John (missionary): 1827–32
Philip, John (visitor): 1825, 1832, 1842
Schreiner, Gottlob (missionary): 1838–42
Smith, Andrew (visitor): 1834–35
Solomon, Edward (missionary): 1851–57
Thompson, George (visitor, Griquatown): 1823
Thomson, W.Y. (missionary): 1843–48
van der Schalk, C.J. (missionary): 1849–50
Walker G.W. (visitor): 1839

Introduction: The Kok dynasty and the Griquas of the Transorange (1713–1825)

In 1713, a number of Cape slaves deserted and made for St Helena Bay and Piketberg on the fringes of white settlement, with the intention of reaching Namaqualand or, ultimately, Portuguese territory (the present Mozambique). On being recaptured by the authorities, they were charged not only with the crime of desertion but also with various acts of theft and violence committed during the time they were at large, and among the charges laid against the 30-year-old Thomas van Bengalen, a slave belonging to the farmer Christoffel Esterhuijs,[1] was that at some unspecified time in the past *"hij seekere jong Claas Kok gen[aam]d, die van sijn meester gefugeert was, eenige tijt met voedsel onderhouden heeft"*.[2]

Thomas van Bengalen was hanged, and his accomplices sentenced variously to be severely scourged and have their Achilles tendons severed or to be broken on the wheel, while their ringleader, Tromp van Madagascar, escaped impalement only by hanging himself while still in prison.[3] This was the violent and bloody world of Cape slavery in which the Kok family appear to have had their origins.

As regards the "boy named Claas Kok who had escaped from his master's service", the term *"jongen"* ("boy") was widely used for male slaves and gives no indication of his age, and the first name Claas was extremely common among Cape slaves. The fact that a Dutch name, later to become a family name, was attached to it instead of the more customary toponym is, however, unusual. The name Kok may have been arbitrarily borrowed from some unknown Dutchman or German or represent the surname of Claas's actual or putative father, or it may equally well have been a nickname, suggesting that he was at some stage employed as a cook. No more is known about him, but according to Ross he was "reported to have been among a group of slaves who had reached the Guriqua, and seems neither to have been captured by the whites nor to have returned voluntarily to his master".[4] It is by no means impossible that he could have reached the Guriqua, a Khoi tribe leading a scattered but independent existence in the vicinity of the Berg and Olifants Rivers in the south-western Cape,[5] and that he was sheltered by them and survived there in freedom, for in 1738 the name of the "Hottentot Claas Kok" occurred in connection with an expedition to the Orange River.[6]

While this somewhat nebulous figure cannot be identified with certainty as the progenitor of the later Griqua Kaptyns, it is noteworthy that during the 1750s a "Hottentot" called Adam Kok obtained burgher rights in the Cape Colony and owned grazing rights on the farm Stinkfontein in the neighbourhood of Piketberg, in the region formerly occupied by the Guriqua,[7] and that the grandson of this Adam Kok stated to Andrew Smith that his great-grandfather had been a slave."[8]

In a period when race was not yet of such importance as a determining factor in South African society as it later became, such an independent state was not unheard of for a man of colour, but it was nonetheless unusual. Adam Kok therefore soon gathered about him various groups and individuals who had difficulty in maintaining themselves socially or economically among the white colonists, most notably the increasingly detribalised Guriqua, as well as Basters ("Bastards", "Bastaards"), sons of white fathers and Khoi or free black mothers, who were normally dispossessed by their legitimate white half-brothers and led a somewhat ambivalent and precarious existence on the fringes of white colonial society. To contemporary whites the disparate members of Kok's following, whatever their individual racial origins, soon became known generally and collectively as "Basters". In particular Kok became associated with the Pienaars, through the marriage of his son, the later Cornelius Kok I, with a daughter of Jan Pienaar, "a Dutch Bastard",[9] and with the Barends or Berends clan by the marriage of a daughter to Klaas Barends (also known as "Klaas Baster"). In later years both these associated families were to play a leading role in the affairs of the Transorange, and the Pienaars would be prominent in the Philippolis Captaincy.

Before long Adam Kok had acquired such a retinue and possessed such authority that he was accorded the status of a Khoi "Captain" or *Kaptyn*, a title used by the Dutch as early as 1686 to indicate the headman of any large group of Khoikhoi, whose authority was then formally acknowledged by the VOC by the presentation of a staff of office.[10] The latter is described as "a cane (*rotting*) with a copper grip that bore a stamped imprint of the Company's coat of arms".[11] The office of Kaptyn, dependent though it was on recognition by the Cape Governor, was

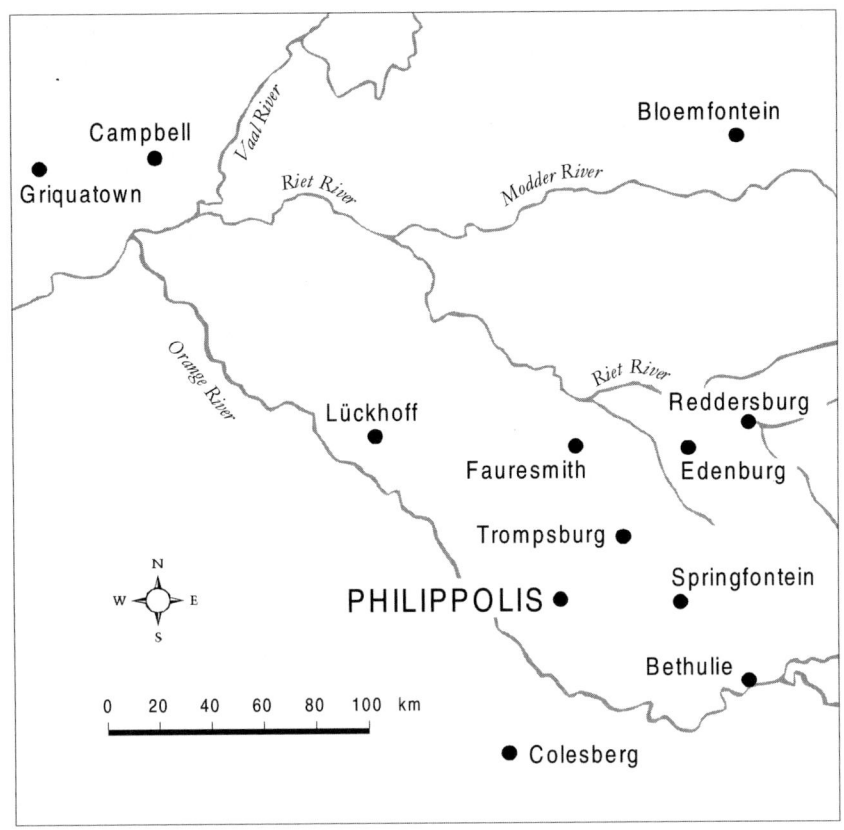

Map showing the main places in the Orange-Vaal area mentioned in the book.

traditionally hereditary,[12] and in this manner Kok became the founder of a dynasty and was in due course to be known as Adam Kok I. In practice his position was most likely in part that of a traditional tribal Chief and partly similar to that of a patriarchal white farmer surrounded by legitimate and illegitimate offspring, slaves, servants, and dependants and hangers-on of various races.

As white pastoralists continued their inexorable movement into the Cape interior during the latter half of the eighteenth century, members of mixed and other races were, however, forced to give way before them, retreating to more remote areas such as the Cedarberg and the Olifants River to the north and the Bokkeveld and Roggeveld to the north-east, and even deeper inland to Namaqualand.[13] Adam Kok held his farm in the Piketberg region from 1751 until 1771, when he lost it to a white settler,[14] and initially withdrew with his followers across the Olifants River to the Kamiesberg region of Namaqualand, where there was still considerable scope for people of mixed origins. Gordon noted in 1779, "From Groene Rivier there are nineteen stock farms in Namaqualand. Of these five are married farmers; the rest mostly take a Hottentot woman or two, which, so I hear, they marry according to their custom",[15] and other notable Baster groups such as the Engelbrechts and Cloetes settled here too.

From their new base in Namaqualand the Basters undertook regular exploring, hunting and trading trips further into the interior and because of their knowledge of the area were frequently asked to accompany white hunters and explorers as guides. Klaas Barends was one of the "twelve Hottentots of the Gerigriquas nation" who accompanied the farmer Jacobus Coetsé from Piketberg and his party on an expedition across the Grootrivier or Orange River in 1760, and later acted as guide to both H.J. Wikar and R.J. Gordon in the late 1770s,[16] and Lichtenstein stated that Cornelius Kok "always made one of Colonel Gordon's suite".[17]

Increasingly too the Basters began to settle for longer or shorter periods in the vicinity of the Orange with their cattle, and Cornelius Kok I declared in 1790 that his father had been granted winter pasturage on the Orange by the Cape authorities "more than twenty years ago".[18] According to Lichtenstein, Gordon had found "a little colony established here of Bastard-Hottentots",[19] and this may refer to Klaas Barends, who by 1779 is known to have been living at Kakais (modern Breësand) on the river, to the west of modern Pella.[20] By 1790 the white farmer Petrus Pienaar, residing in the Hantam on what was then the Northern Frontier of European settlement, could describe the region along the Orange, albeit with some exaggeration, as "opgepropt van Basjtaars en oorlamse Hottentotte".[21] Willem van Reenen in 1792 heard of "Bastard Hottentots" bartering with the Damara in the present Namibia,[22] and Cornelius Kok probably spoke for most of them when he stated in 1790 that he, his father and his brothers had always supported themselves in this region by breeding cattle, selling cattle to the accredited butchers of the VOC, and shooting elephants and disposing of the ivory to Company.[23]

In the course of this movement the Basters made contact not only with the Bushmen, who at this stage were still widely scattered across the interior of South Africa as independent hunter-gatherers, but also with the Korana, a pastoral Khoi people established along the Orange River in scattered small groups,[24] and the Batlhaping and other large tribes of Tswana cattle-owners living beyond in the direction of the present-day Kuruman. The fact that they were in possession of guns,[25] horses and wagons meant that they soon came to be accepted as powerful allies and patrons, and a good deal of interaction and assimilation took place. Campbell in 1820 noted on his second journey into the interior that most of the Griquas in his party were able to speak to a Motswana in his own language,[26] while George Thompson found that Adam Kok II spoke Setswana "with fluency".[27] Campbell records both Adam Kok II and Barend Barends interpreting in Kora in church, the latter "with a natural oratory extremely interesting",[28] and August Gebel in 1834 describes Hendrik Hendrickze acting as Kora interpreter at Philippolis.[29]

Bushmen, Korana and Batswana also attached themselves to the wealthier Basters as dependants or servants, partly under pressure of persistent attacks by the bandits of Klaas Afrikaner and other raiders in the area, and the Dutch missionary Kicherer, who worked among the Basters briefly in 1801, stated, "We found the Corannas and Namaquas mostly in service with the Bastard Hottentots, who are very rich in cattle here."[30] Campbell adduces the specific example of Cedras, one of the earliest Tswana converts of the missionaries, who was employed as a boy of 12 to tend the sheep of Adam Kok II, a son of Cornelius Kok: "He was well treated by Kok; and besides his food and clothes, he received five sheep or goats annually as wages."[31] In 1813, Campbell visiting the kraal of Adam Kok's brother, later Kaptyn Cornelius Kok II of Campbell, found there "of persons who speak the Dutch language, and who are called Orlams, 215; Corannas, 180; Bushmen, 30; total, 425".[32]

For many years Cornelius Kok seems to have visited the Orange River area on a seasonal or irregular basis, but he afterwards told Campbell that he had established himself—by implication permanently—at Bethesda in 1795. This was the name the LMS gave to the mission it founded in 1813 for Kok's people, which was described at the time as "formerly called O[o]rlam's Kraal, on the Great River, about mid-way between Griqua Town and Pella";[33] it is probably the same place elsewhere called Kokskraal and seems to have been situated in the vicinity of the modern Keimoes.[34] To this information Campbell added, "For many years after he resided on the Great Orange River [Kok] sowed nothing but tobacco, supporting his family and dependants by hunting and by the milk of his cows; but at length he procured from some Boors in the Colony the seeds of the water-melon, pum[p]kin, Indian corn and beans."[35] In 1820, Kok could inform Campbell that "all his children except two, and all his numerous children's children, have been born on the Great River and in Griqualand."[36]

Kicherer described Cornelius Kok as "the Chief and possessor of considerable property",[37] while Borcherds stated that he owned 45 000 sheep,[38] although this calculation may include the flocks of his followers, and Lichtenstein in the same period mentioned his being "the oldest and most noted among the Bastard-Hottentots".[39] Although he had succeeded his father as Kaptyn and received his staff of office,[40] he does not, however, seem to have involved himself directly in the government of his scattered followers along the Orange, and early in the nineteenth century he moreover withdrew again to Namaqualand, leaving Provisie Kaptyns (Acting Kaptyns) or deputies to represent his authority on the river.

According to a later statement by Andries Waterboer, not necessarily an impartial witness:

> When the Griqua people lived on the banks of the Great River they were governed by Piet Barend and Lucas Hans in the name of old Cornelius Kok, as his deputies; these men dying, Jan Hendrik and Klass Berend were appointed by the people to govern. This happened about the time, or shortly after, the people settled at

Griqua Town, but that did not continue long, for a party of the people began to rebel against them; and about the same time there came a letter from old C. Kok, who at that time resided in Namaqualand, in which he said it was not according to his wish that those persons should rule in his name, and at the same time appointed his son Adam Kok [II] and his sister's son Berend Berends to rule over the people.⁴¹

An approximate date for these developments is provided by the fact that the death of Piet Barends is recorded by the missionaries at Klaarwater in a journal entry under 16 May 1807, where he is described as "one of our captains".⁴²

This seems to agree basically with the information Cornelius Kok himself afterwards gave to Campbell, who may have set it down in a somewhat garbled form: "When his sons arrived at manhood, and one of them (Adam) was appointed and acknowledged a Captain of the Griquas, [Cornelius] went to the western side of Africa, where he obtained a farm called Silver Fountain, situated on the limits of the Colony in that direction. Having some of the blood of white men in him, like them he seemed to have a predilection for being a Colonial Boor."⁴³ His status in frontier society would indeed appear to have been that of a wealthy cattle farmer, largely unaffected by considerations of race, and Burchell called him "a Half-Hottentot Boor in the Kamiesberg in Namaqualand";⁴⁴ he is said to have owned five farms, including Silwerfontein and Oliewenfontein, and 5000 sheep.⁴⁵ His son, Salomon Kok, was described by Lichtenstein in much the same terms as being the "most substantial personage" in the settlement of Rietfontein in the Transorange and having "entirely the appearance of a Colonist: he was well made, and spoke the Dutch language tolerably correctly, and with tolerable purity."⁴⁶

To all intents and purposes the Basters along the Orange formed an independent community or a number of loosely interconnected communities, supporting themselves by means of cattle farming, hunting and trade with the Tswana tribes of the interior. "About half of our people set out today for the Briqua Tlhaping country," the missionaries stationed at Klaarwater were to report typically enough in 1807, "with beads, sheep, goats and dogs, to exchange for elephants' teeth, cattle and skins."⁴⁷ Ivory, ostrich feathers and animal skins were in turn exchanged with white frontier farmers for items to which the semi-westernised lifestyle of the Basters had accustomed them, thus preserving some nominal contact with the Cape Colony, while official contacts with the Colonial authorities were likewise preserved, as the Basters were entirely dependent on them for permits to acquire the gunpowder and guns essential for their way of life. This was done most notably through the nearest field cornet, Floris Visser, who lived in the Roggeveld near the Sak River and had some personal knowledge of the Orange River area.[48] Lichtenstein, visiting the Transorange in 1805, wrote that "Certain Bastard Hottentots have even been in Cape Town unrecognised once, where they have bought arms and powder more advantageously; but experience has taught them that it is better to give the higher price and be spared the fatigue and expense of the journey."[49] Basters from the Transorange are known on occasion to have undertaken trading trips to Cape Town, however, and William Burchell, preparing for his expedition to the interior in 1811, noted in his journal:

> The party of Hottentots which had long been expected from Klaarwater arrived at Salt-river with their waggons and oxen. It consisted of about twenty men, with an equal number of women and as many children; besides three waggons and families left behind at Tulbagh.
>
> These people were nearly all of the mixed race of Hottentots.[50] Their object in making this long journey to Cape Town was principally that of exchanging ivory and cattle for such manufactured articles as their present mode of life leads them to regard as necessaries. These were chiefly gunpowder, muskets, lead, flints, porcelain, beads, knives, tinder-boxes and steels, tobacco, woollen jackets and trowsers, horses and waggons. The quantity of ivory which they had now brought to town was about a thousand pounds weight, which was sold to English merchants at the rate of seven schellings a pound, Dutch weight;[51] their cattle had been sold by the way to the Boors as they passed through the colony.[52]

In other contemporary sources coffee, sugar and needles are mentioned as goods much in demand among the Basters of the Orange River.

The arrival of the London Missionary Society (LMS) to begin work at the Cape in 1799 was probably seen by the Basters in general as an opportunity to bring about an improvement in their unsatisfactory situation, for the broad division in Colonial society had hitherto been between whites and Christians on the one hand and non-whites and heathen on the other, and acceptance into the Christian church seemed at the same time to imply admission to the social and other privileges enjoyed by the whites. In spite of their isolation, the Basters were therefore eager to preserve some elements of Christianity, as well as some fragments of literacy. The Moravian missionaries who recommenced work for the Khoikhoi at Genadendal in 1792 had already discovered that their station attracted a number of Basters "who wish to come here and learn",[53] while Cornelius Kok is said to have been baptised by "a minister of the English Church" while on a visit to Cape Town some time between 1801 and 1805,[54] and he was subsequently to be known for his generous hospitality and assistance to missionaries travelling northwards through Namaqualand. Again, writing of an epidemic of measles at the end of 1807, the missionaries working at Klaarwater mentioned the death of "a woman called Old Dortze" (probably "Doortje"), of whom they wrote, referring to their arrival some six years earlier:

> her father was a European—she was about 45 or 50 years of age, one of the most useful among the females, not only for her needle, but as a midwife. She was baptized when a child, and had received a little instruction, so that she could read and write. When Brother Anderson and Brother Kramer came here, they found five whom she had taught to spell.[55]

The main body of Kok's people along the Orange came in touch with the LMS through the station called Zak River (near the modern Fraserburg), which was founded in 1799 for the Bushmen beyond the Colonial frontier, in the area under the authority of field cornet Visser. In 1801 the missionaries were encouraged by Baster visitors to the station to move further into the interior and begin evangelisation beyond the Orange River, and as their work among the Bushmen did not seem promising, they responded without much hesitation. Their object here was nominally the Korana, but in practice they found themselves working among a disparate group of refugees from the raiding bands of Klaas Afrikaner and others lower down the river, and their earliest followers were described as consisting of

> heathens of different nations, such as Hottentots, Corannas, some Namaquas (whose general residence is to the north-west), and some Briquas [*Batlhaping*], who reside in the north-east, and that numerous class of men called Bastards. (…) [The missionaries] were afterwards induced to remove from this place by the repeated applications of a considerable number of Bastard Hottentots and others, who lived about eight days' journey lower down the Great Orange River, and who were very desirous of being instructed in the way of salvation (…).[56]

The chief consideration in this change of plan was probably that the other tribes did not prove particularly receptive to the message of the missionaries; from a purely practical point of view also, the Basters had the advantage of being Dutch speaking, so that there were no problems of communication or interpretation, while many of them already had some knowledge of Christianity.[57] What their exact condition and circumstances were at this time is not clear, although they were later described as "a herd of wandering and naked savages, subsisting by plunder and the chase" and "wholly abandoned to witchcraft, drunkenness, licentiousness and all the consequences which arise from the unchecked growth of such vices".[58] This description has been quoted so often that it has acquired a certain authority, but it is as well to remember that it appeared in a book by Dr Philip, superintendent of the LMS, at a time when he was trying energetically to assert the missionaries' control over the Griqua mission stations and the Griquas' dependence on the mission.

As the life of the Baster cattle farmers was closely connected to the availability of water and grazing, it was essentially nomadic, but by 1805 six relatively stable centres of Baster settlement had come into being in the Transorange along a series of fountains in a line stretching roughly north-east between modern Niekerkshoop and Griquatown. That year the two itinerating missionaries responsible for the earliest attempts to evangelize the Basters of this area, William Anderson and C.A. Kramer, settled at a place described as being situated between Leeukuil and

Klaarwater, where they erected houses and a church and laid out gardens, and this was the beginning of what was to be known as the mission of Klaarwater, later Griquatown.

At Klaarwater mission work was begun on a more regular basis than had hitherto been possible, and the baptismal register, commenced in 1807, records no fewer than 43 adult baptisms during the first three years of its existence.[59] The individuals thus received into the church, all of whom appear to have been mainly members of the Baster group, included a number who were to play a prominent part in the affairs of the mission and of the Griqua people: the most notable surnames to be found here are Kok, Barends, Hendriks, Pienaar, Jood and Davids, together with members of the Waterboer family.

Prominent among these early converts was Cornelius Kok's brother-in-law, Klaas Barends, who in 1801 already had been described by Kicherer as "a seal on our missionary vocation. He possesses a sound judgement, reads the Bible reasonably well, and is mostly occupied in prayer or in meditation from morning till evening";[60] his son, the later Provisie Kaptyn Barend Barends, was baptised in 1807 at the age of about 30, became a deacon in 1813, and was appointed "native agent" of the LMS the following year. [61]

Andries Waterboer, who was baptised in 1808, is even more worthy of attention, however, for he was a complete outsider not related to the Kok-Barends family complex, and Hendrik Hendrickze later referred to him scornfully as "a Bushman Hottentot who had come along [to Klaarwater] as an after rider of Adam Kok and was acting as messenger of the court".[62] He soon gained the favour of the missionaries, however, and rapidly acquired a position of some prominence, being appointed native agent in 1814 as well; in the annual report published in 1820 it was stated that the missionary conducted the school "assisted by the native teacher, Andrew Waterboer",[63] and Campbell during his visit shortly afterwards heard him give an address in the church, "with seriousness and at times with energy, and what I understood was simple and Scriptural, but he continued too long."[64]

It was largely by people from Klaarwater that the Philippolis Captaincy was to be established in 1826 and it was the institutions of the earlier polity which were to a great extent duplicated by them. In order to obtain a clearer understanding of the Philippolis community, and to compensate for the inadequate information on its early years, some attention must therefore be paid here to Klaarwater.

In the winter of 1811, when the English traveller W.J. Burchell visited the settlement, he stated that the population of Klaarwater and its various out-stations had two years earlier numbered 784,[65] and the Kaptyns could muster more than 200 armed men.[66] The fledgling settlement itself he described as "merely a row of half a dozen reed cottages" and the church as "a barn-like building of reeds and mud";[67] elsewhere he mentioned 25 "Hottentot houses" (presumably mat huts) in the vicinity of the church and the missionary dwellings, and the same number some distance away; the inhabitants owned about 3000 head of cattle and 80 or 90 horses, many sheep and goats, and a "sufficient proportion" of dogs.

The main occupations of the men were hunting and trading, and Burchell described a hippopotamus hunt on the Vaal River by a group travelling in ten wagons, in which he himself participated,[68] and noted Barend Barends setting off with a party of about a dozen men, two or three wagons and some of their best horses on a two-month expedition into the interior "to hunt elephants, for the purpose of procuring ivory for their next journey to Cape Town";[69] twelve elephants were shot.[70] With regard to cattle trading, he wrote, "By barter for beads and tobacco they annually obtain from the Bachapins [*Batlhaping*] (called Briquas or Goat-men in the Hottentot language) a number of oxen, most of which they sell in the Colony at the average rate of twenty rixdollars each."[71] Thompson twelve years later described members of the Kgalagadi tribe on their way to Griquatown "to barter mantles of wild-cat and jackal skins for beads, buttons, etc.".[72]

"Two or three people work as blacksmiths, although in a very bungling manner," noted Burchell,[73] and described the local manufacture of wooden bowls and jugs (*bamboes*).[74] "All are exceedingly fond of tea (...): next to tobacco and brandy they esteem tea the greatest luxury as a beverage. Their chief food is milk, game, together with mutton or beef, which latter is rarely killed, their principle dependence being on game, of which they bring home no trifling quantity." Some wheat was also sown, and ground in hand mills.[75]

Burchell gave detailed descriptions of the "aboriginal Hottentot dress" he saw at Griquatown—leather or jackalskin aprons for men and women, leather shoes or sandals, jackalskin karosses, bracelets of beads, copper or leather thongs, earrings and rings—and the anointing of the body with fat scented with buchu; Campbell too, visiting a kraal at Ongeluksfontein to the north of Griquatown in 1820, found women "covered with beads, and with brass, copper and ivory rings round their arms and legs".[76] Burchell, however, added, "Many of the Klaarwater people are clothed in the mode above described; but more than half of them imitate the dress of the Europeans",[77] and the prevalence of Western clothing had already struck him in the party of Barend Barends' people with whom he had travelled up from the Nuweveld:

> Most of them were armed with muskets, and clad, generally, in jackets and trowsers, either of woollen cloth or of tanned sheep-leather, with shoes of raw hide. Many had cotton shirts and hats of Cape manufacture; yet the kaross, a genuine Hottentot dress, made of sheepskin prepared with the hair on, was pretty much used by both sexes. Their women and children constituted a third of the number. The younger of the latter were half naked; but the women were decently clothed, some in gowns and aprons of printed calico or leather, neatly made up in the Dutch manner. All had their heads closely bound up with coloured cotton handkerchiefs.[78]

The degree of superficial westernisation to be found on the mission station at Klaarwater is indicated by the fact that Burchell could make Adam Kok II an acceptable present of "a blue jacket, a saw, and some linen which I purchased for him at Graaffreynet",[79] while Kok's wife was "highly pleased" with the gift of "a piece of chintz cotton, a quantity of needles, thread, tape, buttons, brandy, pepper, &c.",[80] that the people of Griquatown, according to Campbell, desired the institution of some form of currency "by which they could purchase any small articles such as knives, scissars [sic], clothing, etc.",[81] and that Barends, according to the same writer, spent Rds4400 during a visit to Cape Town on "tea, coffee, sugar, Cape brandy and some articles of dress".[82] Similarly Burchell noted that the sermon on Sundays was "interpreted in the Hottentot language" for the benefit of those who do not sufficiently understand Dutch; but these hearers constitute a very small portion of the congregation",[83] and remarked of Barends' party, "There were but very few who did not speak the Dutch language fluently, being nearly all Hottentos of the mixed race, and in the yearly practice of visiting the Colony."[84]

However eagerly the outward trappings of westernisation were welcomed by the missionaries and other European observers the process was, nevertheless, only partial, and John Campbell could write revealingly of a church service at Klaarwater, "Several of the Griquas were dressed much like the common people in England. (...) Most of the people sat on the ground, for they are not accustomed in their houses to sit upon seats. Those who had seats, at least some of them, appeared to be tired by sitting so long in that posture."[85] In many respects, and especially in more essential matters, the people clung to their traditions in spite of the vigorous efforts made by the missionaries to abolish or replace them. "The restrictions which it had been endeavoured to lay upon their former customs had rendered the missionaries rather unpopular," reported Burchell;

> and the law for reducing the number of wives from two, often three, and sometimes four, to one, in a nation consisting of more females than males, did not meet with many advocates in either sex. However, since its first introduction, about a hundred, as I was informed, had submitted to it.[86]

In the winter of 1813, John Campbell arrived at Klaarwater in the course of an official tour of LMS stations in South Africa, and became responsible for a significant further step in the development of the Baster community; for at his prompting they decided to change their name, calling themselves Griquas after the Guriqua tribe from whom they claimed descent, adopt a set of laws, and change the name of Klaarwater to Griquatown.[87] At a meeting held on 7 August 1813 it was decided that the Provisie Kaptyns, Adam Kok II and Barend Barends, described by Campbell as "the two native Captains or Chiefs", "should continue to act as commanders in things requiring the public safety against foreign attack".[88]

By this time Griqua pastoralists were scattered over a wide area in the Transorange, and in addition to the existing villages a number of outposts had gradually come into existence. According to Waterboer, Kort

Adam Kok,[89] a brother of Cornelius Kok I, was sent to occupy Knoffelvallei, 45 kilometres to the east, "as an out-station of Griqua Town", "with three of his own brothers, viz., William Kok, Gert Kok and Abraham Kok, also two of his brothers-in-law, Dirk Boer and Jager Boer, and likewise a nephew of his named Adam Bailie [=*Balie*]".[90] The settlement they established here, soon to be renamed Campbell, was thus clearly a Kok family preserve from the outset, and a collection list for the Auxiliary Mission Society at Campbell in 1820 gives almost exclusively the names of members of the Kok, Boer and Jagers families.[91]

In spite of the attempts of the missionaries to persuade the people to attach themselves to the developing settlements of the area and devote themselves to agriculture, the Griquas continued to be basically a nation of nomadic cattle farmers living around the widely scattered sources of water and grazing in groups known as "kraals" or "werfs". Although Burchell noted the presence of Adam Kok's mat hut at Griquatown, Campbell in 1820 found him on the Orange River with his retinue: "From the number of huts composing Kok's *krawl*, the people who inhabit them must be upwards of a hundred, which removes the stillness of the wilderness, along with the lowing of oxen [and] the barking of the numerous dogs."[92] He likewise wrote of "Berend's Kraal" (the subsequent Daniëlskuil),[93] "several Griquas and Bushmen came from their huts to give us a hearty welcome. Berend, it appears, has cultivated a considerable portion of land in this place."[94] Campbell described "Jan Kar's [*i.e. Kars*] Kraal, at Kramer Fountain", some 80 kilometres beyond Griquatown, as "the most northern residence of any of the Griqua nation".[95]

That some degree of progress was nonetheless made by the missionaries in their work among the unsettled people of the Captaincy was indicated in 1814, when the five "native agents" who were "publicly set apart"[96] during the mission conference of the LMS at Graaff-Reinet to act as missionary assistants included Kaptyn Barend Barends, Andries Waterboer and Jan Hendrik of Griquatown and Pieter Davids of Hardcastle (a mission post near the modern Niekerkshoop), and further promising developments were soon to take place. The travels into the interior which Campbell undertook from Griquatown during his visit in 1813 led in due course to the founding of a mission to the Batlhaping to the north, and in 1815 the veteran missionary James Read came to establish a station to be known successively as Lattakoo and New Lattakoo and eventually as Kuruman. For the Griquas this was an event of some importance, as he was accompanied by a number of Khoi or "Hottentot" converts from his congregation at Bethelsdorp, 15 men and 14 women, "several of whom have taken with them their families"[97]—educated, literate and largely westernised people who spoke a form of Dutch and had strong ties with the LMS. They were soon employed on an extensive scale as teachers, catechists, itinerant preachers and interpreters in the Transorange region, where they were generally called "Basters" and formed a group distinct from the Griquas already settled there and acknowledging at least in theory the authority of the Kaptyns. Their ranks swelled by steady additions over the years—which included the fifth native agent of the LMS, Jan Goeyman, and the zealous lay evangelist Cupido Kakkerlak— they soon became an important factor in local affairs, both through their prominence in the work of the mission and their direct links with the Cape Colony.

Another significant development in the early history of the Griquatown Captaincy was the fact that Cornelius Kok I decided to move back to the Transorange with his immediate followers from Namaqualand. Visiting him at Silwerfontein in 1813, Campbell found that he "had it in contemplation to retire to Griqua Town, to end his days with his sons and other relations who live there",[98] but his eventual removal to the Transorange may well have been inspired more directly by the difficulties experienced in implementing the elementary constitution adopted at Campbell's urging. Although the "magistrates" provided for had duly been elected,[99] a considerable section of the Griqua community resented their authority and control and in 1815 removed demonstratively to the neighbourhood of the Harts River, where they became known as the Hartenaars:[100] according to the subsequent account of John Melvill, the nucleus of the group of malcontents established there consisted of "A. Hendrik[s], his two nephews, Gert Goeyman and his three brothers, with several others",[101] names which were to reappear later in Griqua history. At the end of July 1816, William Anderson at Griquatown, informing the LMS that Kok and his people had arrived "last week", added, "Old Kock, having heard before he came here the sad behaviour of the most of the people, sent me word he approved of the regulations introduced by Mr Campbell and when he came would endeavour to force the people to submit. He has great influence both among the people here and among the Boetzeanders [*Batswana*].(...) At present no attention is paid to the rules nor do the persons appointed to hear causes attend."[102] Whatever calming influence Kok may have had on the rebellious Griquas, it was exerted unobtrusively, for he made no attempt to establish himself as Kaptyn at Griquatown, but settled at Knoffelvallei or Campbell, where so many members of his family were already living, and where he led a retired life, dying in 1822.[103]

The main effect of Cornelius Kok's removal to the Transorange was perhaps to assist still further in forming Campbell into a centre of authority rivalling that of the missionaries at Griquatown. His arrival was, moreover, accompanied by a mass influx of his relatives and followers which is stated to have included "many persons" from Kokskraal or Bethesda on the Orange River, where the LMS had shortly before established a mission:[104] this may help to explain the remarkable increase in the number of baptisms recorded in the Griquatown register during 1816 and the early part of 1817, as well as the reception into the church there of several individuals who had been baptised by the missionary Christoph Sass at Bethesda.[105] A notable number of these entries (at a rough count, about 40) involve members of the Kok family, including married women whose maiden names are listed as Kok, and given the fact that it was customary at the time to have many children and that polygamy was not uncommon among the Griquas, the descendants of Adam Kok I may well have numbered a thousand or more at this stage. Certain Christian names such as Adam, Abraham, Cornelius and Griet had already become common among them, making the identification of individuals difficult and requiring the use of patronymics and nicknames: there are, for instance, references to Adam Nicolaas, Adam Johannes, Adam Vink, Kort Adam, Dik Adam and Dam Kok in the register during this period.

As is clear from the examples given above, the surnames recorded in the mission registers of Griquatown and in other, similar sources of the time were predominantly Dutch. Apart from those already cited, van der Westhuizen, Cloete, Balie, Fortuin and Goeyman occurred regularly; as regards first names, Piet (Pieter, Petrus), Klaas (Nikolaas), Gert (Gerrit) and Jan were common among the men, and Griet (Margaretha), Tryn (Catryn), Trui (Geertruida), Fytjie (Sofia), Elizabeth, Anna and Lena among the women. There were also a number of Biblical names such as Pharaoh (possibly of slave origin), Salomon, Rachel, Lea and Sarah.

John Campbell, on a second official visit to South Africa, seems to have found the progress at Griquatown satisfactory when he arrived there early in 1820. "There are at present three houses builded by natives at Griquatown at least 30 feet by 12 or 14," he reported,

> of stone, two apartments, and three or four windows. They are built almost as well as European houses, the walls are finished, and timber brought from the Great River is lying before them for roofs—there are several other inforced[?] stone houses inhabited by the natives, and two or three that have remained for a long time not two feet above the foundations, the proprietors of which had not the perseverance to continue the buildings.[106]

At the out-station at Campbell he found "that the natives had daily regular meetings for worship, conducted by Abraham Kok, son to the old Captain; and at Upper Campbell by Cornelius, another of his sons."[107] At "Berends' Kraal" (Daniëlskuil) he noted, "A Griqua female keeps a school here every day of ten young Griquas."[108]

George Thompson during his visit in 1823 merely recorded the fact that a number of the people at Griquatown were cultivating corn, adding, "The food of the inhabitants consists of milk and flesh, and occasionally a few pumpkins."[109] He estimated the population of the settlement and surrounding out-stations as 1600 with about 1000 more living at a distance, and stated that they were in possession of about 500 muskets;[110] during his visit the Kaptyns claimed that they were able to muster approximately 200 armed and mounted men at short notice to repel the invading "Mantatees" at Dithakong. "Though neither disciplined nor accoutred like regular troops," wrote Thompson, "and dressed in a garb both motley and ragged, yet, with their glittering muskets and bold bearing, they had a very martial appearance."[111]

There was a not inconsiderable degree of prosperity among the Griquas, and the LMS report published in 1814 stated of Griquatown, "One individual in the settlement had 200 head of cattle, and several had from 50 to 100, so that in the last year[112] the colony of the Cape had been supplied from Klaar Water with about 500 head of cattle, in return for which they brought back waggons, horses and other articles."[113] Campbell in 1829 wrote of Jan Goesa Kars or Karse of Kramersfontein, baptised at Griquatown in 1808, "He possesses a new waggon, for which he gave seven hundred rix dollars at the last Beaufort [West] fair."[114]

Since Anderson and Kramer had begun their work along the Orange River, the missionaries had exercised a significant measure of control over the local Baster community, which had been strengthened when the mission at Klaarwater became the centre of Baster settlement in the area and when the Griqua polity came into being under missionary guidance in 1813. The extent of their influence became clear over the period 1820–21, when the zealous young Robert Moffat was stationed at Griquatown for some months and commenced a drastic reform of the congregation later described by his son as "wielding the pruning knife": "In a few months after Robert Moffat's arrival a course of stern discipline had purged the little community."[115] His autocratic methods gave rise to considerable unrest and dissatisfaction in the Griqua community, however, with far-reaching results.

It is likely that Christianity had already begun to cause some degree of divided loyalty and disunity among the Griquas, and that the tenuous authority of the Kaptyns had moreover been weakened by their own absenteeism. Although Adam Kok had a home at Griquatown, for example, Campbell during his second visit was concerned to find him on the Orange River with his cattle and his retainers, as recorded above, and Hendrik Hendrickze later declared that "old Dam Kok left the government of Griqua Town to his uncle, Adam Kok, commonly called 'Kort Adam', and went up a little higher on the Orange River to a place called the 'Slypsteen'", and that Kort Adam himself neglected his duties as a Provisie Kaptyn.[116] John Melvill referred from hearsay to "some disorders that prevailed, and the old Chiefs who resided at a distance from Griqua Town neglecting to use means to restore order",[117] while according to Waterboer's not impartial account, "The Captains Berend and Adam were several times brought before the Council and people and spoken to respecting their neglect of duty."[118] According to the journal of the missionary Heinrich Helm for 1820, Adam Kok had already left Griquatown by then, although he acted in Barends' place during the latter's absence, and Barends himself was reprimanded by the people of Griquatown as early as March that year for "not taking care of his office".[119]

The result of this mounting dissatisfaction was that in December 1820, the people, under the guidance of and possibly also under pressure from the missionaries, elected the local schoolteacher and mission protégé Andries Waterboer as their successor in the course of what might be described as a coup d'état by the mission party. How clearly Waterboer realised his dependence on the LMS appears from his subsequent obsequious statement to them on the question of the Griqua Captaincy, which does not agree with what is known about indigenous institutions.

> I consider the Captainship among the Griquas as originating with the people of the missionary station and recommended by the missionaries as a necessary step to preserve order at the station. I likewise consider the whole of the power of the Griqua Captains as a delegated power, to be assumed for the benefit of the people and the spread of the Gospel in the country and among the heathen beyond the Griqua country.[120]

Sometime during this period Adam Kok retired to Campbell, where his father and other members of his family were living, and where George Thompson found him in the winter of 1823.[121] Waterboer later declared that "Captain A. Kok threw away his Captain's staff and immediately removed from the place [*Griquatown*] with his whole family to the Great River",[122] but this seems to be telescoping and distorting the developments of four years. Barends retreated to Daniëlskuil, and in 1823 to Boetsap, some 90 kilometres further to the east, in the vicinity of the Harts River, where Wesleyan missionaries established the station known as Buchuaap for his people five years later. In 1833, however, he and his followers took part in a mass migration from that region to the Caledon River valley and settled around the mission station Lishuani between the modern Excelsior and Modderpoort. They generally continued to be known as Griquas, but they were to play no significant further part in the affairs of Griquatown, Campbell and Philippolis.

The resentment felt by Kok and Barends—the "Old Captains" as they were called—against Waterboer and the missionaries of Griquatown was to be the cause of considerable further division in the Griqua community: it was all the more effective because on leaving Griquatown they by no means relinquished their authority as Kaptyns, and a compromise seems in fact to have been adopted by those involved. According to the later Government Agent John Melvill, who arrived at Griquatown on a private visit from Cape Town on 2 May 1821, "A general meeting of all the Captains and a large body of the people took place soon after my arrival, at which the appointment of A. Waterboer at Griqua Town, A. Kok at Campbell and B. Barends at Daniel's Kuil was agreed upon; and these proceedings were confirmed by a letter addressed to me from the Colonial Government dated 4 October 1821."[123] In January 1823, according to the same source, "a union of the three Chiefs was effected, and at a meeting held for the purpose a plan was adopted for the government of this country, and some useful regulations were made which were approved by His Excellency the Governor";[124] according to Andrew Smith, writing more fully:

> a code of regulations for the management of the various districts was unanimously agreed to, and one of them provided that the Chiefs should alternately assemble at their respective residences at least once every month for the purpose of settling the general affairs of the country, while the more immediate concerns of each district should be managed by the presiding Chief and his Councillors.[125]

The confusion with regard to authority in the Griqua polity is illustrated by Thompson's description in 1823 of the brothers Adam, Cornelius and Abraham Kok of Campbell as "three of the hereditary Chiefs or Captains of the Griqua tribe, being sons of old Cornelius Kok".[126] While Abraham Kok was a prominent supporter of the mission and is often mentioned by visitors to Campbell, he does not seem to have had any further ambitions; the status of Cornelius Kok II, however, remains ambiguous, and Thompson mentions that Adam Kok, Cornelius Kok II, Barends and Waterboer jointly commanded the Griqua forces against the "Mantatees" at Dithakong.[127] This may possibly be explained, however, in the light of a much later statement by Hendrik Hendrickze in the course of an account which is as biased and confused as any other relating to Griqua affairs. According to Hendrickze,

> [Cornelius Kok I] appointed his son Adam [Kok II] as ruler over the entire Griqua nation and its grounds, and his son Cornelius Kok [II] became head of the family tribe, called the "Koks": this occurred in accordance with Griqua laws and customs. It was then

likewise acknowledged by the British Government, for the former received a Government and the latter a family staff, that is a large cane with a golden knob from the British Government.[128]

The missionary T.L. Hodgson, visiting Campbell in 1822, mentions the presence there of Adam Kok, but states at the same time, "The Captain's name is Cornelius, in whom is vested the power of acting by his brother Adam",[129] which gives the impression that Cornelius acted as Adam's deputy, and Melvill, referring to the events of the same year, likewise writes of him as "deputy chief of Campbell".[130]

Up to now the Griquas in the Transorange had apparently shown little interest in the region to the east of them, the area between the Orange and Vaal Rivers now known as the Free State, which will be for the sake of convenience be referred to here as the Transgariep.[131] Although the present Northern Free State seems to have been known to the Korana, Campbell in 1813 found that the Vaal and the Riet Rivers "had only lately been known to [the Griquas]; of course they had no names for them, except of this as the Mud and the other as the Black River".[132] In 1816, however, a mission to the Bushmen was established under the catechist Piet Sabba at Ramah, near the northern bank of the Upper Orange (on what is now the border between the Free State and the Northern Cape Province); he was under the nominal supervision of the missionaries at Griquatown, and Campbell in 1820 found him living there with two Griqua families as "companions and helpers", while a further thirty Griquas or Basters had settled around him,[133] which seems to indicate that Griquas had already begun moving into the region.

According to Waterboer it was only in 1820, after he had himself become Kaptyn, that Gert Goeyman received permission as the first of the Griquas to move into the Transgariep, "for the purpose of breeding sheep, as he said,"[134] and Jan Pienaar also remembered that "Gert Koeman was the first who migrated".[135] Possibly permanent settlement is meant here, as distinct from casual seasonal migration, but even so it seems unlikely that the ex-Hartenaar Goeyman would have sought official permission for such a move or that it was even required, and Waterboer's statement may possibly be seen as a retrospective attempt to assert his own authority over the migrants. The arrival of Goeyman in the region is significant, however, for he was a member of the church at Griquatown, having been baptised at Griquatown in 1813 at the age of about 27,[136] together with his wife and children; according to Andrew Smith[137] he was a cousin both to Waterboer and to the native agent Jan Goeyman, who was in 1822 to be placed in charge of a further station for the Bushmen in the Transgariep. Quite apart from his leading role in the Hartenaar rebellion, he was therefore a prominent member of the Griqua community, and well suited to forming a minor local centre of authority and discontent.

By the end of 1822, the Wesleyan missionary Hodgson, travelling from Graaff-Reinet to Griquatown, encountered in the vicinity of the Riet River a not inconsiderable population of people he usually described as "Bastards": these he judged by the standards of a nineteenth-century English Christian, in a manner typical of the white travellers of the time, and found sadly wanting. The company outspanned on the banks of the Riet (which he called the Modder River, in the manner of his time), "where many of the Griquas and Bastards from Campbell dorp had, with their cattle, taken up their residence", and the following day, which was a Sunday, he wrote:

> At our morning service many attended, men, women and children at least to the number of sixty. Most of the latter were nearly, and some entirely, naked, and many of the former had only karosses to cover their naked persons, and some of the stout women as they sat had a most disgusting appearance. They appeared attentive during the service, but applications were immediately afterwards made to purchase beads, tea, etc., at which I was much surprised, as most of these people have heard the gospel many years, and have doubtless been instructed to regard the Sabbath, and must have known that we were missionaries. (…)
>
> To see the Bastards living in idleness and almost naked, when a little industry would furnish them with decent clothing and abundance of bread is grievous; but to see them desert the means of grace[138] and suffer their children to be without instruction under the pretext of not having sufficient grass for their cattle, when they might entrust them to servants or a part of the family, and by sowing corn etc. remain stationary at some of the missionary institutions, is truly awful, as it shows they have no relish for the gospel or desire to improve the rising generation.[139]

In the meanwhile the general dissatisfaction at Griquatown seems to have increased: Adam Kok and his followers later told Andrew Smith "that when Waterboer first was constituted a Chief he was without experience, headstrong and fiery to the extreme; that wherever he thought blame to lay he punished without enquiry just upon mere belief".[140] His cousin Gert Goeyman is also stated to have developed a grievance against him after having left Griquatown, which according to Smith "arose from [Waterboer] having punished his brother according to his idea unjustly".[141] When a further number of Griquas left the Captaincy, apparently at the end of 1822, in dissatisfaction with Waterboer and the newly appointed agent of the British Government, John Melvill, they joined Goeyman in the Transgariep: Melvill himself specifically mentions the names of the ex-Hartenaar rebel Andries Hendriks, Jan Hendriks, Hendrik Hendriks (Hendrik Hendrickze, later Government Secretary in the Philippolis Captaincy) and Hans Goeyman.[142] Gert Goeyman was by this time most likely living at Goeymansberg, in the hilly area to the south of the modern Lückhoff, from which he and his followers soon acquired the name "Bergenaars", and the place names Goeymansberg, Sleutelspoort and Skanse, which still exist in what is now the south-western Free State, all date from this time and serve as reminders of their presence.

Their numbers swelled by subsequent additions from Griquatown, the Bergenaars allied themselves with various groups of Korana along the Orange, Vaal and Harts Rivers, most notably those under the leadership of the half-castes Jan Bloem Jr and Abraham Kruger, and, armed and mounted as they were, they began raiding with considerable success among the surrounding tribes and groups: Waterboer and the Batswana to the west, the various Sotho refugees from the Difaqane in the Caledon River valley to the east, amaXhosa on the fringes of the Cape Colony, and Bushmen wherever they were to be found. "When the Griquas and Korannas became Bergenaars, they fired on the Basutos and took their cattle," one of their number, Jan Pienaar, later recalled, "and thereupon Waterboer fired on them, and they returned the fire. These Bergenaars lived from Schansen up to Boomplaats, Sannah's Poort and about that country."[143]

Most notably the Bergenaars stole cattle, which were then exchanged illegally for firearms with the white farmers on the Northern Frontier of the Cape Colony, but there was also a lively trade in young children who were seized and sold into semi-slavery. As Dr Philip of the LMS wrote after his visit to the mission post at Philippolis near Bergenaar territory in 1825,

> At this station the reports I had heard of the nefarious traffic of the Bergenaars was confirmed. The ford through the Orange River I had lately crossed was that by which they kept up their chief communication with the Colony. They had taken possession of the greater part of the fountains in the neighbourhood, and at these fountains they were in the habit of collecting their stolen cattle previous to their being driven across the river. When their different hordes were got together, a signal was made, and they soon found plenty of traders to relieve them of their booty.
>
> In their plundering expeditions they seldom made prisoners of females above twenty years of age, and the boys they took seldom exceeded fourteen or fifteen years. The stolen cattle were exchanged in a regular manner; but they generally had recourse to a certain degree of finesse when the traffic had a relation to human beings. The purchaser, after examining the person he wished to have, was in the habit of spreading before the seller a certain quantity of gunpowder or other articles. When the seller was satisfied with the price, he had to thank the purchaser and pretend to make him a present of the boy or girl for whom he had expressed a predilection.[144]

The Bergenaars and their successors and imitators continued these operations for many years: in 1831, Barend Barends was to lead a disastrous raid in Bergenaar style against Mzilikazi and his amaNdebele to the north, in the course of which Gert Goeyman was killed,[145] while two years later another group penetrated deep into the Cape Colony and carried out a successful raid in the vicinity of the modern Queenstown.[146]

It was at this stage that Adam Kok II left Campbell and moved across the Vaal into the area along the Riet River, under circumstances which are not completely clear. Melvill later declared that Kok had formally resigned his office as Kaptyn (presumably of Campbell) to his brother Cornelius "at a regular meeting, and which measure was approved of by Government",[147] and more specifically that in May 1824 "a council was held at Griqua Town, at which C. Kok was chosen Chief instead of his brother Adam, who resigned".[148] Abraham Kok also, in the course of a somewhat muddled statement made more than forty years after the event, when he was close on 80, stated with regard to Adam Kok, his eldest brother, "In 1819 he again left Campbell finally with the intention of taking up his residence in the Philippolis district, and for this reason before my eldest brother departed he came here [*Griquatown*] and on the occasion of a general meeting of Councillors and the public, my said brother Adam Kok resigned to the late Captain Andries Waterboer, who was unanimously chosen by the general votes as Griqua Chief, the government of Griqualand, including Griqua Town and Campbell."[149] This may well include reminiscences of the proceedings referred to by Melvill.

Waterboer for his part linked Kok's resignation to the difficulties encountered in trying to maintain his authority at the time of the Bergenaar rebellion: after an unsuccessful campaign by Kok and himself against them, said Waterboer, Kok "publicly and entirely laid down his office as Captain, for reasons, as he said, that he felt convinced that he was unfit for such a great work, and that the Griqua affairs were hopeless. His office and staff and work he gave entirely to his brother, Cornelius Kok, who accepted them."[150] On another occasion, however, Waterboer claimed that he himself had appointed Cornelius Kok as his Provisie Kaptyn at Campbell "to preserve order in the country and to promote the interest of the missionary labours in that district",[151] while Abraham Kok likewise declared, "in the year 1824 my late brother Cornelius Kok was appointed by the late Chief Andries Waterboer as his Provisional Captain at and over Campbell and districts-land to the eastward".[152]

The deduction which may tentatively be made from these divergent accounts is that in 1824 Adam Kok, probably as a result of difficulties caused by the Bergenaar insurrection, resigned his authority in the area of Griqua occupation to his deputy, his brother Cornelius, and moved eastward across the Vaal into the Transgariep. Whatever the exact circumstances of his appointment and installation were, however, Cornelius Kok II appears to have established his authority at Campbell very soon, and to have become in fact an independent Kaptyn, while Adam for his part seems to have had his own motley following of Griquas and Korana who either accompanied him or gathered about him subsequently, and who were prepared to recognise him for practical purposes as their leader.

The composition of this group was probably fluid, but some indication of its nature is given by the names of the individuals who in 1825 expressed their willingness formally to acknowledge Adam Kok's authority.[153] They seem to have been mostly Griquas, most notably members of the Kok and Hendriks families, but there were a large number of Korana, among them Piet Witvoet, acting Chief of the Regshande or Right Hand Korana, six members of the Skerpioen tribe,[154] and Martinus Velmink of the Karoshebbers tribe, several of whose relatives had been baptised at Griquatown, while the Lucases also appear to have been of Kora origin.[155] Likewise they included a number of men designated explicitly as Batswana, who must have been refugees from the interior driven from their homes by the "Mantatee" invasion or the amaNdebele. Typical of these scattered Tswana groups was Lephoi, a petty Captain of the Batlhaping and subordinate of Mahura, who later claimed to have joined forces with Kok in 1825, and left some additional information, probably slightly garbled, on this development. "When I came out of my country, I came to Dam Kok. Dam Kok was fleeing, and I met him at Daniëlskuil, between Kuruman and Griquatown. Dam Kok was going forward when I was going to the Vaal River—while I was still on the Vaal River, Kok came to the Riet River, and after that I also came to him to the Riet River, and from there we moved along the river to here [*Philippolis*]."[156]

Adam Kok was not directly associated with the Bergenaars in the Transgariep, but he had many contacts with them and there were nominal followers of his among the group, including his then or later son-in-law, Hendrik Hendrickze, who was to become Secretary to the Philippolis Captaincy; Piet Witvoet also had become a notorious raider by the early 1830s, if not before, and the Karoshebbers tribe to which the Velminks belonged had connections with the Springbok Korana of Jan Bloem. However, in the conditions of the Transgariep allegiance was an arbitrary matter of practical convenience, and no clear distinctions can be drawn among the various groups of Griquas, Basters, Korana and Bergenaars inhabiting the area around the confluence of the Harts, Vaal, Riet and Orange Rivers in the early 1820s. The amount of confusion existing even among contemporaries in this regard may be seen in Jan Pienaar's statement, "There was no Chief of that country there. I cannot say who was the head of the Bergenaars, but Gert Koeman was the first who migrated (...)",[157] and from an entry in the journal of Captain Charles Warren of the 55th Regiment, who visited the Transgariep on a hunting expedition in the winter of 1825:

> We next went to the banks of the Mud River (Cradock),[158] where we came upon what are called the Burgonars, and passed a saltpan. The Burgonars are Griquas, and say that they came from Swartland[159] originally, and from thence to Little Namaqualand, and thence to Griquatown, and then scattered themselves over the country. At present the Old Captains of the Griquas or Bastards have let them join them in consequence of quarrels between them and Waterboer, and of the Government Agent[160] wishing to make them prevent the Burgonars going on commandoes against the Bojismen [=*"Boschesmen"*] and other tribes to steal their cattle. They have wagons, horses, sheep, and imitate the Boers. They have, some of them, as Adam Kok, good houses built in the same manner as the Boers['], but wander about, and live in huts made of mats, which they pack up upon a bullock and serve as tent.[161]

In the Cape Colony the developments beyond the Northern Frontier had been followed with considerable attention, and in December 1824, John Melvill, the Agent at Griquatown, in the course of a long report to the Colonial Government, gave the following warning about the potential threat posed to the Colony by the Bergenaars, albeit with some degree of exaggeration:

> A great part of them are provided with fire-arms and horses, and have a sovereign contempt of danger; they despise the [white] farmers; they are all sharp-shooters, and accustomed to bush-fighting and well acquainted with the country, and by flying before a powerful commando they would wear them out, and while they were harassing them in their retreat, they could spare a sufficient number to retaliate on the families and cattle kraals of the farmers absent on commando. They would not only have their own strength, but by their influence on other tribes, the Bechuannas, Corannas and Bushmen would be brought into a state of hostility against the Colony. They would have it in their power, by watching proper opportunities, to supply themselves with ammunition, and might,

at times the least expected, carry terror and distress into every part of the frontier, from the Tarka to the mouth of the Orange River.[162]

Towards the end of 1824, the landdrost of Graaff-Reinet, Andries Stockenstrom, had been despatched to the Transgariep to make contact with the Bergenaars and attempt to pacify them, and he was to undertake a second visit in the winter of the following year. As the Colonial authorities, however, were both unable and unwilling to spend any significant amount on establishing law and order beyond the frontier, Melvill submitted an alternative solution for their consideration.

> I am satisfied from what has come under my own observation during a residence of two and a half years as Government Agent at Griquatown that the only means of civilizing the savage tribes and preserving the peace of the frontier is to encourage the missions beyond the Colony. I have no doubt that if those missions fail for want of a check upon the Bergenaars, the whole of that part of the country on the frontier will be infested with robbers and murderers. The missionaries have always allayed the spirit of irritation and prevented contests between the Colonists and the savage tribes, their presence preventing the former from dealing unjustly with the savages, and the latter from retaliating when ill-treated by the Colonists.[163]

These statements were over-optimistic, and moreover strongly coloured by the fact that Melvill himself was a warm friend and supporter of the London Missionary Society who had accepted a difficult and unremunerative post for idealistic reasons and was soon to offer his services to the LMS as a missionary.[164] By his recommendations, however, he presented a significant opening to this body, which had recently begun to move into the Transgariep in the course of its attempts to establish a mission among the scattered Bushmen tribes surviving there.

This was the situation when Dr John Philip, Superintendent of the LMS in South Africa, arrived in the Transgariep in the winter of 1825 to visit the mission stations of the interior.

1. Dr Philip in the Transorange (1825)

Since the beginning of its work in South Africa, the LMS had tried to found stations for the Bushmen beyond the Colonial frontier. The missionaries, however, found it impossible to gain any influence over these people, and their attempts to do so often involved them in conflict with the white farmers moving into the areas in which they were working.

One after another the attempts were abandoned, and by the beginning of the 1820s all that remained of the Bushman mission was two "school places" in the Transgariep: one at Ramah, where the Baster Piet Sabba, formerly of Griquatown, had begun work as a teacher in about 1816, and the other at Philippolis, which was under the superintendence of another Baster, the native agent Jan Goeyman, formerly of Zak River, Graaff-Reinet and Bethelsdorp. At both these stations small Baster colonies soon gathered around the missionary assistants who had settled there.[165]

Goeyman had been placed at Philippolis in the autumn of 1822 by young Ds. Abraham Faure of Graaff-Reinet, an enthusiastic supporter of the LMS. Being particularly concerned about the fate of the Bushmen, he had on behalf of this body established a new mission post for them in the Transgariep, 30 kilometres beyond the Orange River, opposite the main ford from the Cape Colony; the foremost white pastoralists had at the time only begun to reach the river, and the area still had a large Bushman population. In his isolated situation, however, and with little practical support from the LMS, Goeyman was unable to exercise control over the Basters who had joined him, nor was he able to protect the mission against Bergenaar and Kora raiders. By 1825 nothing much had been achieved here, and when Dr Philip arrived at Philippolis on 18 August, he appointed a white artisan, James Clark, to take charge of the mission in Goeyman's place.

The condition of the Bushmen at Philippolis was a matter of some concern to Philip, which he had discussed on the way there with Andries Stockenstrom, landdrost of Graaff-Reinet. In the course of his two visits to the Bergenaars in the previous ten months, Stockenstrom had been particularly troubled about their attacks on the Bushmen, and like John Melvill at Griquatown he was inclined to seek a solution in the presence of missionaries; "but then," as he wrote some time afterwards,

> I consider these worthy men in the outset more as protectors than as teachers, at least to the present grown-up generation of Bushmen. By the high respect in which they are held among the Griquas, Bergenaars, [and] Coxdannas [*sic*] (far worse enemies to the Bushmen than ever the Boers were), they will restrain these from injuring such as belong to their institutions, and by the communication which they may keep up with the Government and the magistrates, they will effectually check all attacks on the part of the Colonists.[166]

With these ideas Philip seems to have been in full agreement, and by the recommendations of officials such as Stockenstrom and Melvill the way was therefore prepared for the LMS to take the initiative in the affairs of the region.

Besides his concern about the condition of the Bushmen and the future of the work at Philippolis, Philip was troubled by the dissension among the Griquas at Griquatown, which weakened the Griqua polity and did not reflect particularly well on the authority of the missionaries there or add to the prestige of their protégé Waterboer, and he now evolved a plan by which he hoped to solve these several problems. He seems to have regarded Adam Kok as the leader of all the dissident elements who had moved into the area between the Orange and Riet Rivers, or else as the most suitable person to act as their spokesman, and he accordingly proceeded to establish contact with him. The results were to be far-reaching both for Kok and the Griquas.

Of the various accounts Philip later gave of his visit to the interior in 1825, that which appeared in his *Researches in South Africa*, published three years later, was, all things considered, probably the most factually accurate, although he exaggerated his own role as initiator of the developments he describes and seriously misunderstood and oversimplified the situation he encountered in the Transgariep. Referring to the accusations of slave trading against the Bergenaars already quoted,[167] he went on,

After what I had heard and witnessed of the effects of this dreadful system, and seeing no prospect of its being terminated by any active enterprise on the part of those whose duty it was to have prevented it or to have checked it at its commencement, I addressed a letter from the station to the acknowledged Chief of the Bergenaars [*Adam Kok*], requesting him to meet me with the people on the Alexander [*Lower Riet*] River. The place at which I had appointed them to meet me might be about eighty miles from Philippolis. The messenger I despatched on this occasion[168] was acquainted with the party. He went on horseback, and after an absence of some days he returned and informed me that he had found them nearly fifty miles above that part of the river at which I had proposed to meet them, and that I might expect to meet the Chief and as many of the men at the place of rendezvous as could conveniently attend. (…)

On the evening of the 24th of August we reached Rama, a place which had for some time enjoyed the labours of a native teacher. (…) From Rama to the place where I had appointed to meet the Bergenaars is a distance of about 50 miles, over one of the most dreary districts in Southern Africa; and we were informed we should find no water till we should arrive within a few hours' journey of the Alexander River.

Being supplied with fresh oxen accustomed to the road, and with relays sent to meet us by the Chief Adam Kok, we travelled at a rate of not less than four miles an hour. It may seem ridiculous to boast of such speed in England, but we have not English roads and English mail-coaches in Africa.

(…)

On the 28th [August], on my arrival at the Alexander River, I found the leaders of the Bergenaars and between twenty and thirty of their people waiting for me. They were soon after joined by a number of Corannas who had been united with them in their plundering expeditions.

I spent two days among them, reasoning and remonstrating with them on the iniquity of their practices and on the consequences which were likely to follow from a continuance in them. They were far from appearing such hardened monsters as might have been expected by those conversant only with the annals of English depravity. In reasoning with a people of their description on deeds of atrocity, you have an advantage over them by the novelty of your arguments which is lost upon those who have had to overcome the force of those arguments upon their consciences before they could familiarise themselves with a life of crime. They ingenuously acknowledged the charges I exhibited against them, admitted the evil of the system they had been pursuing, and only slightly mentioned, in extenuation, the temptations they were under to commence and continue that system. Availing myself of their admissions, and of the temper they discovered, I now took higher ground, [and] plied them with every topic, human and divine, that appeared to me calculated to deepen the impressions already made upon their minds; and many of them were moved to tears.

It was now necessary to propose some remedy for the evils which had entailed so many calamities on the unoffending tribes who had suffered so much from their depredations, and for the calamities which the aggressors were bringing upon themselves by persisting in their present manner of life; and with that view I proposed that they should meet me at Griqua Town at a general meeting to which the surrounding tribes were invited, when it was my intention to endeavour to settle their differences and to lay before them some general plan for their future government.[169]

This was the beginning of an ambitious project on Philip's part by which a chain of mission stations, guarded by armed and mounted Griquas, was to be established to protect the indigenous tribes of the interior against white encroachment from the Cape Colony, and the Colony against possible incursions by Mzilikazi and other invaders from the north. As this project developed over the following decade, Philip's desire to retain control of it led him to emphasise increasingly the dependence of the Griquas on the missionaries and the authority of the LMS over the Griqua stations of Griquatown, Campbell and Philippolis, so that his various accounts of what happened in 1825 became increasingly distorted, and this fact must be borne in mind when examining them.

In 1832, in the course of a dispute with the Wesleyan Missionary Society, who were attempting to establish themselves at Daniëlskuil to the north of Griquatown, Philip described the events of 1825 with some significant addition of detail.

> In 1825 I found our Bushman Mission at Philipolis in a precarious situation and standing in need of protection. The farmers who had been recently settled on the Colonial side of the Orange River had already begun to occupy the country around the station with their flocks and herds and to frighten away the Bushmen, and from the north-east they were threatened and persecuted and murdered by the Caffres. Passing the Modder [*Lower Riet*] River, I was strongly solicited by Adam Kok to allow him to settle with his people in that district. The proposal required due consideration before I could give an opinion upon it, and I then told him that I should think of this matter when I came to Philipolis[170] and then give him my ultimatum. After mature deliberation I employed Mr Wright, now at Griqua Town,[171] to inform the Chief Kok that he had my permission to come with his people to Philipolis on this *condition*, that he was to protect the Bushmen.[172]

The following year, in a letter to the Acting Governor, Lieut. Col. Wade, which subsequently appeared as an appendix to the report of the Aborigines Committee appointed by the British Parliament, Philip wrote with reference to the "Berghannas" or Bergenaars of the Transorange:

> In 1825 I visited that country, and tried what persuasion would do with them; they met me on the Alexander River, where I spent some days among them, reasoning and remonstrating with them on the iniquity and impolicy of their conduct, and they made many promises at that time that they would abandon their evil courses and settle at a missionary station; but I was not so sanguine as to expect that they were all sincere in their declarations. (…) It was on this journey that the Chief Adam Kok solicited leave to settle with his people at the missionary station of Philippolis, and to this I gave my consent for reasons I need not now enumerate. The conditions on which these arrangements were agreed to on my part were that his residence in that place should be approved by the Colonial Government, and that he should protect the Boschmen.[173]

In 1842, seventeen years after the event, Philip gave what may be probably regarded as his definitive version of these events in a document titled "The tenure by which the Griquas hold the lands at Philippolis".

> The Bushmen mission at Towerberg [*sic*], now the site of Colesberg, was commenced in 1816.[174]
>
> In 1818 the missionary was recalled within the Colony. This was done by order of the Colonial Government on the complaint of the farmers against the missionary. The site of the mission, however, and the country around it was still considered by the Government as belonging to the London Missionary Society, and when that country was added to the Colony in 1822,[175] the ground on which the mission premises had stood was still recognized as belonging to the Society and the Bushman Chief [Uithaalder], who had become a Christian. His family and a few of his people, who had derived benefit from the labours of the missionary, were still allowed by the Government to occupy that portion of his lands which was left him.
>
> Many applications were made by the farmers who now filled the surrounding country to the Government for this particular place, but they were told by the Landdrost Stockenstrom in reply to their petitions that their requests could not be complied with, it being the site of a missionary station belonging to the London Missionary Society.
>
> This affair having been brought under the review of His Majesty's Commissioners of Inquiry,[176] in answer to a letter of theirs to the Landdrost on this subject so late as 1824, that functionary stated that the lands in question were still considered as belonging to the London Missionary Society.
>
> In my journey into the interior in 1825, I conversed with the Landdrost on this subject, and was told by him that the springs of water and a considerable portion of the land around them were still reserved for a missionary station, and that we might occupy them for that purpose when we pleased.
>
> In 1820 the Revd. A. Faure, then minister of the Dutch Church at Graaf Reinet, visited that part of the country and, commiserating the miserable state of the Bushmen, recommended to me the

establishment of a mission for that unfortunate people on the other side of the Great River and at no great distance from Towerberg or Colesberg, as it is now designated,[177] and this gave rise to the missionary station of Philippolis.

The district of Philippolis was then a Bushman country and occupied by Bushmen, and it became a question with me whether I should re-establish the mission at Towerberg or remove the small remains of the Bushmen still hovering about it to our new station on the other side of the river.

These poor people get[t]ing notice of my arrival on the site of the mission came out of their hiding places (for the surrounding country was at that time occupied by the Boers, and the ground still left for their use no longer afforded them any protection), and came to my wagon to make me acquainted with their miserable situation and to entreat me to furnish them with a missionary to teach them.

This part of the country had belonged in the district of Graaf Reinet and had been formed into a separate jurisdiction, and the attention of the Government having been directed to that place as the only one in the neighbourhood for the seat of the new magistracy, I was willing to meet the wishes of Government as far as it could be consistently done with the duty I owed to the miserable objects then about me, and I was the more willing to do this in the hope that the Government would in return be the more ready to assist us in protecting our people at our new station in the district of Philippolis, an assistance likely to be required from the contiguity of the Boers who were now separated from them by the breadth of the river only.

After hearing the statements of the people, I stated to them that it did not appear to me desirable to remove our mission at that place [*Philippolis*], and they having agreed to remove to Philippolis, I took them with me and fixed them at that place, giving up Towerberg, now Colesberg, to the Government.

On my arrival at the Bushman station of Philippolis I found that the Boers who had recently settled in the new district so lately added to the Colony had found their way across the river, and were beginning to annoy those who had the conducting of the mission and to oppress the Bushmen, under the pretext of searching for stolen cattle and runaway Bushmen and children who they had alleged had been contracted to them and promised them by their parents. The missionaries were set at defiance, the statements of the Bushmen were disregarded by the Boers; their [*sic*] was no authority in the country to decide such questions, and the Bushmen were unable to defend themselves.

Proceeding northward I came to the residence of Adam Kok, one of the Griqua Chiefs and the father of the present Chief of Philippolis, whose territory lay next to the lands of Philippolis, and who proposed to protect the Bushmen against the aggression of the Boers provided that I would permit him to reside at Philippolis. To this proposal I gave my consent, on this condition that he was not to dispossess the Bushmen of such land as they might require nor consider himself or his heirs as having any right to sell any part of the country or to give a lease of any part of it except to his own people, and that he and they were merely to have the use of the lands as belonging to a missionary institution.

There was nothing strange to him in this proposal, as it was agreed upon by the Griqua Chiefs after they had been reclaimed by the missionaries from their wandering and savage life and begun to locate themselves in particular spots for the purpose of cultivating the soil, that they should all hold their lands by this tenure.[178]

This arrangement with Kok was agreed to and afterwards sanctioned by General Bourke[179] on his accession to the Government, and it is fully admitted in a letter of recent date from the present Chief of Philippolis, in which he stated that neither he nor any of his people had any right to dispose of the lands of Philippolis to the Boers, by sale or by leases granted for any term of years.[180]

The Boers have, however, found their way into the Philippolis district to the amount, it is supposed, of 700 or 800, and they consider themselves secure in the possession of it, as many of them have leases to show which they had obtained from the old inhabitants, giving them what they regard as a legal right to the grounds they respectively occupy.

There are two flaws in these titles. In the first place, as has been shewn, the people had no right to dispose of the grounds they occupied in this manner, and in the second place those who disposed of their land did so in opposition to a law enacted by the late Chief and his Council which prohibited any of the people disposing of them by sale or otherwise, excepting among themselves, and these leases were granted without the knowledge of the present Chief, except in one instance of the occupation of a remote part of his territory under peculiar circumstances for a term of three years, and in this case as well as in the others the Boers have expressed a determination to keep possession and to resist any attempt the Griquas may employ to remove them.

The question at issue is as to what is to be done in this case, and how to prevent the parties from taking up arms to settled the point in dispute, an event to be deprecated from the calamitous state in which it might place this Colony. At my suggestion the Griquas have agreed to refer the arbitration of the matter to the Colonial Government, and the Boers having virtually done the same thing, having collected and sent their leases to the Government,[181] a fair opportunity is now afforded Government of settling these differences so as to prevent the evils to be dreaded from a war between the parties, to which the question might otherwise give rise.

The lands claimed by the Chief of Philippolis are bounded on the south east by those of the missionary institution of Bethulie, on the south and south west by the Cradock [*Orange River*] to Ramah, where they are bounded by Waterboer and his Griquas on that side of the river to its confluence with the Vaal. In 1825 and '26 I found the old Chief Kok and his people occupying the Modder or Alexander and the Riet Rivers stretching as far to the south as the ground on which the missionary institution of Bethani[e] now stands,[182] but I am unable to say how far the territory to which they laid claim extended towards the sources of these rivers. It was then a part of the Griqua country and held by the Chief and his people on conditions which have been specified and which he had his people assent to before they were permitted to occupy the district of Philippolis, which afterwards gave its name to that portion of the Griqua country claimed by the Chief Kok and on which Kok and his people were residing when I visited them in 1825.[183]

The tenor of this statement was undoubtedly affected by the fact that details of 99 farms under the jurisdiction of Philippolis leased by the Griqua owners to white farmers had been submitted to the Colonial Government the previous April, as mentioned by Philip, together with a "treaty" concluded with the Griquas in 1840 (actually a declaration by the Kaptyn and his *Raad* or Council concerning the rights of the white settlers in Griqua territory) and a covering letter signed by 63 white farmers living between the Riet and Modder Rivers, protesting their loyalty to the British Government.[184] In these circumstances it was not only necessary for Philip to establish the authority of the LMS in the territory, but to do so specifically with regard to the claims of the farmers.

After his discussions with Kok and his followers on the Riet River, Philip proceeded to Griquatown and Kuruman, and it was at Griquatown on his return journey that the projected meeting of the various Griqua leaders and other interested parties duly took place which he described as follows in his *Researches*.

> The general meeting of the Griquas and other tribes was held, according to appointment, on the 20th of September [1825]. The men assembled on this occasion from different parts of the country might amount to between three and four hundred. I regret that it did not occur to me at the time to take their exact number, with a list of their names.
>
> The first three days were spent in hearing their differences and in endeavouring to reconcile the parties to each other. After this difficult task had been effected, in a manner which exceeded my previous expectations, a few simple regulations congenial with their own notions and the progress they had made in civilization and general knowledge were proposed at a meeting of all the parties, discussed, and adopted by acclamation. At the passing of each resolution all the men stood up and held up both their hands. While they were yet standing, in passing the last resolution, with their hands lifted up, "That they would all unite in suppressing all commandos against Bushmen and Bechuanas, and in putting an end to the nefarious system which had been carried on by the Bergenaars", I addressed them as follows:—"Your hands are now lifted up in the presence of God and angels, before whom you have solemnly

pledged yourselves that you will keep this resolution; and if this solemn engagement is violated by you, I shall appear as a witness against you on the day of judgment."

The scene was altogether one of the most solemn and interesting I have ever witnessed; and the manner in which the people were affected after this public expression of their sentiments may be conveyed in the language of a Coranna Chief, who exclaimed, "My heart is glad! My heart is glad! A few days ago, when we saw each other at a distance, and did not know to what party we belonged, we were glad to creep behind the bushes. We were afraid to meet, but now we can travel over the country in peace; we have nothing to fear, we can go from house to house, and in every house meet friends!"[185]

As far as the arrangements made specifically with Adam Kok are concerned, Philip wrote in the statement of 1832 which has already been quoted:

Adam Kok, the Chief of Philipolis, had for some time before expressed his anxiety to have his eldest son, since dead,[186] made a Chief, and he made several applications to me on the subject. After one of the public meetings which took place on that occasion between 5 and 6 o'clock p.m., Adam Kok, the Chief of Philipolis, his son whom he wished to be made a Chief, Berend Berends and others retired with me into a small hut I then occupied, to come to a settlement on the subject. After having conversed with the young man and received the testimony of the people in his favour, I consented to recommend his appointment to the Colonial Government, and on that recommendation the Colonial Government sanctioned his appointment.[187]

A considerably less idealistic or optimistic account of the proceedings at Griquatown was given shortly after the meeting by the Government Agent, John Melvill, in an official letter to the Government Secretary in Cape Town.

I have the honour to acquaint you, for the information of His Excellency the Governor, that some of the Bergenaars and the two old Chiefs, Barend Barends and Adam Kok, have been to Griqua Town and made peace with Cornelis Kok and A. Waterboer, the two Chiefs of the missionary stations Campbell and Griquatown. The Bergenaars and some others expressed a desire to put themselves under Adam Kok, who resigned his office as Chief about a year and a half ago, and I understand they intend making regular application to Government to have him regularly appointed again as Chief.

It appears probable that the two old Chiefs and their adherents will entirely separate from the other party, and leave the Griqua country to reside opposite the Nieuw Hantam,[188] which is about ten days south-east of Griqua Town. The separation will no doubt tend to promote peace in this quarter, but whether the Bergenaars will cease to plunder the Bechuana tribes is very doubtful, for about ten days ago I received information, and the report has since been corroborated, that a large party of them went out on a marauding expedition, and that only two of them have returned, the rest having been cut to pieces by the people they attempted to plunder.[189]

In a less formal letter to the LMS written two days after the above, Melvill expressed his opinions about the events more openly.

You will no doubt be informed by Dr Philip that he has lately visited this country, and that he has attempted to bring the Bergenaars and Waterboer's party to terms of peace. There was a meeting here and about 200 persons were present, but there were only five Griqua Bergenaars and about 20 Coranna belonging to their party. Some good regulations were proposed by the Doctor, and everyone professed to be satisfied and promised to adopt them. However, knowing the character of the people and their deep-rooted enmity to each other and natural deceitfulness[?], particularly as there exists no power to enforce the regulations, however good they may be, and as I am certain that the Chiefs hate each other [as much if not][190] worse than formerly, there appears to me very little hope that the two parties will be united.[191] Indeed, the two old Chiefs had very long ago formed a plan of settling with their followers and the Bergenaars about ten or twelve days south-east of Griqua Town, on the Cradock [*Upper Orange*] River, and since Dr Philip left this, we have heard that one of the old Chiefs is now removing thither. It was long my opinion that after a peace was established a separation would be better for both parties, and tho' I did not think proper to propose such a thing, I naturally wished the party opposed to Waterboer and Cor[neliu]s Kok would leave the country.[192]

A highly critical view of the meeting was expressed by one of those directly involved, Kaptyn Andries Waterboer of Griquatown, in a declaration made some three years later.

> When Dr Philip arrived at Griqua Town, he informed me that he had seen the Mountaineers [*Bergenaars*], and that they would be here by the time he returned from Lattakoo [*Kuruman*]. It occurred accordingly: A. Kok and B. Berends, together with the Mountaineers, came to Griqua Town, and carried [*behaved*] themselves in the first instance towards me and my people very unfriendly; and now, without my being made farther acquainted with anything that was about to take place, or whether I was willing or not that Dr Philip should interfere between me and the other parties, or whether I would sanction the proposals that were about to be made or not, I was called into the church, where all the Mountaineers were assembled, to defend myself against several ungrounded complaints that were brought against me. The individuals who made the complaints were employed and prompted by A. Kok and B. Berends, this is a fact well known, and those two individuals took good care not to come into the meeting during the time these complaints were brought forward. There were complaints also made in the same way against Captain C. Kok, but we were able to meet them all and to justify ourselves, except in the case of Sibinell,[193] and in that case I think it is already evident where the fault lay, and as I have also stated, we intend in that case to make satisfaction.
> When I and Captain C. Kok saw how things were going on, and being fully convinced that all the proceedings had been prepared beforehand without our knowledge, and thinking that it did not become Dr Philip as missionary to interfere in our governing

affairs, and that the Mountaineers in a great measure were our people, who had left us and rebelled against us without a sufficient reason, we considered such conduct an outrage on Captainship and Government and on all laws and order. We refused to accede to everything respecting that meeting, and would on no account acknowledge the mediator, nor would we sanction any proposal that had been made. We farther made it known to A. Kok and B. Berends and the Mountaineers, and to everyone that were [*sic*] in any way dissatisfied, that we should always be glad if they would personally and openly come to us with their complaints, and that we doubted not but that we should always be able to settle the difference between us to their satisfaction. But notwithstanding, the business of the Mountaineers was proceeded with, and against our wish and will A. Kok was appointed Captain of the Mountaineers, and thus were our own people encouraged in their rebellion against us and in an unlawful and never before heard of improper way torn out of our hands. We can well appreciate the good intentions of our friend, Dr Philip, in this affair, but he was much too ignorant of the real state of things amongst the Griquas to effect anything that could turn out good or useful, and we are at this time heavily suffering the effect of his improper conduct.[194]

The most destructive account of the proceedings comes, however, from another missionary, the censorious and outspoken Robert Moffat of Kuruman, who had accompanied Philip back to Griquatown, and who was no particular friend either to him or the Griquas. Writing confidentially to his parents-in-law in England two months after the events he described, he sharply criticised Philip's conduct while at Kuruman, and continued:

Before touching on what took place at Griqua Town, I shall first premise by noticing that the Doctor, without consulting with the missionaries, [and] without the sanction of the Government or their agent, Mr Melvill, on his way from the Colony called the Mountaineers together, inquired into their grievances, heard their complaints, and fixed a day when all were to appear at Griqua Town, when he would rectify the former abuses and devise new plans for future peace, etc., etc. Accordingly, when we reached Griqua Town, nearly all the parties were collected.

On Wednesday, Thursday and Friday long meetings were held in the church, when discussion took place of the most ridiculous nature, and proposals were made equally inconsistent with the professed character of their author. I was not present, having given my unqualified disapprobation to the interference, but Mr Bartlett's interpreter[195] gave me the minutes of what took place, which was such as to display the folly and weakness of man, for, as the Griquas themselves remarked, grievances could not be settled without first being heard, and plastering over a sore was not healing it. The Doctor, feeling that one mean could not succeed, had recourse to another, and endeavoured to persuade the party disaffected that all was settled. "But on what ground?" enquires a Chief, which threw the Doctor back where [he] began.

In this way it went on till the Doctor was completely baffled (and no wonder), and feeling that neither his name nor popularity could succeed, he had recourse to another expedient. On the Wednesday evening he requested me privately to call the Captains (with whom I was familiarly acquainted) to his lodging, and he should treat them with a glass and settle differences between themselves. I pointed out the pernicious results of such a step, and refused compliance. However, on the evening following he took the Captains or Chiefs to his room (their subjects or men followed, and were spectators!), and, as if determined to make a peace which would last till he left the precincts of the town, he took the most likely means. A Griqua refusing to drink a pint of spirits might be considered a miracle. But, marvellous to say, two of the Chiefs[196] actually refused to drink what the Doctor had poured out. Leaving you to imagine what would follow, I shall only add that next morning the two old Chiefs came up to me when I was standing with the Doctor, and requested me to say that they did not feel themselves accountable for what they had said the night before!!! Mr Melvill witnessed all these scenes with heartfelt sorrow, and it was a subject of criticism and diversion for the two India gentlemen mentioned in my last,[197] who had waited to see what the Doctor would make of them.

(On glancing over what I have written, I feel half inclined not to send it. What I have written is, alas! but too well attested facts, and have been so glaring that a proposal has even been made to send a united letter demonstrating the profanity of his conduct on this side of the Orange River. To such a proposal I could not agree, and what I have written is to enable you to judge for yourself when you see eulogiums written and encomiums passed and fine varnished speeches delivered so fostering to pride and vain self. What I have written is for your own information.)[198]

The various accounts of the events of 1825 here quoted, with their varying emphases and judgements, form a graphic illustration of the disunity existing in the Transorange at the time, even within the ranks of the London Missionary Society. The immediate practical upshot of the arrangements was, however, that the Bergenaars were to place themselves under Adam Kok II, pending the official approval of the Governor of the Cape, and that he and his people received permission to settle in the Philippolis area on the sole responsibility, it would appear, of Dr Philip. It was not without reason that the Wesleyan missionary James Archbell exclaimed rather testily in the course of the dispute about Daniëlskuil seven years later, "What right had the Doctor to go into that country at the first and to claim possessions there? What right had he to take the Griquas there? Who were the original proprietors of the soil as claimed? Did Dr Philip or his agents purchase it? Where are the documents?"[199] It would appear, however, that the Colonial authorities, at a loss for any practicable solution to the problems of the Transgariep, were only too willing to sanction the steps taken by Philip on his own authority, the more so as they were in conformity with the advice of their own agent at Griquatown. According to Philip's statement, "When this measure was laid before General Bourke he approved of what I had done, and sanctioned the continuance of Adam Kok and his people in that district, on the condition that he would protect the Boschmen."[200] After the conference at Griquatown, Adam Kok II was in October 1825 moreover formally elected Kaptyn by the Griquas, Bergenaars and Korana willing to acknowledge his authority, and 110 individuals appended their names or marks to a memorial to the Cape Governor requesting that he be formally appointed,[201] which further strengthened Philip's hand.

The affairs of the Transorange having been settled to his own satisfaction, Philip promptly departed for the Cape and for England, where he was to spend several years championing the cause of the Khoikhoi, his major preoccupation at this time, not returning to South Africa until the end of 1829. The implementation of his improvised plans for the Transorange area was left to his protégé and confidant, Peter Wright, who had been working as a mission assistant at Theopolis in the Eastern Cape, and whom Philip on his return to in Cape Town providentially encountered there, on his way back to England for the sake of his wife's health. Wright was persuaded to remain in South Africa, ordained, and appointed resident missionary at Griquatown with special responsibility for the affairs of Philippolis.[202]

The mission assistant James Clark gave the following account of developments at Philippolis in the immediate aftermath of Wright's arrival, in a letter written in September 1827, apparently to Andries Stockenstrom at Graaff-Reinet. The "Hottentot inhabitants" mentioned by him were the Basters who had originally settled there around Goeyman some years before.

> Immediately on Dr Philip leaving this country for England, the Hottentot inhabitants of Philippolis began to build for themselves a considerable number of good houses and *other works*, both on that station and the neighbouring fountains arround. They also began to cultivate a considerable quantity of corn. But several months afterward (now 16 months ago)[203] Mr Wright, missionary at Griquatown, arrived at Philippolis on his way to the Bergenaars then lying at the Moder River,[204] and informed me that he was appointed their missionary, that Dr Philip had requested that he might endevour to bring *them back to Griquatown*, but that in the event of their refusal, he was at liberty to form a station among them where they choosed, even at Philippolis, and in that case I and my people must commence a station for Bushmen at the Caledon River.
>
> Mr Wright proceeded to the Bergenaars and gave them Dr Philip's authority to occuppy Philippolis, which they consented to do. Soon after this an outpost near Philippolis was attacked by a party of Caffres, which threatened very soon to return, and not doubting Mr Wright's authority, we called in the Bergenaars to

Philippolis, and I even gave them the station over *in writting*,[205] in order that they might be inclined to protect it. The Bergenaars were not, however, inclined to protect it, but left it and went towards the Griqua Country (where, by the by, as above mentioned, Dr Philip originally wished them to go),[206] and they requested Adam Kok, their *Kaptein*, to accompany them, which he refused to do.[207]

Official approval of the election of Adam Kok II as Kaptyn of the people in the Riet River area had been given by the British authorities at the Cape on 10 January 1826, and Wright obviously intended to put into effect the tentative arrangements made by Philip a few months before. As he subsequently wrote to Clark with reference to the developments sketched above: "This state of things at Philippolis, together with finding such a immense population connected with A. Kok of upwards of 300 families of Griquas, Coranna and Bechuannas on the banks of the Modder [*sic*] River without any abiding place, destitute of the Gospel, desiring the means of grace and pleading to go to Philippolis, induced me to make the communication to them that they had Dr Philip's authority to proceed to that station."[208]

Before anything further could happen, however, Boesmansfontein, a farm some 10 kilometres to the north-west of Philippolis belonging to the mission, was attacked by a party of what contemporary documents describe as "Caffres", presumably Sotho refugees or scattered amaXhosa living in the vicinity of the Orange River. Believing that they had tracked cattle stolen from them by raiders to Boesmansfontein, they carried out a retaliatory raid on the settlement one night in May 1826, in which 31 people were killed or burned to death when their houses were set on fire, and Clark, panic-stricken, summoned Kok and his followers to Philippolis to defend the station against possible attack.[209] They had arrived by the middle of July, and in order to ensure that they would remain, Clark formally made over the station to them. As Wright put it in his subsequent letter to Clark, which is the main source of information on this transaction:

From the document put into my hands which you gave to A. Kok dated 22 July 1826, consisting of four separate strange articles, I find you have not only ceded the *station* to all intents and purposes to the Captain and his people, which is an act neither you nor the Missionary Society had power to do, but you ceded the *missionary also*, whoever he may be, for ever, so that by your paper he is become to all intents and purposes a subject of the Captain of Philippolis.[210]

On the arrival of Adam Kok and his people, the mission station became the capital of the new Griqua Captaincy, and after this there were two distinct groups at Philippolis, the original Baster members of the congregation (the "Old Inhabitants"), and the Griqua followers of Kok, who may have included Christians, but had no strong allegiance to the church or the mission and were not inclined to accept the authority of the LMS or its missionaries. For many years there was to be a struggle for power between the Old Inhabitants and the later Griqua incomers, to which almost all the missionaries successively stationed at Philippolis fell victim. Peter Wright, who died there in 1843 shortly after having been transferred from Griquatown, was in fact the first missionary not to have been driven from the station by local intrigues.

As regards the Bergenaar and bandit elements who had nominally accepted Kok's authority, the alliance improvised by Philip very soon proved to be unstable, and a portion of them reconsidered their decision, withdrew their allegiance and retreated to the Orange River; according to Andries Waterboer, he was told by Kok "that the whole party of Bergenaars had in a very angry manner left him, and that they were at that time threat[e]ning to shoot both him and his children. (...) A. Kok informed me that he would never have anything to do with them again, that they were too wicked and ungovernable."[211] However, former Bergenaars remaining in the Philippolis Captaincy, together with their sympathizers and supporters, continued to influence local affairs, and this group was responsible for what may be called an "anarchic" element in the early history of the Captaincy, represented most notably by the Government Secretary Hendrik Hendrickze.

The high-handed and arbitrary methods by which first Dr Philip and subsequently Clark disposed of the Philippolis territory seem never to have been questioned. When he appeared before the Aborigines Committee of the British Parliament in 1836, Andries Stockenstrom was asked with regard to the Transorange in general, "Are you aware whether any possession was taken of any part of that country in the name of the London Missionary Society?", to which he replied, "Philippolis and Griqua Town are now both London Missionary stations." The Committee continued,

> You were understood to say that at Philippolis the missionaries of the London Missionary Society had taken territorial possession of the country?—The establishment as a missionary station was ceded by Dr Philip to the Griquas. The Griquas established themselves there and cultivated the soil, and most of the Bushmen disappeared.
>
> Do you mean that the possession of the soil was ceded by Dr Philip to the Griquas from the Bushmen?—Yes; a paper was shown me by Mr Melville at the time I visited the place in 1830 or 1831.[212] (…) I recollect perfectly that there was a strong representation made by me, as I disputed the right of Dr Philip to dispose of that land at all.
>
> Did you dispute the right of Dr Philip on behalf of the British Government?—Not at all. I said that the Bushmen had a right to be there.
>
> Were your remonstrances attended with any effect?—It is a Griqua establishment now.
>
> (…)
>
> Do you know whether Dr Philip claimed a proprietory right to the site of Philippolis, either personally or on behalf of the Society?—I do not know upon what grounds he claimed it, but he did act, for I saw the paper. The missionaries Melville, Rolbe [*Kolbe*] and Clarke can give the best information about this paper.
>
> (…)
>
> What paper do you allude to?—A paper shown me by the missionary then upon the spot.
>
> What was the nature of it?—In the name of the London Missionary Society he authorized those Griquas to be there.
>
> To what extent of territory did that authorization extend?—That paper did not specify; it spoke only of the establishment at Philippolis.
>
> Do you know within what bounds that establishment was comprised?—I cannot say.[213]

The Bushmen for whom the mission at Philippolis had been established and for whose protection the Griquas had been encouraged to settle there seem to have been oppressed by their protectors as much as by any other group,[214] and the Bushman mission continued to languish. In 1828 James Clark and his charges were obliged to remove to Bushman School (subsequently to be named Bethulie) near the confluence of the Orange and Caledon Rivers.[215]

2. The early years of the Captaincy (1826–1832)

Not only was Bergenaar raiding in the vicinity of the Orange River to continue for some time after the developments described in the previous chapter, but for several years there were also complaints of attacks on the Griqua settlers and cattle raiding by the Bushmen in the area. The Griquas were, with Dr Philip's active encouragement and the blessing of the Colonial Government, moving into territory traditionally occupied by the Bushmen, and in 1827 John Melvill, noting that a number of Bushmen had been punished by the Griquas at Philippolis for cattle theft, described one of them as "a man who formerly lived on this station" and added, "It appears that the spring of Philippolis belongs to this Bushman Chief."[216] In 1843, when the Boers were disputing the area with the Griquas, they saw fit to produce an affidavit from Piet Kraankuil, "Bushman Captain", declaring "that the greater part of the country now occupied by the Bastards was, previous to the encroachment of these people, inhabited from time immemorial by our nation".[217]

The Koks themselves were traditionally known as protectors of the Bushmen, but their followers were often less well disposed, and the mutual relationship of the two groups seems for the greater part to have been one of open enmity. Andrew Smith, travelling from Philippolis to Campbell in 1834, remarked in his diary: "The Hottentots, Bastards and Griquas are afraid to travel singly and unarmed in these parts. They state that the Bushmen are very evilly disposed and will often waylay one or two persons proceeding along the road. They will not attack where there is a wagon because they cannot be certain of what is in it, nor of the weapons with which these people may be supplied."[218] In his journal he added, "Henrick Henricks considers the Bushmen of the Reit and those of the tract between that and the Black River[219] as almost the worst disposed; and though he maintains that he is much respected by all Bushmen, yet he is forced to confess that he fears those of whom we are at present speaking."[220]

If the Bushmen in the Philippolis territory were abnormally aggressive, one can only imagine that there were good reasons for this, and

Andries Stockenstrom, who was greatly concerned about their lot, reported in 1830 on a number of specific atrocities on the part of Griquas, in which Hendrickze was also implicated, although some may well have been the work of Bergenaars and Korana not under Kok's authority.

> I had discovered that a kraal of Bushmen living among the migratory Boers (...) were attacked by a commando of Griquas of Dam Kok's party, who killed fifteen, left two for dead badly wounded and carried off the only survivors (three children), after offering them for sale to the [white] Farmers. (...) In another kraal fourteen were killed by a party of Griquas under the command of Kok's son-in-law, Hendrik Hendriks, and other outrages against the Bushmen were related of which I have no proof.[221]

The main threat to the peace of the fledgling Captaincy of Philippolis was constituted, however, by the Kora raiders of the Transgariep, who had already established themselves firmly, and were not inclined to subject themselves to Kok and his Griquas: the names of Piet Witvoet, of Abraham Kruger, the son of a white hunter and adventurer, and of a leader known as Willem are often mentioned in early accounts.[222] In practice these raider bands were probably very mixed groups not easily to be distinguished from the Bergenaars; they had at any rate already achieved a considerable degree of wealth, power and even sophistication, and Dr Philip, meeting a group of them (Abraham Kruger's people, as subsequently appears) for negotiations at Ramah during his visit in the winter of 1825, wrote:

> I expected a horde of naked savages, and I found a number of smart young men, dressed quite in the style of the most respectable farmers in the Colony. The young men had generally white fustian jackets, leather pantaloons, striped waistcoats, white hats with broad edges, shirts, neckcloths, stockings and shoes; and the Chief was dressed in a handsome surtout with silk facings and edgings.[223]

Andrew Smith reported a few years later that when Kruger's people came to Philippolis to conclude peace with the Griquas, "they gallopped into the town about 200 in number, each with a gun".[224]

For several years the Griquas attempted to subjugate the Kora raiders,[225] and in the course of one of these sporadic expeditions an incident occurred which long afterwards gave rise to one of the earliest known testimonies by a Griqua woman, Tryn Isaac. The events described probably took place in 1830.

> Hostilities broke out between Adam Kok and some Bitterbush Korannas in his district. The men of our "werf" were my husband David, Piet Isaac, Jan Isaac, David Isaac and Hans Isaac, my four brothers, Cobus Isaac and Paul Isaac, my nephews. My sister[s?] Anna, Letta and Lys were also there.
>
> My brothers Jan and David Isaac went to join Adam Kok's commando. After a time one Jan Kok returned from the commando and brought us news that my brother David Isaac was wounded. The way it happened I heard was this: Adam Kok had beaten the Korannas at Schietmakaar,[226] and David was returning homewards with others when Jan Kok fired a shot at a vulture near to Opperman's farm.[227] Some Korannas in the neighbourhood, hearing it, lay in wait for them at a ridge. Setebe, a noted headman among the Korannas, led the party, and was seen and recognized before a shot was fired. He fired, and hit my brother David Isaac below the left knee; my brother staggered, and Setebe cried out, "That hit you!", but my brother took aim, fired, and shot him dead; upon which the Korannas carried him off, and our people also carried away my brother David Isaac for some distance in a "brayed" hide, till he became too weak to carry further, and Jan came on to tell us.
>
> On the news arriving, the wagon was prepared, and we started that evening, travelling the whole night. We crossed the Riet River at the junction [with the Modder], and went up along the road on the south side. It was dawn when we crossed, and about eight o'clock when we reached the place where David Isaac lay, adjacent to the river and to the left of the road. Those who accompanied me in the wagon were Jan Kok, Piet Isaac, Cobus Isaac, Paul Isaac and my husband David; the women were Anna Isaac, David's wife[,][228] Fytje, and I. We made a bed for him under the wagon and put mats around it for shelter. He had been wounded in the

left knee, as he was kneeling on the other knee to shoot, and the leg bones were split open downwards. About eight o'clock the next morning he died, and he was buried in the afternoon in a grave dug with a spade we had brought. We returned home the next day.[229]

"I washed the bandages of his wound and gave him the last cup of water he drank just before he died, for which he thanked me," Anna Isaac's Bushman maid Fytje recalled on the same occasion.[230] Many years later the exact location of David's Graf, which had become a local landmark, was to be of some importance in the Diamond Fields dispute.

By 1834 Adam Kok could still complain to the Colonial authorities "that the [white] farmers encourage the Corannas, a most unruly and numerous people, to plunder the neighbouring unprotected tribes of their cattle", and that "the Corannas are now becoming so daring from the encouragement they have met with, that for his own protection, and to prevent his own people from becoming as lawless as the Corannas, he must have recourse to arms towards the Corannas, which he is very averse to, as the war will be a very serious one."[231]

By this time, however, as already indicated in the above quotations, a greater problem was facing the Griquas of Philippolis in the shape of white Colonists moving into the area from across the Orange River.

In September 1824 the Upper Orange River had become the northern boundary of the Cape Colony, bringing the area of official white settlement into the immediate proximity of Philippolis, and in November 1825, during a period of drought in the Colony, Andries Stockenstrom, landdrost of Graaff-Reinet, permitted white farmers to move across the river temporarily to obtain grazing in the Transgariep. Occasional seasonal migrations soon became a regular institution, and within the next few years a large number of white farmers or *trekboers* settled on a semi-permanent basis at fountains in the Philippolis area and in the neighbourhood of the Riet and Caledon Rivers.

Not only did these trekboers dispute the scarce natural resources with the Griquas already living there, but in practice they often refused to recognise the authority of the Captaincy or the rights of the Griquas themselves, establishing their own authority by means of superior force and numbers. A notorious example of an intractable white immigrant was Ockert Schalkwyk, whom the missionary Hodgson had encountered near the northern boundary of the Colony in April 1828. "This man lives in a most uncomfortable manner," he wrote at the time,

> his wife being separated from him on account of his conduct. He has since taken a Bastard as a wife, by whom he has had one child, the mother of which is dead after experiencing most cruel treatment. He has also had a natural child to one of his slaves. He was once one of the richest farmers in the neighbourhood, and, when sober, is generous and friendly, but when drunk is the terror of the neighbourhood, beating his dependants in the most unmerciful manner and, being a very strong man, compels all who are with him to drink to excess.[232]

According to several sources, Schalkwyk settled in the Captaincy later in the same year, and he was subsequently described as "the first Boer to settle North of the Orange River", by which formal settlement with permission of the Griqua Raad is presumably meant, unless he had earlier undertaken prolonged visits on a seasonal basis.[233] By 1831 he was charged by the Kaptyn and the missionaries with violent behaviour and supplying drink to Griquas,[234] and ordered by the Cape authorities to return within the Colonial frontier, but the order does not seem to have been effective, for in 1834 Andrew Smith could still describe him as "a dangerous person to live beyond the Colony",[235] and in 1849 Ockert Johannes van Schalkwyk, presumably the same individual, leased two farms in Griqua territory for his "Bastard or Griqua children" Tobias and Ocker.[236] Schalkwyk may well have been an extreme case, but men of this type were by no means uncommon along the frontier, and he serves as an example of the violence and unruliness with which the Griquas were obliged to deal with the inadequate force and authority at their command.

By January 1829 Adam Kok and his Raad were already compelled to protest formally to the Cape Governor about the presence of white farmers in the Captaincy,[237] and the following year a letter of complaint appeared in an unidentified Colonial newspaper under the heading "Oppressions of the Griquas". It is by no means impossible that it was indeed composed in Dutch by a Griqua as alleged,[238] in which case the most likely author would have been Hendrik Hendrickze, who had by that time settled down and was already a member of the Griqua Raad, for he was an eloquent and educated man, and not particularly well disposed to the missions or to Christianity. It is a remarkable expression of the Griqua viewpoint as formulated by a particularly articulate spokesman, and as such it deserves to be quoted in full.

> I have heard that the Hottentots have permission to write to you, Sir, and that you are a good friend to all oppressed men. We have also heard that the great King of England has made all the Hottentots free,[239] but we do not believe that the King knows how it fares with us in this country, otherwise he would likewise take care of us. Please to say, Sir, whether we can not remain free in our own country, and have farms, the same as other men. The spot where the Cape stands and all about it has been the land of our forefathers; there they have pastured their cattle and sheep in peace and freedom, and had it not been for the Christian men we would be to this day in that country.
>
> It was not agreeable to our inclination that we have come so far; the white people have pressed on, that we have now at last come to reside in this country over the Great River, and we thought that nothing now was required to escape from the Christians. You will have heard, Sir, that three or four years ago the Boers had gone everywhere in this country. They said at first that it was on account of the drought; but now when there is so much grass within the Colony, we see that there is another aim, and we have become suspicious. They say it is Bosjesmen land and therefore they have a right to occupy that country. I say also that it is Bosjesmen land. But, Sir, where is not Bosjesmen land? From here all along the Great River to the great sea ocean is Bosjesmen land, and Graaff Reinet and everywhere where the Boer resides is also Bosjesmen land. Where are we to go now and not live in other men's land?
>
> It is the fault of the Christians that we are not at this day in our own land. We can no longer go to the land of our forefathers with our cattle and sheep; the people have seized all our grass and springs; where then shall we go? We cannot reside between heaven and

earth. If we could go to the moon we would fly there, in order to be free of the Christian men and see there for land; but that is too far.

We have resided here already four years and remained in peace and friendship with the Colony; wherefore must we be plagued and annoyed incessantly? Are we not also creatures who are destined by the same God of us all to remain on the earth? Wherefore then must we suffer continually so much from the Boers as to compel us to fly further into the interior? If we go further inland they may afterwards say again that we reside in other people's country and therefore they must drive us again away, and so on till they drive us out of the world. But, Sir, if that is right, then I think, according to my simple understanding, that the Namaquas, Coranas, Bosjesmen and Griquas have the same right to go with their cattle and sheep into the Colony, and they can say they do it because it is Bosjesmen land. We think then, Sir, that we have as good a right to that land as the Boers have to the country on the other side of the River and other parts of the Colony. I think, Sir, that the Christians ought to restore first our country and that of the Bosjesmen, and then they can talk about this land.

Sir, we have heard that the Great River is the boundary line of the Colony; can it not remain so for ever? Why must it always be altered when the children of the Boers grow up and when their cattle breed so very much? I will ask you, Sir, whether the people of England also alter often their boundary lines when their children grow up and their cattle increase? But there in England will not be found Hottentots bordering on it so that they can take land from them.

Sir, is it true that it is the will of the King of England that all the people in the world shall build houses and plough and sow and make gardens? In old times we have pastured our cattle and hunted; but since we have come to this country we have taken fifty farms in hand, have led the water out, have ploughed, sowed and made gardens. I think, Sir, that the King will be glad if you tell him that Hottentots have done all this; and, Sir, you must come yourself to look at our farms. We were also of intention to do more; but we have now been quite discouraged, from the intrusion of the Boers;

for we think on the manner of old times when the Christians seized the places of our forefathers.

Last year a Boor [*sic*] took one of our places,[240] and has built houses, ploughed and sown; his name is Hendrik Batenhuisen. Other Boers have also said that they will take places. In 1828 we wrote to the Governor about these things,[241] and also about the beatings from the Boers, because we have heard that he takes the part of the oppressed. He has written a handsome letter to us, that he will take care that we are not oppressed, and has given orders to the Boers to return to the Colony; but the Boers have only returned in the months of February and March of this year, and at present there is abundance of grass in the Colony; but notwithstanding this they come again over into this country sorely to plague us. The cattle of the Field Cornet[242] have always grazed on our ground; we have complained, but it is of no use. We have sent three letters more on that subject to the Governor, but we cannot think that he has seen them, otherwise he would help us.

Please, Sir, to tell these things to the Governor, that the Boers may be prevented from coming over. We cannot agree with them, and we are not of intention to remain in the same country together with them. We have a long time since contemplated going into the interior of the country, but we wait yet to see whether the Governor can help us.

I also thought that you, Sir, could help us if you please before we go away into the Bechuana country. If we go there we must do the same which the Christians always do; we must seize (*afvat*)[243] their country. I think then how it will be with us if we go so far from the Colony. We are accustomed to clothing, and receive many other things from the Colony; we shall become very savage and wild in the interior, without clothing and other things; but, Sir, we think it is better to be naked and free than to wear clothes and be oppressed.

You will have heard many things of us that are not good, but I believe, Sir, you will not give implicit faith to all that our enemies say of us. A man will not hear good from his enemy, and as a crow pecks on the sore of an ox, so he seeks to touch on the worst business. Our doings have not always been good, but our black spot is made tenfold larger than it is, and we are accused of things which are far from the truth. All that our enemies say is picked up to bring in something against us, and even without giving us an opportunity to speak on our behalf. Sir, is this right? What would the gentlemen of the Colony say if I had heard bad things of them and would talk everywhere of them and say, I have heard very bad things of the gentlemen of the Colony? But I shall at present not tell anything of it to you, Sir. I trust then, Sir, that you will not give faith to everything about us, but that you had better come yourself to see and hear with your own eyes and ears. And if the Governor could come to hear and see himself, it would be much better than to hear everything from our enemies, who look at everything in a wrong view and relate everything wrong. But I think that the Governor will not judge about a people so summarily (*zoo maar*).

With regard to our bad things, Sir, I say myself that we have cause to be ashamed about some things, we must improve yet, we are still half savages and not so as civilized men. I think that men require many years to become properly civilized, but, Sir, it is a pity that the Christians do not get better, considering that they are so long a time Christian men. We have learnt many things from them that are not good. Some of us have made in former times commandos with them and shot Caffers and Bosjesmans, and I hear that continually commandos go against the Caffers and bring out thousands of cattle, and that guiltless [people?] are shot. Have you not heard, Sir, of the great commando which went some months ago against the Bosjesmen at Bamboosberg?[244] They have killed many Bosjesmen. The Bosjesmen had only taken horses.

Sir, I think according to my simple understanding that people who will pick up our faults must first remove these things and give a little example to us, for they are Christian-men and they can speak about us. Pray, Sir, please tell the Governor to come hear, or otherwise to send an Englishman, the Boers are a great deal too bad, they frighten us when they speak with us about a thunder cloud which will break over us. Sir, you must advise us and tell us whether the King of England will be offended if I write him a letter about these things. But I entreat you, Sir, to insert this letter in your paper, in order that the Governor can see how the people do with us, and if I see you one day I will give you my thanks, Sir.

The people who have come here are Arnoldus Pienaar, Dou Stein, Andreas Visagie, Hans Logenberg, Piet Niemand, Hendrik van Heerden, Piet Schalkwyk, Jan Schalkwyk, these are come from the New Hantam. There are more people come, but I do not know their names.

This letter is sent by an Oppressed Griqua. Philippolis, 14th August 1830.[245]

Whatever the origins of this letter, the sentiments it contains, though expressed with greater fluency, agree in substance and in tone with the various official statements repeatedly made by the Kaptyn and Raad in this regard over the next thirty years. By January 1834 matters had already deteriorated to such an extent that Kok could propose to Lt. Col. Henry Somerset, Commander of Kaffraria, "that an intelligent Government servant or officer should be sent up to reside at or near Colesberg or over the Orange River near Allemall's [*Allemans*] Drift for some time to order the Farmers away, and to establish order and peace and to see the Government's orders enforced".[246] In October of the same year, Dr Philip, as part of a wider and more ambitious scheme for stabilising the region, suggested "that an officer with 25 or 30 of the Cape cavalry should be stationed at Philippolis", recommending Lieutenant H.D. Warden of the Cape Mounted Riflemen for the post,[247] and this suggestion would eventually be put into practice in 1846.

According to Griqua custom, land could not be alienated, and Adam Kok III later stated that a specific law in this regard had been made at an early stage in the history of the Captaincy, "in 1830, in my father's time",[248] but illegal land transactions by Griqua subjects were nonetheless regrettably common. As Gottlob Schreiner wrote from Philippolis in 1842:

> The greater part of the farms thus disposed of have never been cultivated, not would they [bc] by the Griquas on account of the distance from the station and, I must in truth add, the indolence of the owners. This being the case, they were of course of not much real value, and the Farmers offering them from two to six and eight hundred pounds was too strong an inducement for them to

resist. Added to this it was sufficiently evident that the Boors, once in the land, were determined to remain; they were in actual possession of many of the unused fountains, and made no secret that they were willing to remunerate, but remove they would not. (…)

The working part of the population retain their farms and will do so; the others live as they did before, from their flocks, and buy their corn, so that they have lost nothing temporally as yet, but whether they are destined to furnish another melancholy proof of the black man withering away before the white remains to be seen. God forbid that it should be so, but recent occurrences in other parts of the country make me tremble.[249]

As mentioned by Philip in his statement of 1832,[250] Adam Kok II at the time of the negotiations at Griquatown in 1825 already intended to resign his authority, and he was soon—apparently in the course of 1826—succeeded by his son, Kaptyn Cornelius Kok III.[251] The latter died in 1828, however, and on 1 January 1829 Melvill wrote to the Secretary of the LMS in London in the edifying phraseology of the time:

> It may not be improper in this p[oint?] to give a short account of the death of Cornelius Kok, the late Chief of this place and son of our old Chief Adam Kok, which took place a short time ago. He was about 32 years of age. He was brought up and baptised by Mr Anderson, former missionary of Griqua Town, and was a member of the Church at that station, but afterwards fell away, and appeared very indifferent about the concerns of his soul until shortly before his death. He was superior in understanding to most of the Griquas, and was anxious to improve in knowledge. He exerted himself to promote the welfare of the mission, and was very favourable to civilization,[252] but unhappily he did not possess the wit or natural disposition to gain the affections of the people, and owing to this and other causes was very unpopular.
>
> Being dangerously ill of the stone, he was advised to have an operation performed, and was proceeding to Graham's Town for that purpose, but died on the road. About a fortnight before [he] left the station he began to be somewhat concerned for the salvation of his soul. When he took leave of me, he requested I would

remember him in my prayers, and committed to me the care of his children, expressing his earnest desire that they should be brought up religiously. Although when in health his heart was altogether set upon his worldly property, consisting in much cattle,[253] a very great change took place just before he departed, and his mind seemed altogether taken off from it and fixed upon the things of eternity.

I was informed by his brother, who accompanied him a day's journey, that he continued a whole night in conversation with him upon religious subjects, and among other things made the important remark that *the grand business of Man's life should be to secure a place in heaven*. He frequently exhorted his father on the road to engage in prayers, and could not bear to hear his wife and sisters, who attended him, speak upon worldly subjects. His sister told me that he was continually either engaged in prayer or speaking of the Lord Jesus. She remarked that he frequently spoke in a strain quite above her comprehension, that he enjoyed a confident hope of being saved, and looked forward to the hour of his departure with pleasure.[254]

In the margin of his letter Melvill added, "The Old Chief had resigned the Chieftainship to his son Cornelius, which was sanctioned by the Colonial Government, but has again resumed his authority", and Adam Kok II was to govern the Captaincy for a further seven years. The German missionary August Gebel who accompanied Andrew Smith to Philippolis in 1834 described Kok as "a rich man and well disposed towards all missionaries",[255] but he was not a strong or assertive personality nor did he make a particularly favourable impression on observers. In all fairness, however, it must be borne in mind that he was an elderly man, described by Smith as "old and infirm",[256] who obviously had little inclination for his responsibilities as Kaptyn in a situation which was becoming increasingly complex.[257]

Recording his visit to the Transgariep in August 1834, Smith wrote concerning his reception by Kok:

When we reached Philippolis he was absent, not having returned from Colesberg, where we first made his acquaintance, but by noon of the following day he paid us a ceremonial visit—I say a ceremonial one, because in reality it was such. Both his manner and appearance were on this occasion very different to what they were when we first met him. They were then indicative of goodness of nature and openness of heart; they were now characteristic of sullenness and reserve. The extraordinary change caused us much surprise, more especially as his welfare and that of his subjects was dear to our hearts, and therefore we were disposed to view his conduct as evincing an indifference to our friendship. Reflections, however, proved the conclusion to be unfair, since he had yet had no peculiar testimony of our favourable disposition towards him, and consequently no particular reason to regard us as friends.[258]

After a few weeks' sojourn at Philippolis, Smith summed up in a letter to the Cape Governor, Sir Benjamin D'Urban:

I have had a good deal of conversation with old Kok, and must confess he appears to me a very undecided and weak person; but I am satisfied were he to be properly supported by Gov[ernment] he would act with more decision and by no means unjustly. His subjects are of a very heterogeneous description, and by no means united. Whenever a crime is committed there is always a party ready to support the accused, and if he belongs to a division which is strong, he escapes the punishment he merits, merely from there being not sufficient power to enforce it. He is aware of what is wanting, and says that had he more directly the countenance and support of the Colonial Government, he would not only enforce order and peace in his own territory, but also ensure absolute protection to the whole of the frontier in his direction.[259]

The real power in the young Captaincy was the ex-Bergenaar Hendrik Hendrickze,[260] who soon attained a position of importance in the Captaincy and had already become a member of the Raad by January 1829.

Hendrickze's origin is unknown, but he is said to have been born about 1795,[261] and he himself later declared, "I was present in the year 1811 with the first trek of the Griqua nation from the Kamiesberg in the Cape Colony to over the Black River [*Orange*], to a place later called Griqua Town."[262] He was not, however, very strong on dates, as his account of Griqua history shows, and he may in fact have been referring to an earlier migration. One Hendrik Hendriks received baptism at Klaarwater in 1808 at the age of 38, and he and his wife Elsie Kaffer had children baptised by the missionaries there regularly, the eldest having been born in 1797, while Elsie herself was baptised in 1814;[263] these may have been the parents of the later Griqua Secretary. A certain "Andrias Hindriks" was accepted as a member of the Griquatown congregation in 1813 "on his confession of faith", presumably as an adult, but his age has been left blank in the register, and this may have been Hendrickze's uncle, subsequently to attain notoriety as a Bergenaar leader. [264]

The baptismal register likewise records the baptism of one Hendrik Hendriks, Hendrik's son, as an adult, on 26 January 1817, an entry which may well refer to the later Government Secretary himself, for he is known to have been a member of the church at Griquatown. He is said to have had a brother called Andries, and a child of Hendrik Hendriks and Elsie Kaffer was baptised at Griquatown by the same name in 1810, while Charles Bell in the caption to the portrait of Hendrickze he made in 1834 described him however, as "brother of David and Andries Hendriks the Bergenaars".[265]

Early in the 1820s Hendrickze left Griquatown with his uncle Andries and unnamed brothers to join the Bergenaars.[266] For the remainder of the decade his name occurs largely in connection with raids on the Bushmen, Basotho and others, although it is also to be found on the petition requesting the appointment of Adam Kok as Kaptyn, and it must have been about this time that he married Kok's daughter Griet. The missionary G.A. Kolbe wrote subsequently of the early period of the Philippolis Captaincy that Hendrickze "had the most influence in the country, although guilty of many enormous crimes".[267] Andrew Smith declared with regard to Kok, "It has been generally stated that the old man is greatly influenced by his son-in-law, Hendrick Hendricks",[268] and Gebel expressed the thought more strongly: "his right hand and his brain is his son-in-law, Henrik Henrik".[269] Elsewhere, referring to the Pienaar faction at Philippolis, Smith remarked, "Letters have been written to them by Hendrick Hendricks, the secretary to Kok, and when they enquired about the subjects of them they found that the Captain was ignorant of such ever having been penned",[270] and to D'Urban he mentioned allegations that "Hendrick (…) was in the habit of writing letters to individuals and also to the Colony which were never directed by the present Chief".[271]

White observers were often inclined to regard Hendrickze with their customary feelings of amused condescension, like the artist Charles Bell, a member of Smith's party, who portrayed him "presented with a worn out pair of Wellingtons boots and sketched while grateful".[272] The Attorney-General of the Cape, William Porter, wrote in a similar facetious strain after a meeting at Colesberg in 1845:

> It would not be fair to expect in a country Hottentot the same degree of fashion in attire which we usually see with Hottentots about town. But I was given to understand that he was upon this occasion got up at great expense. The dirty handkerchief which he wore the day before was discarded, his head, as might be seen through the scant hair, was not, I thought, so very dirty. He wore a large, loose greatcoat of coarse duffle, which, if he had no shirt (as I suspect was the case) was so folded round the body as to hide the want. His crackers[273] were in tolerable order, except in regard to length, but they certainly (to my taste) showed more of his naked and not very well washed legs between their bottoms and his veldt shoes than was desirable.[274]

The fact that Hendrickze had been among the earliest of the rebels to leave Griquatown and his reputation as a Bergenaar were weighty arguments against him, and Gebel described him as "a warrior famous and to some extent also feared throughout the Colony".[275] The missionaries at Philippolis looked on him with somewhat mixed feelings, and he initially did not make a good impression on Andrew Smith, who first saw him at church.

> Hendrick Hendricks was present, and during the service he displayed a demeanour indicative of great self-conceit and conceived importance. Upon conversing with Mr K.[276] as to the character of this person, he assured me that the opinion I had formed was perfectly correct; that he was vain and conceited, and considered himself a person of no trifling consequence. He states him to be a most plausible person, and of so accommodating a temper that when the Captain gets displeased with him and rejects his councils,

he gradually ingratiates himself again, and is never for any long time out of favour. He is much respected by the Corannas and Griquas, but treated with indifference by the Bastards.[277]

After closer observation during his sojourn at Philippolis, Smith described Hendrickze as "the oracle of the Council", and added, "The Cape Town newspapers regularly reach Philipo-land, and the reports of its Legislative Council and legal proceedings are studied at least by the Secretary, who is never backwards in quoting them as precedents",[278] while Gebel remarked after attending a session of the Raad, "I must admit myself that his form of expression, his insight and his naivety won my highest admiration. Because of his wild life he was formerly one of the greatest scourges of the mission; for the past six months, however, says Kolbe, he has joined the lambs in the pasture of the Gospel."[279] Kolbe himself at the same period described in a letter to Dr Philip as "one of those active minds that must always have some employ",[280] and in his letter to D'Urban some weeks later, Smith, while admitting that Hendrickze was stated to be "a man of bad character", added that he was nonetheless "a man of great acuteness and very considerable information", and gave a summing-up which was remarkably favourable.

> As regards his character I have had little opportunity of judging. Mr Kolbe informs me that within the last six months he has improved very much; that before that he was much addicted to drink and some other evil practices, but now he can discover no cause of complaint in him. His character will never stand high as long as the Farmers etc. shall be the only medium through which it shall be known. He is too sharp for them, too much of a lawyer not to be able to expose their acts of injustice, which consequently makes him a person not at all desirable for Griqualand, and therefore as a man to be represented as a character upon which the Gov[ernment] ought never to depend. If I had not long ago been acquainted with the ideas of the Farmers in regard to the Hottentots and aware of their malicious proceedings towards them, I would just have written down verbatim the words of Hendrick. I never heard the truth more fairly and distinctly told, and if he could be heard in the House of Commons he would produce an impression which

even time itself would scarcely efface. I cannot pretend to decide whether he is a man of principal [*sic*] or not; he is eaten up with vanity and ambition, and I would almost fear that to cherish the one he might sometimes be disposed to forego the other. If properly managed, however, he might be rendered a most useful person. Any individual acquainted with the workings of human nature might make anything of him. I merely in common justice complimented him upon the accuracy of his observations, and expressed my wonder at his being so well acquainted with the contents of the Colonial newspapers, and that was quite sufficient to give me such influence upon him as to enable me to lead him as I wished.[281]

Writing unofficially and informally in his diary some months later, Smith gave much the same summing up, stating,

Some days ago he astonished me with some remarks concerning the proceedings of the Government functionaries. (…) Such an oration would have done no discredit to the British House of Commons, and I am sure had it been delivered there it would have produced a sensation far beyond what even the most eloquent pen could have excited if wielded by any but a person who had actually laboured under the smart arising from an ill directed policy.[282]

Captain A.B. Armstrong of the Cape Mounted Riflemen, who had visited the Transgariep the previous year on an official mission to investigate the unrest in the area, described him as "a man who reads and writes well and is one of the most intelligent colored persons I ever met with, but an unprincipled fellow",[283] while William Porter too, in spite of his derogatory description of Hendrickze, admitted that at Colesberg he delivered "very fluently a long and really able speech".[284]

Initially it would seem that Hendrickze represented the remnants of the old Bergenaar group in the Captaincy. It is significant, for example, that the missionary Kolbe by his own account incurred Hendrickze's wrath by preaching against the raiding expedition in true Bergenaar style which was undertaken against the Ndebele of Mzilikazi in the interior in the winter of 1831 by the former Bergenaar leader Barend Barends, supported by the Bergenaars Gert Goeyman and Abraham Kruger and a considerable number of individuals from Philippolis.[285] Through the disproportionate influence he exerted on Griqua affairs for a period of some twenty years and the perpetual unrest of which he was the main source, Hendrickze caused considerable problems in the Captaincy. Whatever his failings may have been, however, he was also an extremely gifted man, as even his enemies were forced to acknowledge, and probably one of the most gifted individuals in the public life of South Africa during the first half of the nineteenth century.

3. The development of the Captaincy (1832–1843)

The first clear indication that the Griquas of Philippolis had a mind of their own and were less amenable to guidance from the missionaries than the people of Griquatown was given in 1832, when Dr Philip, in the course of a second journey to the interior, once again tried to interfere in the workings of the Captaincy. Philip's attempt and the signal failure which attended it were recorded graphically in the missionary Kolbe's journal.

22 October [1832]. Received information this morning that Dr Philip had arrived at the Great River. I rode off immediately on horseback to meet him, and fell in with his wagons about 15 miles from this station. The Doctor invited me into his wagon, and we had much conversation on the state of the Griqua missions etc. About 4 miles from the station the Chief met us with his horse wagon and conveyed us in it to Philippolis. In the afternoon Dr P. conversed with the Chief and the people.

23 October. Many of the people collected together to speak with Dr Philip. The Doctor gave them excellent advice, and they all agreed to sign a number of resolutions, promising obedience to the present law and Government, and for this to use all their endeavours to rectify the existing law and to support the authority of the Chief and of the Council. (...)

28 October, Sunday. Dr Philip preached to the people in the morning on the blessings and advantages of religion. I preached in the afternoon, and the Doctor again in the evening on the necessity and benefit of temperance societies.

29 October. Today the Chief called a general assembly of the people. Dr Philip advised them in a most kind and amiable manner to promote their own happiness and welfare by fearing God and acting justly.

30 October. Dr Philip left us this afternoon and proceeded on his way to Griqua Town. (...)

20 December. Dr Philip arrived here from Griqua Town. During the Doctor's absence one of the Old Griquas[286] had exerted all his influence to eradicate the good counsels of Dr P. from the minds of his countrymen. He had collected a party of all the worst of the people to unite themselves together, and they deposed the principal counsellors, subverted the laws and acted as they judged proper. The Chief tacitly allowed them to act in this manner. The Bastaards or New Griquas and all the members of the Church expressed their abhorrence of such conduct, and steadfastly adhered to the law. These people with their Chief, who solemnly professes by oath to defend the law and Government, wanted to subvert them. What can be said of the character of such men?

25 December. Dr Philip, perceiving that through the folly of the people his remaining any longer here would be of no service, left today (much to our sorrow) this station. I accompanied him as far as Colesberg.

The ingratitude with which the Old Griquas have repaid Dr P. for all his kindness and laborious exertions in their behalf evidently show[s] that they despise their best friends and benefactors.[287] On the contrary, the new inhabitants of the country, the Bastaards, were thankful to the Doctor for his good advice and exhortations. About 50 collected together at the river to see the Doctor safe through the water, and saluted him with many discharges of musquets.

28 December. I took my leave of the Doctor from Colesberg. I felt very much at parting with this Christian friend. His kindness and condescension during his short stay with us and his edifying conversation endeared me much to him [*sic*]. I felt as if I was parting from a father, and now while writing, memory recalls the pleasant hours which I spent in his company, and the tear of Christian affection is involuntarily starting from mine eye[?].[288]

As far as is known, the only indication of the feelings of the Griquas on this matter is provided indirectly in a précis by a modern researcher of material in Philip's archives subsequently destroyed by fire. The somewhat enigmatic note in question reads:

Philippolis—Dec. 24, 1832. Free translation of a letter sent to Mr Kolbe (…) by the Griquas to be read to the two counsellors Cornelius Niels and Lodewyk de Bruin telling them that the Griquas have done with them and will not recognise them as judges over them. The Griquas are in general contented with the Counsellors last chosen, and also with a part of the former Council, namely [?].[289] There follows a list of the persons who had sent this letter. It had been done by the burghers of the country.

A general meeting enacted certain laws, a copy of which was sent to Fairbairn,[290] and these were signed by the same people as above. They undertake to support the Chief and Government as it now is, but they wish to amend the laws so that justice might be done to all.[291]

Philip himself, describing these events in a subsequent letter to Acting Governor, T.F. Wade, was at great pains to emphasise the disorder still existing at Philippolis because of Kok's lack of control over the Bergenaar and Kora elements in the population.

> On my arrival at Philippolis I found the missionary and his family, and all the respectable part of the people, in very great distress. (…) At my solicitation the Chief, Kok, sent for the principal men of the banditti, and they came to Philippolis to meet me, but my arguments had not the same effect upon them which they had in 1825. I could make no impression upon them; and it was evident to me from the reception they received from the Berghannas [*Bergenaars*], and the manner in which they associated with them, that the people of Philippolis were correct in the suspicion they entertained, that they were in league with them.[292] (…) I did everything possible while I was among them to induce them to lay aside any evil designs they might have against the peaceable and respectable part of the community, and the Chief, Kok, promised to protect them; but he is entirely under the influence of Hendrick Hendrick, his son-in-law, who is one of the leading men among the Berghannas, and the worst and most dangerous man among that party. Hendrick is clever and he is plausible, but he is a thorough scoundrel, and such is his power over the old Chief that whatever resolution he

may form, in half an hour Hendrick can make him change his mind.

The present is the most favourable opportunity that can possibly occur for putting an end to the disorders of that country, and putting the affair[s?] of the northern part of the Colony upon a good footing. The great body of the people at Philippolis are sound at bottom, and will be very glad to be included within the limits of the Colony, or to have any system the Colonial Government may think proper to establish among them that will deliver them from the present Chief and afford them security. They will be very happy to be placed upon the same footing with the Kat River,[293] and to pay their taxes the same as the other Colonists pay theirs.[294]

Philip's indignant reaction to the thwarting of his plans for Philippolis was to recommend that Joseph de Bruin, described by him as "a man of good sense and courage", be appointed nominal Kaptyn at Philippolis in the place of Adam Kok, that Abraham Kok be appointed in the place of his uncle, Cornelius Kok II, at Campbell, and that both these Captaincies be made subordinate to the tractable Andries Waterboer of Griquatown.[295] Why Abraham Kok should have been regarded with such favour is not clear, but De Bruyn was a prominent member of the Baster group at Philippolis and a leading member of the congregation, and this suggestion was an unabashed attempt by Philip to gain control of the Captaincy for the LMS; it does not seem to have been considered seriously by the Cape authorities, however, and the Griquas were left to find their own solutions for their problems.

Two things seem to have happened at Philippolis to cause this sudden and unexpected check to Philip's plans. The first was that Hendrik Hendrickze had after Barends' disastrous campaign against Mzilikazi in 1831 obviously decided to withdraw from participation in Bergenaar raiding and the use of violence and turn to more peaceful measures, and had made a successful attempt to shape the policy of the young Griqua state through the use of argument and persuasion. This hypothesis is borne out by the fact that Andrew Smith, in discussing the possible succession to the Captaincy during his visit to Philippolis in 1834 later could observe, "Hendrick Hendricks denied [Adam Kok's] right to dispossess

[Abraham Kok],[296] but now that he sees the voice of the people is for him, he has turned also",[297] which indicates likewise that Hendrickze had withdrawn his support from the Bergenaar raiders, who supported Abraham Kok, and allied himself, whether realistically or opportunistically, with the more established Griqua faction at Philippolis. In the second place, moreover, the Griquas had begun to distinguish between the Captaincy and the mission at Philippolis, or at any rate between their own interests and those of the missionaries, and to take control of their own affairs. By the end of 1832, there was obviously a group in the Captaincy independent enough to dissociate themselves from the LMS and be swayed or used by Hendrickze, and large enough to influence the course of events. In spite of continued advice and active interference on the part of the local missionaries, of Peter Wright at Griquatown and of Philip himself, which they sometimes requested and sometimes also followed, as they saw fit, the Griquas would henceforth increasingly take their own decisions. After this Hendrickze was to become steadily more prominent in the affairs of Philippolis, and in practice it must to a large extent have been he by whom the policy of the Captaincy was determined.

The feebleness of the young Griqua polity in the face of the many dangers confronting it seems to have been realised from the beginning, and as early as January 1827, James Clark, writing to Stockenstrom about the threat posed by the Korana, went on, "I have further to mention that I am authorized to state by Adam Kok (the oldest and original Griqua Chief) that he is quite willing to enter into any terms with the Colonial Government that may be agreeable to both."[298] This idea was now revived, as mentioned by Philip in his letter to Wade, no doubt encouraged by the fact that preparations were being made for a treaty between Andries Waterboer and the Cape Government, which was finally signed in Cape Town on 11 December 1834, and with the approval of the Griqua community themselves it was decided that the Philippolis Captaincy would seek a similar alliance. Not only would this imply the recognition of their polity and assure them of the nominal protection of the British Government, but it would secure for them at least a limited supply of the gunpowder they required in order to maintain themselves in the difficult circumstances of the Transgariep and assist the Kaptyn in maintaining his precarious authority.

By August 1834 these plans were so far advanced that Kolbe could write to Philip:

> I had much conversation with the Chief and Hendriks as to that delicate business of their submission to the Colonial Government, and they readily entered into your views. First a private then a public meeting of Council, including their influential men not Council[lors], was called to take this matter into consideration. The result was that the Chief, Hendriks, Gert Ko[k?], the Council and the people unanimously agreed to place themselves under the protection of the Colonial Government. Old Dam is very sanguine in this respect. He sees that he cannot govern the people, and they all perceive that it is the only means to prevent their being crushed by the Boers who continue daily to come into the country. (...)
>
> At the request of the Chief I shall draw up a petition to His Excellency stating the desire of the Griquas to be under the protection of the Colonial Government, provided the lands and farms granted to them by the Chief and lawfully purchased with his approbation be guaranteed unto them by that Government. They also trust that their places [*farms*] will be measured free of expenses.[299]

In connection with this, Kok planned to meet the then Governor, Sir Benjamin D'Urban, in the Eastern Province, and Gebel wrote from Philippolis in the same period, "on the occasion of the Governor's impending visit to Kat River some form of defensive and offensive alliance will probably be concluded between the Captain and the Governor".[300] D'Urban's visit was cancelled at the last moment, however, and when the Sixth Frontier War broke out in January 1835, a meeting on the Eastern Frontier became impossible. Adam Kok was accordingly invited to Cape Town, and travelled there in the winter of 1835, accompanied by a party of twelve people which included his sons Abraham and Gert Kok, and Hendrik and Griet Hendrickze. As the Governor had meanwhile left for the seat of war, they spent some months here waiting for him, but Kok's failing health finally compelled him to return to Philippolis with the purpose of his expedition unaccomplished. He did not survive the journey, dying on the Berg River near Paarl on 12 September 1835.[301]

Upon this followed a somewhat protracted interregnum in the

Philippolis Captaincy, and it was not until 26 January 1836 that Abraham Kok, the eldest surviving son of the former Kaptyn, was elected to succeed him. The election appears to have taken place under some pressure from the Colonial side, and the Civil Commissioner of Graaff-Reinet, W.C. van Ryneveld, travelled to Philippolis for the occasion, together with five field-cornets and a number of burghers.[302]

It was a rather unexpected choice, for Abraham Kok does not seem to have been regarded with much favour by any observer. Andrew Smith noted in his diary in 1834, "The eldest son of [Adam] Kok is a hasty, imperious character, and even when they are trying cases does not hesitate to rise up and beat a witness. He is not respected by the people, and they object to him as the successor to the Captainship. They consider his not being able to write a great objection."[303] When Adam Kok was absent from Philippolis on a visit to Kat River at some time prior to Smith's visit, it was not Abraham who was appointed to act in his place, but his younger brother, the future Adam Kok III, and this must have caused some dissatisfaction on Abraham's part, for shortly afterwards Kolbe wrote to Dr Philip, "the Chief had a private interview with Abraham, and he now is perfectly reconciled to the place. I cannot but feel for poor Abraham, perhaps through your kindness something may be done for him. He is now Commandant of the country, a situation I think well befitt[ing] him."[304] By the Cape Colonial Secretary, Col. John Bell, Abraham was described as "Dr P[hilip]'s *un*favourite",[305] which is confirmed by Philip's icy description of him at this time as someone "wholly unfit to succeed his father, and this was felt and acknowledged by the father himself".[306]

The election of an illiterate Kaptyn at this sensitive point in Griqua history when negotiations with the Colonial authorities were still in progress might perhaps be interpreted as the last successful attempt at self-assertion by the unregenerate Bergenaar element in the Captaincy, the representatives of the traditional Griqua ways and lawless existence of the past, as opposed to the educated and westernised Griquas, now including Hendrickze, who were seeking rapprochement with the Colony.

At first Abraham Kok followed the policy already laid down by his father, and on 7 January 1837 a meeting with Andries Stockenstrom, by now Lieutenant-Governor of the Eastern Province, took place on the banks of the Orange River concerning a possible alliance with the Colony; the missionaries Theophilus Atkinson from Philippolis and Peter Wright from Griquatown were also present. The subsequent Griqua councillor Piet Draai later spoke of "that time Sir George Napier and Sir Andries Stockenstrom were on the pont on the Orange River",[307] although his memory was at fault as far as the presence of Napier is concerned, while Atkinson recorded at the time that the meeting took place "at the Float".[308] "And there in the presence of all," wrote Atkinson,

> His Honour recognized the sacred right of the Griquas to the country they occupied, and stated the determination of the British Government not to interfere with these rights. He made it known also that all who came into their territories must be subject to their laws, and if they offended must be punished accordingly, and that if they considered any individuals injurious to their interests they must take them into custody and set them over the river. (…) The [Lieutenant-]Governor, however, recommended them first to form an alliance with Waterboer, which was also in contemplation before, stating that he could not enter into a treaty with them till they were first united among themselves. This is one great object that Mr Wright has in view in his present visit, and from the state of feeling among the people, there seems every prospect of carrying this desirable plan into execution, and then the treaty with the Colony will be ratified.[309]

"Since their interview with the Governor," Wright could write from Philippolis on 1 February 1837 to Mrs Jane Philip in Cape Town,

> the Chief [*Waterboer*] and Councillors have been fully engaged in preparing the public mind for the proposed arrangements, in which they have been hitherto quite successful. Yesterday a general meeting was held, when a union with Waterboer and a treaty with the Colony were fully approved of by all. This is a great point gained; it is an important matter so far accomplished which I never expected to see, and I do hope the things will now meet with no further difficulties so far as it regards the ratification of the treaties. But the working of the new arrangement of things—in this we shall meet with serious difficulties, because with regard to both the Chief and a great majority of the people (in this affair), they are

raw, and it will require much that good Mr Atkinson does not possess to secure the establishment of a peaceable and prosperous state of things in the country.[310]

A delegation which included the Kaptyn's younger brother, Adam Kok, and Hendrik Hendrickze, was sent to Griquatown to negotiate a treaty, and an agreement with Andries Waterboer was "drawn up and ratified" at a public meeting held there on 25 February 1837.[311] Through the medium of Peter Wright the Kaptyns also expressed their eagerness for a treaty to be duly concluded between the Philippolis Captaincy and the Colony, with special reference to the necessity of "permission for their subjects to purchase ammunition and firearms in the Colony".[312]

As far as Abraham Kok was concerned, however, his interests lay elsewhere, and it is significant that he took no active part in concluding the treaty. The organised emigration of disaffected white farmers from the Cape Colony later to be known as the Great Trek had recently started, and early in 1837 Mzilikazi and the amaNdebele living beyond the Vaal River, who were long-standing enemies of the Griquas, had been routed by Trekkers whom they had attempted to attack. By March 1837 Abraham Kok was planning to take advantage of their disarray by launching another raid on them with his uncle, Cornelius Kok II of Campbell, his father's old ally, Barend Barends, and the Kora leader Jan Bloem Jr; the raid duly took place the following winter, but much had changed over the preceding decade, and Abraham found his expedition violently opposed by a notable section of his own people.

This was a period of intense activity in and around Philippolis, with a great deal of plotting and counterplotting involving not only the various groups in the Captaincy but also the LMS missionaries at Griquatown and Kuruman, between whom there was considerable rancour and rivalry. In March 1837, Kolbe had been driven from Philippolis on charges of adultery, after a protracted campaign in which Hendrickze had taken a leading part. Kolbe's colleague Theophilus Atkinson, and Peter Wright of Griquatown had, however, also been extremely active in the prosecution of their fellow missionary, and his affairs became inextricably entangled with those of the Captaincy: Wright alleged that Kolbe "has done his utmost to prevent a union of the two Griqua Chiefs and the treaty with the Colony",[313] and declared that the Chief of Philippolis rendered himself unworthy of further confidence or notice owing to the influence which Mr Kolbe exercised over him. Mr K. induced him to break his engagements and to quit the station, and he joined himself to a [*sic*] banditti in the neighbourhood. Kok then in open violation of his engagements sent out a commando against the people of Masilikatse to steal cattle, and which we are informed was executed with dreadful carnage.[314]

Wright further claimed that Robert Moffat at Kuruman had supported Abraham Kok, while the missionaries at Kuruman in turn accused Wright of being responsible for Abraham's downfall.[315]

Subsequent developments were described in a letter written by Atkinson to Dr Philip which naturally reflects his personal antagonism to both Abraham Kok and to Kolbe.

On my arrival here[316] I found the government in the hands of Abraham Kok (the eldest surviving son of Adam Kok, the former Chief). He remained here till July last [*1837*], though most of his time was spent at one of his farms, and he never attended much to the affairs of his government. In July he went to pay a visit to Mr Kolbe, who was then staying at Mr Pellissier's station [*Bethulie*], and from that time he never came to reside at Philippolis again. He had shortly before this abandoned his former intention of entering into a treaty with the Colonial Government, and had come to the resolution of going on a commando against Mosalekatsi. I endeavoured, as a friend, to dissuade him from the latter and to remove his objections to the former, offering to explain what he professed not to understand in the proposed treaty. The Civil Commissioner of Colesberg[317] had likewise kindly offered to come over and explain the matter still further to him. But this was declined, and all that I could say was without effect.

Soon after his return from the visit just mentioned, and while he was still in this neighbourhood, Mr Kolbe paid him a visit, and a letter was written to the Lieutenant-Governor, stating that he was sorry that his people persisted against his will in going against Mosalekatsi (though he had signed an order for them to go), that he was now perfectly ready to enter into a treaty with the Colonial Government and wished Mr K. to be appointed Colonial Agent. I cannot say whether any reply was ever received to this letter, but there was a strong and determined feeling on the part of the Council here against the appointment in question, which was communicated to the Lieutenant-Governor.

A short time after this Abraham Kok removed to a considerable distance. Several letters and messages were sent to him from the Council to enquire what were his intentions, but no notice was taken of them. He declared, however, that he had done with Philippolis, and should never come to live here again.[318]

After the withdrawal of Abraham Kok from Philippolis, Barend Lucas was elected or appointed Kaptyn in September 1837, and it is significant of the developments within the Captaincy that he had been one of the Bergenaars who had placed themselves under the authority of Adam Kok II in 1825, but had since become a member of the Griqua Raad. This was, however, probably looked on as no more than an interim arrangement, and late in 1837,[319] in spite of the opposition of the Raad, the community at Philippolis determined to elect a younger brother of Abraham Kok, who duly became Kaptyn as Adam Kok III. It is possible that advantage was taken of the absence of Abraham Kok's supporters and the Bergenaar faction to engineer this development, but it is significant that the election of Adam Kok enjoyed the support of Hendrickze.

A highly critical view of these developments was given by the French missionary J.J. Pellissier of Bethulie, who was not only well disposed towards Kolbe, but anxious to preserve the territory of his own station from encroachment by the Griquas. "Two sons survived him," he wrote concerning Adam Kok II. "The elder was chosen by a majority of votes to be his father's successor. But the younger, an ambitious person, had expected to be appointed Captain in preference to his brother. When he saw that this was not to happen, he quickly formed his own party with the purpose of deposing the legal Chief and taking his place. In this he succeeded, and in his present attempts to increase his power, he spares the rights of none."[320] Peter Wright, however, wrote in March 1838, in a letter to Dr Philip concerning the proposed treaty with the Cape Colony:

A younger brother of the Chief named Adam Kok, a man of good principle and talent, disgusted with and ashamed of the conduct of his brother, took upon himself to care for the honor and interests of the district,³²¹ and to endeavour to restore order. By a large majority of the people Adam is called to the government of the district, and Waterboer has determined to support him and enter into a treaty with him.

Since Adam was chosen Chief, the ex-Chief and his banditti have committed depredations in the district, and a skirmish between the parties has taken place. Mr Atkinson informs me that it is well known that Kolbe is the instigator of the whole, that he is doing his best to strengthen the interests of the ex-Chief, in order if possible to have Mr A. driven away from Philippolis and himself placed there again.³²²

As mentioned by Wright, Abraham Kok attempted to reassert his authority in the traditional Bergenaar fashion by raiding the Philippolis outposts with the support of his uncle, Cornelius Kok II of Campbell, Jan Bloem and an indiscriminate following; Atkinson wrote that "the impossible characters by whom he is surrounded urged him on to greater lengths than those to which he might have gone of himself".³²³

The brief Griqua civil war of 1838 does not seem to have been documented fully, but an outline of events may be obtained from the journal kept during this period by Wright at Griquatown.³²⁴ On 12 May, according to this source, Andries Waterboer and his Raad, who were preparing to go to the assistance of Adam Kok, received the news that Cornelius had tried to attack Philippolis but had been "routed and put to flight", and had sent "to fetch the families of Abraham Kok and Adam Kok from Lower Campbell, because they feared that in case of [Cornelius] Kok hastening back to Campbell with his party and be[ing] pursued by the Philippolis people, these families might be involved in confusion." The men of the Griquatown Captaincy were called up, and as Jan Bloem's Korana were threatening to attack Griquatown if Waterboer were to go to Adam Kok's assistance, many people living at outlying fountains fled to the settlement for safety. No attack materialised, however, and at the request of Adam Kok, Waterboer departed at the end of the month for Philippolis with a bodyguard of 50 men to confer with him and his

Raad, discovering on his arrival "that every preperation [*sic*] had been made by them to proceed to the rendezvous of Cornelis and Abraham Kok to take them prisoners and in case they refused to give themselves up to destroy them on the spot".

On 5 June a Joint Council of the Philippolis and Griquatown Captaincies was held at Philippolis, at which it was decided that Waterboer would attempt to act as mediator between Adam and Abraham Kok. Having succeeded in making contact with Abraham Kok five days later, as Wright recorded grandly but rather vaguely:

> The Chief settled all matters between the two brothers, but did not allow them to see each other on the occasion. It is finally settled that Adam is the Chief of Philippolis and Abraham is left to choose under what Chief he will live. The Coranas and a few other wretched characters who had given support to Abraham's cause were ordered to disperse, which they promised to do. Kornelis Kok never showed his face, he remained in his *schans*, never leaving his gun which is now all his confidence, and the Chiefs left him there without noticeing [*sic*] him for the present.

As Waterboer's missionary at Griquatown and the particular confidant of Dr Philip, it was obviously Wright's intention to establish Waterboer as the senior partner in the Griqua confederacy and to assert his authority over Cornelius Kok at Campbell, in accordance with the plan for the "northern part of the Colony" proposed by Philip a few years earlier;[325] if allowances are made for this bias, however, his account is probably correct enough.

After this Abraham Kok seems to have disappeared from view, while Cornelius II, according to the available accounts, was nominally deprived of his Captaincy. His brother Abraham (presumably to be distinguished from the former Kaptyn) later stated,

> that this appointment of my brother Cornelius Kok was on the occasion of the assembling of the united Council of the Philippolis and Griqua Town Governments held at Philippolis in the year 1838, annulled and cancelled. I was present at Philippolis when my brother Cornelius Kok was dismissed at Philippolis, and I have never since

that time heard that he was reinstated in the post or appointment as before 1838. My brother Cornelius Kok of Campbell was himself present on the occasion in 1838 at Philippolis when his post was personally taken from him and cancelled.[326]

This too reflects a bias in favour of the authority of the Griquatown Captaincy, but most likely it is accurate in recording the fact that Cornelius was subsequently put on trial before the Joint Griqua Council.

As regards the Philippolis Captaincy, Adam Kok III was clearly the choice of the people as his father's successor, a fact which seems to have been obvious already at the time of Andrew Smith's visit in 1834, for the latter noted in his diary:

> The body of the people are desirous that Adam, the second son, shall succeed, and the feeling is so well understood that it is universally considered that he is to be the person. He has not yet agreed to assume it, and upon my questioning him on the subject he observed that it was no easy matter to accept, and that it required the most serious consideration. He is described by Mr Kolbe as a firm, determined person, and Mr K. says during the short time he governed for his father when he was absent at the Kat River effected more good than had been done for years before. He administered justice more rigidly, and even went in opposition to his own relations.[327]

In a letter to D'Urban, Smith elaborated on this, adding: "A powerful reason why the people wish to have Adam for the successor is that he can read and write, so that their Chief, they say, will not have to employ Hendrick [Hendrickze] to do it (...)." "His appearance is much in his favour," Smith further informed the Governor. "He is a good-natured, amiable-looking young man, and notorious for his honesty and decision";[328] though in his diary he displayed some reservations, writing: "He is a sensible looking man of about 24 years of age, rather taciturn and diffident. He does not mingle much with the people."[329] Dr Philip, attempting to promote Adam over his elder brother Abraham, described him about the same time as "an intelligent young man, who could read and write, was sober in his habits, and regarded by all the good people in the country as a man of sound judgment and good principles".³³⁰

Backhouse in 1839 depicted Kok as "a young-looking man of plain features and middle size; he was dressed in a drab, duffle jacket, bound and buttoned with black, and trousers that were the worse for wear";³³¹ William Dower, minister to the Griquas at Kokstad during the last years of Kok's life, described him as

> a short, stout, pock-marked man. He was not good-looking, but he was shrewd, intelligent, kindly and hospitable. For a man who had read little and had never been out of the country, so that he might learn from sight what he did not learn from books, he had really a wonderful knowledge of the world and its affairs.³³²

Adam Kok III pursued the policy of co-operation with the Cape Colony already laid down, and on 9 November 1838 a new treaty was concluded with Waterboer, which differed from the first mainly in that a Joint Council was provided to act as Supreme Court for both Captaincies, the previous treaty having called upon the assistance of the Cape courts for this purpose; the change was apparently made on the advice of the Colonial authorities.³³³

In the meantime problems with white intruders in Griqua territory had increased steadily throughout the 1830s. By 1840 the farmers settled in the Riet River area under the nominal leadership of M.A. Oberholster, a former field-cornet in the Colesberg district,³³⁴ were powerful enough to obtain from the Griqua Kaptyns of Philippolis and Griquatown documents which they themselves opportunistically called "treaties", a term which has been adopted by later historians; in fact these seem to have amounted to no more than a formal acknowledgement of the rights and privileges claimed by the whites.³³⁵ While these settlers still recognised the authority of the Cape Government, however, discontented white emigrants from the Colony were at the same time beginning to establish themselves in the area beyond the Vet River, further to the north-east, where the village of Winburg was already in existence by 1842. These people had contacts with like-minded white groups at Potchefstroom beyond the Vaal and the recently established Trekker Republic in Natal, which were all loosely united in what was termed the *Maatschappij*, and their ranks were significantly strengthened after the British occupation of

Natal in May 1842. Large numbers of aggrieved and militant republican-minded Boers then returned to the Highveld, where they became a serious threat both to the loyalist white farmers along the Riet River and the Griquas of Philippolis.

This was the situation Dr Philip encountered when, during the first half of 1842, he paid his third visit to the interior, stopping at Philippolis on his way to Griquatown in March and returning in May, and it necessitated a drastic change in his plans. Discovering that Gottlob Schreiner, the then missionary at Philippolis, had antagonised Adam Kok and a large section of the people by his headstrong and tactless behaviour, Philip had him summarily removed from the station,[336] and Peter Wright, Philip's confidant of the preceding seventeen years, was transferred here from Griquatown. With the large-scale settlement of white immigrants on the Highveld and beyond, this area was to become the centre of future developments in the interior of southern Africa rather than the old "missionary road" through Griquatown and Kuruman: the transfer of Wright to Philippolis is a clear sign that Philip realised the fact, and that Philippolis and not Griquatown would henceforth form the focal point of his policy for the Northern Frontier. Schreiner himself wrote at the time that Philip on dismissing him had stated that this was done "not from any supposed unfitness (...), but my being German and not acquainted with the niceties of the English language, which might make me unfit to do much for the people in *political* affairs",[337] while Wright informed the LMS at the same time,

> You are aware of the importance of this mission not only from the superior numbers attached to it, but from its relative position, and that its destruction would involve the missions and tribes to the northward in serious difficulties, and that a strenuous effort is required which by a blessing may avert such a calamity.[338]

In August of that year Oberholster and his followers, alarmed at the activities of the republicans, sent a petition with 380 signatures to the Cape Government requesting its protection, accompanied by a copy of the Griqua "treaty" and details of 99 farms leased to them by Griquas,[339] and it must have been at this time that Philip composed the statement entitled "The tenure by which the Griquas hold the lands of Philippolis" which has already been quoted.[340] It was an attempt on his part both to safeguard the rights of the Griquas in the Transgariep and to assert the paramount authority of the LMS over the Captaincy.

It was the threat of violence on the part of the Republicans in the Transgariep, the "calamity" referred to by Wright, which finally forced the British authorities to act. Over the new year of 1842–43 discussions with the new Lieutenant-Governor, Col. John Hare, took place at Colesberg, in which Adam Kok, Hendrickze, Peter Wright and Oberholster participated, and at the end of 1843 the long-awaited treaty between the Captaincy and the Cape Colony was finally concluded: it was signed by Sir George Napier on 5 October, and by Adam Kok on 29 November.[341]

For some months Peter Wright was able to guide these developments, but he did not live to see the treaty, for he died suddenly at Philippolis on 14 April 1843 of typhus, and his death at this particular stage in the affairs of the Captaincy was regarded by the Griquas and their sympathisers as a major calamity.[342]

"On the Thursday when my dear partner grew worse," his widow, Margery Wright, later wrote to the LMS,

> the deacons assembled the people together in the church purposely to pray for their dear pastor's recovery. Some of the old members came and knelt at his bedside, and prayed earnestly that the Lord would not remove from them their kind shepherd, who cared for all their interests and who watched over them with fatherly kindness. The last two days of his life were days of weeping and lamentation among the people: they all attended his funeral and wept bitterly over his grave; the service was conducted by one of the deacons, who has taken a deep interest in all our concerns. The other deacon[s?],[343] with the Chief and his principal men, have done all in their power to comfort us.
>
> The first Sabbath after Mr W.'s death the place of worship was a place of mourning; the speakers could not be heard for weeping— they had to stop and mingle their tears with the people. We have had three congregations every Sabbath morning, the chapel being far too small for the Griqua population. When it was filled, the rest were assembled under the trees and addressed by a native.[344]

Wright was buried at Philippolis, and the congregations of Philippolis and Griquatown contributed to the erection of a gravestone which may still be seen in the local cemetery. The elaborate inscription in Dutch reads in part (translated):

> The last 17 years of his life were spent among the Griqua nation, where his labours were blessed to the establishment of peace in the affairs of the country and to the prosperity of the Church of Christ. He ended his days in the execution of a weighty task in the district of Philippolis, where he was the means of enlivening the temporal and spiritual prosperity of the country. He was endowed by the Head of the Church with great meekness, zeal and valour.

James Read Sr of the Kat River, pioneer LMS missionary in South Africa and champion of the Khoikhoi, described Wright's death as "the heaviest stroke in missionary work that has ever been inflicted in Africa",[345] and as no successor with his knowledge or experience was to be found, the involvement of the LMS in Griqua affairs was unavoidably weakened. With his death an era in the history of the Philippolis Captaincy may be said to have come to an end, and after this the Griquas were thrown largely onto their own resources.

1. The *mat hut*, breipaal *and wagon of Adam Kok II, as sketched by the traveller William Burchell during his visit to Klaarwater (Griquatown) in 1811.*

2. *"Griqua huts at Aarnhaan—near Kuruman, 1835", the first of ten water-colour sketches reproduced here by the artist Charles Bell, who accompanied the expedition of Dr Andrew Smith into the interior, travelling through Griqua territory in 1834–35. The houses have been constructed of reeds; the woman to the right, a baby on her back, is stamping corn.*

3. *"Griqua family at home,—1834", judging by the date, a sketch made in the Philippolis area. The women and children are in traditional dress or undress, while the man crouched in the opening of the mat hut is wearing western clothes, a distinction often remarked on by visitors. At the back is a boy on a riding ox.*

4. *"Griqua belles, 1834": women in traditional karosses cooking in an iron pot of western manufacture. The facetious caption was provided by the artist.*

5. *"Griquas on riding oxen—1834."*

6. *"Old David Hendriks—a Chief the Bergenaar robbers about 1830 to 1833. (...) Having ceased to be a light and active horseman, he used a tame riding ox, and it was a remarkable thing to see him mount after this portrait was sketched in 1834."* Hendriks was one of a small independent group of Griquas originally living under Barend Barends at Boetsap across the Vaal who had moved to the Caledon River the previous year, where they settled at Lishuani.

7. *"Philippolis—Capital of Griqualand, 1834"*. The view of the settlement is to the north, along what is now Voortrekker Street, towards the gabled church building. The houses are presumably those built by the Basters who settled around the missionary assistant Jan Goeyman when he began work here in 1822.

8. *"Congregation of Mr Kolb at Philippolis—1834"*. The interior of the church depicted by Bell in the sketch above, with the missionary G.A. Kolbe in the pulpit on the left. The man seated below him to the left is presumably an interpreter.

9. *Kaptyn Adam Kok II, a water-colour portrait by the artist G.H. Ford who accompanied the expedition of Andrew Smith as a draughtsman.*

10. *"Vark Fontein—Griqua cattle farm near Philippolis, 1834"*, where Andrew Smith's party stopped on 28 December, on their way to Campbell. In his diary Smith described the farm, which is situated to the south-west of the modern Fauresmith, as *"the place of a Griqua family with abundance of cattle and a large flock of sheep. They have an immense supply of milk and furnished us with that in great abundance. Spring which furnishes water moderately strong and differs but little throughout the year."*

11. *"Encampment of the Griqua Chief Adam Kok in the Riet Moder [sic] River, Jany. 3, 1835"*, a sketch made on the Riet River while Smith and his party were on their way to Campbell, accompanied by Adam Kok. The vehicles shown include the Kaptyn's own *"light waggon drawn by eight horses"*, whose driver was described by Smith as an *"expert whip"*, and two wagons in which Kok's wife and a number of his relatives were returning from a visit. The sketch apparently shows the Government Secretary, Hendrik Hendrickze, reading to the assembly from newspapers received from the Cape.

12. *"Hendrik Hendriks—brother of David and Andries Hendriks the Bergenaars—son in law of Adam Kok (the Chief) and the able Secretary to the Government of Griqualand—presented with a worn out pair of Wellingtons and sketched while grateful—1834."*
A portrait of Hendrik Hendrickze, one of the most gifted and remarkable men of his day.

13. *Panoramic view of Philippolis from the south-west, by James Backhouse who visited the village in the winter of 1839, with the church partially visible behind the little hill on the extreme left.*

14. G.A. Kolbe, missionary at Philippolis from 1831 to 1837.

15. Dr John Philip, Superintendent of the LMS during the period 1819–49.

16. A view of Philippolis by the French missionary Franz Maeder, ca. 1840, looking northwards along the village street towards the church.

17. Gottlob Screiner, who worked at Philippolis in 1838–42.

18. Theophilus Atkinson, stationed at Philippolis in 1836–40.

19. Peter Wright, formerly of Griquatown, who was transferred to Philippolis in 1842 and died there the following year.

20. *The first of seven photographs from the album of W.B. Philip, who was stationed at Philippolis as minister of the Congregational Church from 1857 to 1861. It shows the same view as that previously depicted by Bell and Maeder (see nos. 7 and 16 above), but the church has meanwhile lost its gable.*

21. *"Parsonage (former mission house)", a typical thatched house of the time. It is also visible on the extreme left of the preceding photograph, and seems to have been on the western side of the main street, close to the church.*

22. *A panoramic view of the village from the hill to the north-east, with the T-shaped church in the foreground to the right and the spruit visible as a diagonal line on the near side of it. The white ridge of the parsonage roof may been seen immediately to the right of the centre of the photograph.*

23. *W.B. Philip with his household. He was a son of John Philip of the LMS.*

24. Group of four unidentified men from Philip's photograph album.

25. Members of the Griqua exploratory expedition (Kommissietrek) to Nomansland in 1860; the original of this photograph has not been traced, and it has been reproduced from a reproduction of poor quality. The men, from left to right, are: Abraham le Fleur, father of the future Griqua leader A.A.S. le Fleur; Adam Muis Kok, a relative of the Kaptyn; Johannes Ulbricht, a son of the German missionary J.G. Ulbricht by his Khoi wife; Frederick Werner; Jan de Bruin, a member of a prominent local family; and Dirk Swartz.

26. *Kaptyn Adam Kok III, a final photograph from the Philip album. Note his embroidered waistcoat, watch chain and staff of office.*

27. One half of a stereographic view of Fauresmith taken in 1861, the year in which the Griqua exodus from Philippolis began. The village had been established by the Boers on the farm Sannaspoort in Griqua territory in 1849 in spite of the protests of the Kaptyn.

28. The main street of Philippolis from the hill near the church, looking south-east; the photograph was taken in 1863, after the village had been incorporated into the Free State; the building in the foreground appears to be the former parsonage (see no.22 above). By this time the thatch of the pioneer period was being replaced by flat roofs, as shown by the neighbouring houses, and these were in turn to become equally typical of the second half of the century.

4. The people of the Captaincy

In April 1827 John Melvill, newly arrived at Philippolis as a missionary, noted in his journal: "The whole population of the country subject to A. Kok amounts to about 60 Griquas and Old Inhabitants together,[346] 150 Bechuannas, 30 Corrannas, and about 30 families of the plundered tribes called Basootoos, making the whole, men, women and children, about 1150";[347] four years later he stated that the population of the "outposts" consisted of 868 Griquas and 840 "Bechuanas", the total amounting to 1860 people.[348] In 1833, Captain Armstrong, concentrating on the number of men capable of bearing arms, gave the estimate, "Griquas and Bastards, about equal strength and amounting altogether to 600 men armed with muskets. (...) There may be from 2 to 300 old men and boys also armed with muskets who must remain at home in charge of the farms &c."[349]

In 1845 Adam Kok III could write to the Colonial Secretary of the Cape:

> My subjects are not all of one tribe, and consist of Grikwas, Bechuanas and Bushmen. Of these the lastmentioned were the original possessors of the country, and the Bechuanas consist chiefly of such persons as sought refuge amongst us from the wars of the interior. Some are, however, the subjects of Moshesh, and are subject to my laws only as long as they reside in my country.[350] There are also some Korannas living in my territory under a subordinate Chief named Piet Witvoet.[351] None of the other tribes are under a subordinate Chief, but live immediately under my rule. The people under my rule amount in number to about six thousand, of whom rather more than three thousand are Grikwas, and the remainder consists of the tribes mentioned above.[352]

In the given circumstances, these figures are not likely to have been more than approximations, but they serve at least to indicate how small the population of the Philippolis Captaincy was and how mixed its origins. This continued to be the case, and in 1879 an official report into conditions among the people who had by that time removed to Kokstad could declare: "The term 'Griqua' in its widest sense embraces Griquas, 'apprentices',[353] Hottentots, Korannas, Namaquas, Bushmen, Barolongs, Basutos and Damaras, all more or less intermixed."[354]

Bushman resistance to Griqua settlement was gradually broken during the 1830s under the force of the incessant persecution they suffered at the hands of all other groups in the territory, which may be succinctly and graphically illustrated by the reminiscence of the ex-Bergenaar Jan Pienaar: "Bushmen inhabited the country about Philippolis. We exterminated them, and Dr Philip gave [us?] the country. We exterminated the Bushmen and Korannas between the Harts and Vaal Rivers, and occupied the country."[355] In 1833 the LMS moreover abandoned the work it had been doing among them somewhat sporadically for 34 years, and the mission at Bushman School was handed over to the Paris Missionary Society and became a station for Tlhaping refugees under the name Bethulie. By 1843 the Bushman Captain Piet Kraankuil could declare formally, albeit at the not disinterested instigation of the Boers: "Previous to the arrival of the Bastards in our land, there were more Bushmen residing in it than there are now Bastards; there are now only two kraals left of Bushmen, containing an inconsiderable number of inhabitants."[356] The status to which they had been reduced in the Philippolis territory is indicated by Kraankuil's declaration, "The reason of my now being in the Colony and working for my food is because the Bastards took away all our cattle and murdered our people."[357]

The lot of the odd handful of Bushmen who still managed to maintain a semi-independent state is vividly illustrated by the case of the three men who were tried by the Combined Griqua Court at Ramah in November 1848 for the murder of a Boer named Karel Kotze or Coetzee: as the matter was formally brought to the attention of the Kaptyn by the British Resident by that time established at Bloemfontein, it was reported extensively in the Colonial press.

The accused in this case were the brothers Old Jacob and Swartbooi, together with Vigilant, who was the son of one of them, and they belonged to a group of whom nine—four men and five women—are identified, all by Dutch names. "My father and brother and the other man stole the cattle, slaughtered them and carried the meat to the mountain," said Windvogel, who was called as a witness. "There were six of us together. When we saw the Boers coming, they sent me to tell the women of the approach of the Boers. I went and told the women, and remained with them." The pursuers were fired on with arrows, and Coetzee was shot "about the kidneys" at a distance of some 100 yards. "I shot because G.C. and Jochen had shot my brother dead after the battle of Touw Fontein,"[358] declared Old Jacob. "G.C. beheaded my brother and threw the head into the water and burnt the body. I was with my brother when G.C. shot him, and when he fell, I fled to the mountain. When the Boers were gone, I returned to the spot where my brother was shot. The body was then burning, and the head lying in the water." Of Swartbooi it is stated in the report of the case, "The prisoner pleads guilty, but craves mercy, as the many grievances which the Boers have occasioned him from time to time, in addition to the murder of his brother, induced him to take such a step against the Boers."[359]

The Bushmen who survived in the Transgariep did so as individuals or small family groups, often as hangers-on on the mission stations in the area or in the service of Griquas or whites, and it is significant that the hunting expedition of Adam Krotz of Philippolis and other Griquas, with whom the French missionaries travelled to the Caledon River valley in 1833, was accompanied by "quite a small army of half-naked Bushmen, who were to look after the draught oxen, saddle the horses, and follow their masters in hunting, carrying the heavy guns".[360] The "Law on Bushmen" promulgated by Adam Kok III in 1846 referred exclusively to thefts committed by "Bushmen who from time to time have deserted from the service of Boers and other inhabitants of my territory".[361]

The Korana raiders who had initially been such a serious threat to the peace of the Transgariep in general and the Griqua Captaincy in particular, disappeared from the scene during the 1830s, most likely as they were increasingly confronted by armed and mounted Griquas and whites who constituted more dangerous opponents than indigenous people with traditional weapons. Kora pastoralists, mainly of the Regshande tribe, were congregated largely along the Riet River in the vicinity of Bethanie—the Buffelboud family was especially prominent—and for some time they also formed a sizeable group at Philippolis itself: Gebel attending an afternoon service in the church there in 1835 "heard the Hottentot language for the first time, when Kolbe preached on the text 'One thing is needful' in Dutch, while the abovementioned Henrik [Hendrickze] translated it for the Korannas who were present".[362] None of the Kora groups was very large, however, and there never could have been great numbers of Korana in the Captaincy. Armstrong in 1833 estimated the total number of able-bodied men under Piet Witvoet and one "Class" or Klaas as 350,[363] adding, "Piet Whitefoot may have about 200 inferior Corannas as servants, herds, &c."[364]

"The Coranna tribes (not connected with this banditti) which I visited had very few articles of British manufacture among them," wrote Dr Philip after his meeting with Abraham Kruger's raiders in 1825, "and they were without the means of obtaining them. They were generally clothed in the sheepskin kaross, and after the ancient manner of the Hottentots."[365] In 1834, however, Andrew Smith, returning from Thaba Nchu, wrote of Korana he encountered near the Modder River, "Some were dressed in leathern trousers and jackets; one or two had cloth jackets; most of them had hats and a number had carosses; some simply had a small piece of skin hanging in front not sufficient to conceal the organs of generation",[366] and his companion, A.G. Bain, noted of the kraals he visited on the Vaal, "The kaross among them appeared to have given way to leather jackets and trousers, and some even enjoyed the luxury of a shirt, but which is never washed from the time it is put on till worn out."[367] "In dress they ape the European costume," wrote Methuen ten years later, "wearing greasy, tattered leathern jackets and trowsers, with a caross frequently thrown over the whole."[368]

In 1834 some members of the Berlin Missionary Society established a mission to the Regshande under Piet Witvoet and Goliat Ysterbek (/ʔurikxʔamma) at Bethanie in the modern Reddersburg district, and on 28 December 1838 the missionary C.F. Wuras and twelve Korana visited Philippolis and the latter formally submitted to the authority of the Griquas.[369] After this they obtained a degree of self-government and made local regulations, but in 1846 they abandoned Bethanie and wandered off in the direction of the Vaal River, ceasing to play any further role in the affairs of the Captaincy; during the 1850s they began to lose their tribal cohesion and identity, and such individuals as survived gradually disappeared among the local population. The Lucas or Lukas family, whose name often occurs in the annals of the Captaincy, would seem to have been the descendants, at least in part, of Klaas Lukas, Captain of the Kora tribe known as the Katte,[370] while the Oersons were descended from Oerson or Ursob, brother of Gert Links of the Linkshande (Left Hand Korana).[371] In spite of some superficial westernisation through their contact with the Griquas, the Bergenaars and the missionaries, however, the Korana seem for the greater part to have preferred their traditional existence, and were specifically not inclined to change their nomadic style of life.

Tswana and Sotho refugees formed a much more significant part of the population of the Captaincy: their origins were, on the whole, probably similar to those of the "Bechuana families" Melvill found forming part of the kraal or *werf* of Piet Sabba in 1827, of whom he wrote in a passage reflecting the current confusion that they were "mostly of the Bashootoo tribe who were plundered by the Bergenaars. From the accounts given by these people they were driven from their native country by a tribe of Caffres whom they call Matabeele, which is probably the Tambookies.[372] After this they were attacked and entirely impoverished by the Bergenaars, whom they followed into this country. Many hundreds have since found their way into parts of the Colony."[373]

The refugees of Sotho origin largely returned to the Caledon River area as stability was restored there under Moshweshwe during the 1830s, but a considerable Tswana population remained at Philippolis and scattered elsewhere about the Captaincy. A number of them also settled at Bethulie and Bethanie, which had originally been established for the Bushmen and the Korana respectively: at all three stations the missionaries soon discovered them to be a promising field of labour, and were delighted with their industry. In 1839 Gottlob Schreiner could write from Philippolis, "The Bechuanas are a peculiar source of joy and encouragement to us, the Lord is indeed showering upon this poor people the rich blessing of His grace."[374] "Since the Bechuanas have been living here," wrote the missionary Wuras from Bethanie in 1848, "the gardens have been enlarged, so that it is a true joy to me to see them when I return to Bethanie",[375] while Inspector Schultheiss reported about the same time, "Now the lovely waters of Bethanie no longer run away unused, as the Bechuana settlers have laid out large gardens. The outside fountains too are being used for agriculture more and more, so that there will soon be no more arable ground (…)."[376]

While their numbers were sizeable and they formed an increasingly important element in the mission, the Sotho and Tswana inhabitants of the Captaincy took no active part in its affairs. One of the very few who achieved local prominence was a Motswana baptised in Cape Town under the name Richard Miles, in honour of Dr Philip's deputy, who accompanied the German missionaries back to the interior in 1835 as an interpreter, but subsequently broke with the mission, acting as the agent of various indigenous leaders—Goliath Ysterbek, Kausob Kausobson, Jan Bloem Jr and Lephoi —as well as the remaining Korana of Bethanie in their final struggle to maintain themselves there; he is known to have owned a number of farms, and was later sometimes addressed by the title "Kaptyn".[377] A similar exception was Jan Julie, a Mosotho who rose to prominence at Philippolis in the 1850s as the protégé of Adam Kok, and whose name appears as a donor of 7s 6d to the Auxiliary Mission Society in 1853; he and his father accompanied the Griquas on their trek to Kokstad, where he seems to have become a field-cornet and "Jan Julie" and "Victoria Julie" were listed as erf- or landholders.[378]

The presence of these various groups in the Griqua Captaincy must be noted, but this work will concentrate on the Griqua and Baster section of the population who, in spite of their divisions, may be said, together with the Bergenaar element, to have formed the "ruling party".

In the terminology of the times the names "Hottentots", "Bastards" and "Griquas" were used loosely and interchangeably. While it might often prove impossible to classify a given individual according to these categories, "Hottentots" properly speaking should be used for the detribalised descendants of pastoral Khoi tribes of the Cape Colony who were increasingly being drawn into the western economy as farm labourers or inhabitants of the mission stations. "Basters" properly refers to people descended from the union of Khoikhoi and whites, who according to Arbousset also described themselves as "Binnelanders",[379] and "Griquas" to such of the Basters as specifically recognised the authority of one of the Griqua Kaptyns. Another common term in the early nineteenth century was "Baster-Hottentots", referring to descendants of Khoikhoi and slaves, with no admixture of white blood; "Oorlams" was sometimes employed loosely for any of these people who had attained some degree of westernisation in their dress and habits, but it merely indicates a degree of acculturation and will not be used in the present work.

The Baster population of the Philippolis Captaincy originated in the group of Christian families from Bethelsdorp who in 1815 accompanied the missionary James Read to the interior, as already mentioned,[380] with subsequent additions: strictly speaking this group was probably made up largely of Christian Khoikhoi and "Baster-Hottentots", rather than "Basters" in the technical sense as defined above. Writing in 1827 of the "Old Inhabitants" resident around the mission station at Philippolis, Melvill could define them as

> five or six families of Colonial Hottentots who belonged to the Bushmen mission, and eight or nine families from the Colony who were allowed to settle here while Jan Goeyman had the management of the station. Some of these came from Bethelsdorp; only part of these persons have regular passes to come beyond the boundary of the Colony.[381]

Regular later additions to their number came from Bethelsdorp and other LMS stations in the Eastern Cape, and from the former Zak River congregation of the missionary Kicherer now living in the Graaff-Reinet area, and they were welcomed by the missionaries as swelling the ranks of church members and mission supporters. John Clark wrote somewhat opportunistically from Philippolis in February 1827, probably to Andries Stockenstrom, that

> we are but few in number here, and that should the Government allow from time to time a few Hottentots of good character (who might be willing) and [to] settle here under the Governmint [sic] of Adam Kok, I have no doubt but that he would be willing (with them and the necessary means) to engage to render every assistance in his power for the defence of the boundary for a considerable distance to the north and south of this.[382]

Still later settlers came from the coloured settlement at Kat River, which was established in 1829, and from the Roggeveld. "[The road] which leads from the Roggeveld is sufficiently beaten, if seen by daylight, to guide a stranger to Klaarwater," Burchell had remarked as early as 1812,[383] and migration to the Transorange increased over the next few decades, as

Baster stock farmers were gradually pushed out of the area by whites. Andrew Smith in 1834 noted the presence of a "Bastard from the Roggeveldt" with 200 goats at Bossiespruit in the Transgariep, which he had bought from Hendrik Hendrickze,[384] and the Wesleyan missionary James Cameron at Thaba Nchu recorded in his diary the regular traffic between the Roggeveld and the Transgariep in 1842.[385] Through its Baster element, the Philippolis Captaincy acquired and preserved regular contact with Bethelsdorp and the Colony, and specifically with James Read Sr and Jr, who both worked at Kat River and who were known as champions of the Khoikhoi. At the same time, however, the Basters were said not to be well-disposed to the Colony or the Colonial authorities, and in 1836 the French missionaries Arbousset and Daumas described them in general as cherishing "inveterate hatred towards the Colonists",[386] which further complicated the already complex internal politics of the Captaincy.

When Van der Kemp had established the mission at Bethelsdorp in 1803, he had still found it necessary to compile a Khoi catechism,[387] but the process of westernisation among the Colonial Khoikhoi seems to have been extremely rapid. The early missionaries were insistent on their converts wearing western clothes and building rectangular houses, and Dutch was the general language on all the LMS mission stations, even when the missionaries themselves were English speaking, as was often the case. The results of this process may be seen from the somewhat jaundiced description of the "Bastaard" given by Arbousset in connection with his visit to Platberg:

> During his leisure time, and of that he has abundance, he finds a pleasure in lounging about the house of his missionary, whither he goes—sometimes with, but oftener without an object. It is seldom, if he be a pious man, that he has not some spiritual malady of which to complain to his religious instructor: "Oh, how my peace is dried up! Oh, how cold my heart is!" Or he speaks of his debts and his loans, or oftener still of his horses and his cattle. And if at the moment the bell summon the worshippers to the sanctuary, thither also he goes most willingly; for all possess a respect for religion, and all are more or less acquainted with its doctrines and its duties, and some, though unhappily their number is limited, love and practise these.[388]

In spite of the unpromising impression they seem to have made on the French missionary, however, it was this group which provided the mission stations of the interior with preachers, catechists and teachers. Prominent examples in the early history of the Philippolis Captaincy were Jan Goeyman and Piet Sabba, both referred to already, or the "coloured woman brought up at Bethelsdorp" whom Backhouse found employed as an assistant in the school at Philippolis.[389] From this category of people the Captaincy also drew many of its officials, such as "Andries Wiese, a Bastard residing in the district of Graaff Reinet", who in 1831 received official permission to settle "under the Chief Adam Kok" at Griquatown (*sic*),[390] most probably the man Andrew Smith encountered as "Wyk master" at Philippolis three years later;[391] or Wenzel Heemro, baptised at Bethelsdorp in 1815 and still living there as late as 1836, who in 1847 was serving as Secretary to the Griquatown Raad and by 1850 in a similar capacity to the Raad at Philippolis, and who subsequently became member of the Raad at Kokstad.[392]

Especially worthy of mention in this regard is the Le Fleur family. Marthinus le Fleur, whose origins are unknown, was a member of the Griquatown church and related by marriage to the Krotzes, a Griqua group, with whom he settled at Ramah in 1863.[393] Of greater significance, however, is Abraham le Fleur, born at Uitenhage near Bethelsdorp in 1826, who was a member of the Griqua Commission trek to Nomansland in 1859, and whose son, A.A.S. le Fleur, was through marriage into the Kok family to become the ultimate successor of the Philippolis Kaptyns.[394]

There were, however, other groups of Basters living in the Transgariep than those within the boundaries of the Philippolis Captaincy, most notably those under Carolus Baatje who had in 1833 settled in the area near the Caledon River, in the present Ladybrand district, which they called "Nieuwland", where they became successful wheat farmers and where the Wesleyans established the station Platberg already mentioned above. This settlement suffered much in the intertribal warfare of the area, and by the beginning of 1853 Baatje was said to have no more than 100 followers.[395] Related to them was a smaller group at Jammerberg on the Caledon, near modern Wepener, in a region which during the 1850s, after the evacuation of Nieuwland, became known as "Baatjes" ("Batis").[396] These groups are of interest here because, unlike those in the Captaincy, they were always clearly distinguished as Basters and distinctly described as such. To them belonged, for example, the little group who settled on the French mission station Beersheba, near the present Smithfield, and were mentioned by Samuel Rolland as receiving instruction there in 1837: Witbooi, aged about 30, who received the baptismal name of Jacobus; Rachel, aged about 40, who had lived at Bethelsdorp under Van der Kemp and at Griquatown; and Frans Coetzee, who had accompanied the French missionary Casalis to the Colony in 1836 and received "extremely good impressions" at Bethelsdorp, together with his younger brother Piet, aged about 28, and their 18-year-old sister Fytjie (Sophia).[397] Rolland gives some details of their religious experiences, and a revealing account of a conversation on religious matters between Witbooi, Rachel and the Griqua David Jansen.[398]

Not always clearly distinguished from the Basters were the ex-slaves or "apprentices" who settled in the Captaincy. In 1834, Kolbe at Philippolis had reported that there were 100 slaves belonging to trekboers in the Transorange,[399] and Backhouse, visiting the Wesleyan mission of Imperani, on the fringes of the territory occupied by whites, in 1839, found there a number of slaves who had escaped from their Boer masters, "having been so oppressed that the man says he would rather die than return".[400] About the same time an escaped slave from the Colony, Frederik Opperman, attached himself to the missionaries at Bethanie, and his son Adam subsequently acquired land in the vicinity of the modern Koffiefontein and became a wealthy man with a considerable following.[401] In December 1834, however, slaves in the Cape Colony were emancipated and apprenticed to their former owners for a period of four years, after which they were fully free, and many of these people subsequently chose to remove from the Colony entirely. Curiously enough, however, it was not until the 1850s that references to the presence of "apprentices" in the Griqua Captaincy begin to occur, as though they had not made their presence felt until then. In 1851, the missionary Pellissier at Bethulie mentioned "some families of Bastards, Bushmen and freed slaves living at some distance" attending services in his church,[402] and in 1856 he referred to "my little congregation of liberated slaves", providing details on the life of one Antonie Potgieter.[403] By 1852 there were 54 "former slaves" at Bethanie, where they formed a third of the population on the station and were said "to feel themselves superior because of their active life to the easy-going Korannas".[404] Edward Solomon, formerly of

Philippolis, mentioned in a lecture on the native tribes of the interior that the original Griquas had been joined by "many people from the Colony, of both what are familiarly called Bastards and Apprentices, and the infusion of these classes among them has been productive of much good to the whole body",[405] and in 1854 the French missionary Prosper Lemue declared that Griqua territory was "occupied to a great extent by liberated slaves".[406] At Kokstad in the 1870s, William Dower found that the "*apprentices* or slave descendents [*sic*]"[407] were still to be distinguished as a group conscious of their own identity, while the Cape Government report of 1879 stated of Griqualand East, "The Apprentices, or descendants of slaves, have always been distinguished by their industry."[408]

As far as the Griqua population of the Transorange is concerned, the earliest followers of the Kok family came mainly from the Western Cape— the Berg River area at first, and later the Olifants River region and Namaqualand—and from a different kind of background, and they consisted of independent or semi-independent stock farmers who had moved into the Transorange with motives very different from those of the mission-orientated Basters. Preserved from undue missionary control by their nomadic way of life and their economic self-sufficiency, they had been able to resist undue pressure to become westernised, and seem to have adopted such elements of the European way of life as they considered appropriate and retained the Khoi customs that remained serviceable to them, to the general disapproval of European observers, as will appear from many of the accounts quoted here.

Gottlob Schreiner, in a letter to missionary friends in Switzerland in 1843, could write concerning Philippolis, "The predominant language there is Dutch, besides which one hears various dialects of the Hottentot or Bushman language spoken, in the last named of which the Word of God etc. have been translated for the old people,[409] but more common is the Sechuana language, without which the missionary is unable to achieve much."[410] The Griquas traditionally spoke Xiri, a Khoi language related to the languages of the Damara, Namaqua and Korana: when it is reported casually of Philippolis that "Hottentot" was to be heard there, and even in many specific references to "Korana", it may in fact well be Xiri which is intended, as when Atkinson wrote in 1838 of the Sunday evening service at Philippolis, "I have lately at the request of several persons who could not so well understand the Dutch had the sermon translated into the Hottentot language".[411] Writing about the Griquas he met at Ramah in 1844, Methuen stated that they "imitate the whites as far as possible, even in their clothing", and added: "their proper language is the peculiar clicking one of the Hottentots, Bushmen and Korannas, but most of them speak Dutch fluently."[412] Xiri survived for a remarkably long time without any formal or official encouragement, and the widow of Adam Kok III is stated to have spoken it by preference to her attendants during her final years at Kokstad in the 1870s;[413] a hundred years later it was said still to be known to older people in the Campbell district.[414]

Because of the strong Baster element in the Transorange, the Griquas were, however, to a considerable extent Dutch speaking: it was in Dutch that the missionaries of the LMS ministered to them, and as contacts with the outside world, and more specifically with whites, increased, so too did the use of Dutch among them. Developing as it did in the isolation of the interior, checked only to a limited degree by formal education, the Dutch of the Griquas underwent influences different from those of the whites, and became eventually "Griqua Afrikaans", a dialect with its own distinct character and idiom, as may be illustrated by two brief fragments recorded in the twentieth century. "Oens vra seetplek veer oens een oense keeners," said Klaas Kok, the 77-year-old grandson of Adam Kok III, at Griquatown; "noe ees oens soos vlieënde vouels, een selwers die Kaffers bevoeiel oens." "Oens ees maar van dieselfde bloedintrek," said one "Mieta", "want hy wat Daam Kook was, ees oens almal se grootoutjie. Lê hyse spôre dan nie aural van Piekeetberg toot hier by Selwerfontein en dauer by Griekwastad nie?"[415] Later Afrikaans writers seem invariably to have found the Griqua dialect quaint and amusing; but it is of course no more or less so than Afrikaans itself.

Insofar as information on members of the original Kok following in the Transorange is available to provide an illustration of their origins, Hendrik Hendrickze mentioned having migrated to the Transorange with the Griqua trek of the early 1800s,[416] while Tryn Isaac, whose brother David was killed by the Korana in the early years, testified later, "I was born not far from Cape Town, near Picquetberg, at the farm of one Willem Burgers, where my father, old David Isaac, lived",[417] and Jan Pienaar, a one-time resident of Philippolis, had been born at Kamiesberg,[418] as had Hendrik Klaas, who served as a driver to A.G. Bain in 1835.[419] Jacobus van Wyk declared many years later, "I was born in the Cape

Colony, in the district of Beaufort West, and while I was still a boy removed with my father to Griqualand, while old Adam Kok (commonly called Dam Kok) was the Chief. When Dam Kok left Griqua Town we went with him and settled down with him at Philippolis."[420]

In practice it would be hard to apply the technical distinction between Griqua and Baster consistently as a means of dividing the two main groups among the subjects of Adam Kok into tidy categories on the basis of origin. All of them were fairly recent arrivals from the Cape Colony and of mixed Khoi descent, and in pragmatic terms there was little or no difference between them. In actual fact the terms "Griqua" and "Baster" served as an indication of loyalties and interests, and in this sense the Griquas may be defined as those individuals who, on the whole, had preserved some degree of independence under the nominal authority of their Kaptyns, were not necessarily Christians, although many had been baptised, had clashed with the missionaries at Griquatown and rebelled against their control, and increasingly saw the need of establishing good relations with the Colony, on which they were dependent for arms and ammunition. The Basters, on the other hand, were generally linked with the LMS, and may be defined as Christians and supporters of the church and the missionaries; in addition, they felt some degree of antagonism towards the Cape Colony, where their experiences at the hands of the white population had been increasingly unhappy, and the fact that many of them were, according to Melvill, in the Transorange without Colonial passes may be seen as an indication of their feelings. It is in this generalised sense, based on common aims and interests rather than origins, that the terms "Griquas" and "Basters" will be used from now on in the present work to describe two distinct factions in the Captaincy, irrespective of the race or background of any of their individual members.

The impossibility of providing the clear-cut definitions beloved of later South African bureaucracy, and of correlating loyalties with ethnic origins in practice, even in the case of the comparatively well-defined groups in the Captaincy, may be gathered from Arbousset's description of the Basters at Platberg in the Caledon River valley in 1836:

> Those who are easy in their circumstances, and picque themselves on their civilisation, dress in European style; but many still wear the kaross, or cloak made of skins of the sheep or the jackall sewed

together. The same incongruity is seen in the structure of their houses; some build them of raw brick or of clay, on a plan which is simple, and not unhealthy, though very incommodious; but others content themselves with a narrow, low and smoky hut formed of mats, and into this the people and their household utensils are huddled together in the most disgusting confusion.[421]

This description could refer equally well to the original subjects of Adam Kok settled at Philippolis. The same blurring of outlines is often to be encountered in individual cases as well, like that of Andries Pretorius Sr, who called himself a "Bushman", though he is also referred to as a "Bastard Hottentot". Born on the Upper Fish River in about 1775, he settled at Bethelsdorp in 1805, accompanied John Campbell on his journey into the interior in 1813, and was baptised by James Read in the Orange River, after which he became a deacon of the Bethelsdorp congregation. He was among the group that helped Read establish a station for the Batlhaping at Lattakoo, and was later connected with the mission to the Bushmen at Ramah. By 1825 he was farming for the LMS between Ramah and Philippolis, subsequently being mentioned as the leader of the "Old Inhabitants" at the latter station. In 1830 Andries Stockenstrom heard allegations that Sybrand Bronkhorst, a Boer, "had cruelly beaten a Bastard Hottentot named Andries Pretorius" living in the Philippolis Captaincy, which may well have been the same person and serves to explain why he and his sons settled at Kat River soon after its establishment, becoming prominent in the coloured community there. In 1848, after the Seventh Frontier War, he returned to Philippolis, where he bought the farm Meyerskraal from Adam Kok III, but he died at Kat River in 1858. The Andries Pretorius of whom Goeyman complained in 1825 and who was mentioned as a Bergenaar in 1827 was probably his son, Andries Pretorius Jr, and so too the member of the Griqua Raad appointed in 1850;[422] another son, Maurits Pretorius, enjoyed some eminence in mission affairs at Philippolis during the 1840s.[423]

Gottlob Schreiner provided an illustration of the distinction made between the two groups along these lines when, on leaving the station in 1842, he reported to the LMS in London:

There were never many of the Griquas in the Church, and those proved themselves not at all worthy of their privileges, and I fear in a short time I might have been obliged of fulfilling the painful duty of excommunicating almost the last, which secured me somewhat of their displeasure already. (...) The Bastards in general do more honour to their profession, but also in adorning their belief by a consistent walk,[424] though it is painful to say that even some of them have been a source of bitter grief.[425]

Schreiner went even further in the way of generalisation when he wrote to Switzerland in 1842: "The Griquas are apparently the ruling people, the Bechuana are despised but blessed by God, the Bastards (*properly*)[426] the dominant party in the church, who look down on all the others, etc."[427]

On the whole the biographies of individual inhabitants of the Captaincy must be pieced together from a wide variety of sources. The most prominent were, of course, the various members of the Kok clan, including Hendrik Hendrickze, but there are a few other individuals who stand out or have retained some degree of identity. At the most one is struck by certain names which acquire a certain familiarity through their repeated occurrence in documents as members of the Raad, delegates, church officials and witnesses, and about whom some sketchy detail is thus available, such as Adam Eta Kok of Sterkfontein, a second cousin of Adam Kok III, for whom he habitually acted as Provisie Kaptyn, most notably during the exploratory expedition to Nomansland in 1859,[428] or Lukas van der Westhuizen, who was to act as Provisie Kaptyn after the death of Adam Kok III at Kokstad in 1875.[429] Jan Pienaar was especially prominent during the 1850s, and appears variously as deacon of the church, field-cornet, magistrate of Philippolis and Provisie Kaptyn;[430] he accompanied Hendrickze to the Cape Colony for meetings with J.J. Freeman of the LMS and Andries Stockenstrom in 1849,[431] and Adam Kok III to Fauresmith for discussions with representatives of the Free State Government in 1854.[432]

Other names which may be mentioned in this regard are those of Petrus Pienaar and Piet Pienaar, two distinct individuals, and in this connection it may be remarked that according to Armstrong the latter was the brother-in-law of Adam Kok II,[433] which may help to explain the role of the Pienaar family in Griqua affairs. David Jansen was mentioned as a member of the Raad in 1829;[434] in about 1836 he was stated to have been captured by the Xhosa bandit Nzwane or "Danster" and escaped to the mission station at Beersheba,[435] and at the same time he was described by the French missionaries as a prominent member of the congregation at the latter place.[436] The name of Piet Draai is another which occurs with some regularity in the affairs of the Captaincy: as early as 1836 the farm Boomplaats was transferred to him,[437] and in 1879 he was to be found at Kokstad, where reference was made to "[his] memory extending over fifty years".[438]

On the women of the Captaincy there is less information, and where their names have been preserved, this is only in their capacity as wives: Griet Kok, the daughter of Adam Kok II, who married Hendrik Hendrickze and travelled with her father to Cape Town in 1835, or Margaretha Kok, the wife of Abraham Kok and subsequently of Adam Kok III, who survived her second husband and was buried at Kokstad. Of Margaretha Kok there is an unexpectedly detailed description by the Revd William Dower, who knew her in her old age:

> She was as pure a specimen of the Griqua woman as was then alive, with an olive complexion, short of stature, woolly peppercorn hair, sleepy eyes, high cheek-bones and small hands. Her type of beauty was not exactly queenly. In truth, she was but a charred, wrinkled piece of womanhood. Of the English language she knew nothing; of the Dutch she knew only a little, but she spoke the old Griqua tongue to perfection. She bore no children to Adam Kok, seldom left her room, and always wore a superabundance of clothing. With her few female attendants who were able to understand and speak with her, she was sociable and talkative. With all others, especially white people, she was shy and taciturn.[439]

The voice of Tryn Isaac has been preserved, with some autobiographical information,[440] together with the voices of a few other women whose evidence was recorded at the time of the Diamond Fields dispute, but the Griqua woman about whom the most information has been found, scanty though it may be, is probably the wife of Andries Wiese who played a leading part in the scandal surrounding Kolbe's departure from Philippolis in 1837. Her name was Elizabeth Johanna Jacoba

Wiese, and she was properly speaking a Baster, the daughter of Jan Goeyman, the "native agent" and catechist of the LMS; he was married three times, and it is not known which of these three women was her mother. She was born on 9 July 1808, presumably at Graaff-Reinet, where she was baptised in the same year, and came to Philippolis with her husband Andries Wiese or Wiesen in 1831.[441] She was the woman with whom Kolbe was alleged to have committed adultery, and the Wieses both left the church after the dissension caused by his removal from the station, and were only reconciled to it in 1841. In 1849 Freeman mentioned the house of "Mr Weise" of the Philippolis congregation between Colesberg and Philippolis, and presumably she is the "Betta Wiesie" and "Bella Wiesie" referred to in the printed lists of contributions to the Auxiliary Mission Society in 1853 and 1854; by that time her husband would appear to have been dead.[442]

Dower in his reminiscences of Kokstad mentions Mietje Jood from Bethelsdorp, stating that she could remember Dr van der Kemp, who died in 1811, and had taught school at Port Elizabeth in about 1820; although she would seem too old, one is inclined to identify her with Eliza Atkinson's assistant in the school at Philippolis in 1838, who is said to have come from Port Elizabeth,[443] and the "coloured woman brought up at Bethelsdorp" whom Backhouse saw there at the same time.[444] "Mietje Jood, formerly Vries", aged 21, is listed in the baptismal register at Griquatown as having settled there in October 1840, with the later note, "To Philippolis again", and as a widow with two children she accompanied the Griqua trek to Nomansland, where she was mentioned as an erfholder in 1875.[445] Nothing is known about her family, but the surnames Jood and de Vries were well known at Philippolis, and Jan Jood and Jan de Vries were both married to daughters of Kaptyn Abraham Kok, who were therefore stepdaughters and nieces to Adam Kok III.[446]

By the time Andrew Smith and his party visited Philippolis in 1834, it appears from the portraits executed by Charles Bell that the leaders of the community were as westernised in their clothing as the white farmers of the interior. This is also reflected in a list of articles which the party accompanying the Kaptyn to Cape Town the following year requested from the Colonial authorities for their return journey, and which probably indicates their actual standard of living rather than their aspirations. Hendrickze's requirements are particularly illuminating.

For Captain Adam Kok. A warm cloak, 8 ells flannel, 6 common shirts, 2 common colored cravats, 1 pair duffle trowsers, 1 duffle jacket & waistcoat, a hat, a pair of shoes, 2 quires writing paper, small box wafers,[447] quart bottle ink, cash £3.

For Abraham Kok. A common cloth jacket & trowsers, 2 common shirts, a worsted undershirt, a pair of shoes, a common cravat, a waistcoat, a hat, 2 ells flannel, 1 piece voerchitz,[448] 4 ells unbleached linen, 2 silk neckerchiefs, a bonnet.

For Valentyn Neimand [sic]. A duffle jacket & trowsers, a hat, 2 shirts, a waistcoat, a pair of shoes, 2 common cravats, a pair of stockings, a pair of leather trowsers.

For Abraham Jagers. Pair of leather trowsers, a duffle jacket, 2 common shirts, a worsted undershirt, a hat, a pair of shoes, 1 black silk handkerchief, 2 common red and white checked cravats, 1 tinder box & steel, 1 packet thread & 1 dozen buttons.

For Gert Kok. Pair leather trowsers, 1 duffle jacket, 2 shirts, a hat, a waistcoat, 2 common cravats, 1 pair shoes, 1 pair stockings.

For Hendrik April. Pair leather trowsers, 1 duffle jacket, a hat, 2 shirts, 2 common cravats, 1 pair stockings, 1 pair shoes.

For Karel Vizagie. Pair leather trowsers, 1 duffle jacket, 2 shirts, 1 waistcoat, a hat, pair of shoes, 2 common cravats, pair of stockings.

For Mrs Griet Hendrickze. A pewter chamber utensil, 10 ells unbleached linen, a pair of shoes, a pair of stockings, 2 common handkerchiefs, a piece of voerchitz, 8 ells of flannel.

For Antje van der Westhuis. A piece of voerchitz, 8 ells unbleached linen, 2 handkerchiefs, 1 pair shoes, 1 pair stockings, 4 ells flannel.

For Stuurman. A duffle jacket and waistcoat, pair of leather trowsers, 1 shirt. For Windfogels & for Salmon the same as Stuurman.[449]

For Hendrik Hendrickze. 1 duffle jacket, 1 pair ditto trowsers, 2 common handkerchiefs, 1 pair shoes, 2 common shirts, a worsted undershirt. The means of purchasing 12 or 14 Rds[450] worth of Dutch books of history &c., 2 pairs common spectacles, a common writing desk.

12 lbs coffee, 4 lbs tea, 50 lbs common biscuit, 1 bag common sugar.[451]

August Gebel, as has been seen, called Adam Kok II "a rich man",[452] and Andrew Smith mentions his "light waggon drawn by eight horses" and refers to "the horses being in good condition and the coachman an expert whip".[453] Visiting the home of the future Kaptyn Abraham Kok, however, Smith wrote, "He has a mat house and no furniture. His wife dressed in leather, and his face painted red[454] to protect it against the sun and wind",[455] and elsewhere, of the same farm,

> The dwellings (…) had nothing in their appearance which indicated any advance towards civilization, and had it not been that their inmates were clothed in dresses of tanned leather, formed after the European fashion, the mere spectator would not have inferred that the inhabitants were in any way removed from what was the original condition of the Hottentots.[456]

Of the people living around Andries van Wyk near Ramah, Backhouse remarked, "The principal traces of civilization among them were in a few cotton garments, and others, made in a European style; but many of the people wore little but carosses and brass rings and beads."[457] Smith on the whole noted a desire for Western dress, writing of the Griquas in general, "All, at least of any respectability, were dressed in European garments, and although the material consisted of imperfectly tanned skins, yet they were made up in conformity to our fashion. The wearers were always desirous of procuring cloth instead, by barter or other means."[458] To which Backhouse adds the interesting information: "The people here have little to protect them from the cold but their skin garments; and these, whether tanned or otherwise prepared, are so much injured by wet that they are reluctant to expose them to rain. This remark applies also to the harness of oxen, and to the shoes and trowsers used by the Boors in the Colony."[459]

On the other hand, John Melvill could report from Philippolis shortly after his arrival there in 1828:

> It will scarcely be credited that all the Griqua women in these parts (with the exception of only about half a dozen) smear and paint their bodies, wear the native dress, and load themselves with beads. In this respect they differ nothing from the Corannas. The men,

however, differ in this particular, and without exception wear some kind of clothing,[460] and some are even decently dressed. The Coranna men also very generally wear leather trousers of their own making. [461]

The "Griqua family at home" portrayed by Charles Bell in 1834 are probably typical in this respect: a man in Western dress, women in karosses and bracelets and a boy on a riding ox, in front of a traditional mat hut; his "Griquas on riding oxen" and "Griqua belles" likewise depict people in traditional costume and traditional situations.[462]

With regard to the westernisation of the Griquas, it may incidentally be noted that Melvill's report continues with the remark, "Heathenish dancing, with its attendant immorality, is not uncommon, and sorcery is also still occasionally practised among all the tribes in these parts." As late as 1853 the church at Griquatown could still exclude two of its members on charges of "heathen singing, dancing and probable adultery" while on a trading trip in Namaqualand.[463]

5. Life in the Captaincy (1826–1843)

"The more civilized part of my subjects reside with their families at separate farms," declared Adam Kok III to the Colonial Secretary in 1845; "others who do not possess fountains live together in what are called 'werfs' or 'kraals'."[464] There were a large number of such settlements in all parts of the Griqua territory, and between Philippolis and the Modder River Smith noted many of these "villages", as he called them,

> one of which was exclusively inhabited by Corannas, besides several farmhouses. At neither of these, however, was there much to indicate the existence of any degree of industry. The inhabitants seemed chiefly devoted to pastoral life, the care of small flocks and herds constituting their only occupation. To such a choice the nature of the country might have forced them, as we could discover but few facilities for tilling the ground.[465]

Travelling onwards to the Vaal River and Kuruman some months afterwards, he likewise noted:

> Where there was sufficient water even for domestic purposes we generally found Griquas settled in greater or less numbers, all of whom appeared entirely to depend for existence upon their flocks and herds. (…)
>
> Nothing removed from the usual form of the Hottentot hut was observed during this portion of our journey, and the many Griquas we reproached for a want of consideration for their dwelling places replied that they would readily construct better ones after the European fashion could they feel convinced that the waters where they were established would continue permanent. The uncertainty of that we are prepared to admit may have an influence upon them, but we are rather inclined to consider the excuse as only advanced under the idea that it will be less censured

by strangers than if they ascribed their neglect to its true cause: disinclination to labour or a feeling that their present description of houses is equally as comfortable as those of a better construction.[466]

James Backhouse in 1839 elaborated further on the "mat huts" of the Griquas:

> they were framed of a few arched sticks stuck into the ground, so as to form a hemispherical framework; over these, mats were spread, leaving a small entrance, which, when occasion required, was also closed with a mat. The mats were formed of rushes strung side by side, so that they neither excluded light nor air. When rain came on, it beat into the huts, but the rushes soon swelled so as to exclude the wet. Persons accustomed to these habitations complained of the closeness of houses. Mat huts are easily packed, either on oxen or in wagons, the sticks being tied in bundles and the mats rolled together; they therefore suit the convenience of a people who have often to remove for the sake of better pasturage or in order to plough or sow at their different fountains.[467]

"A mat hut requires only about two hours to take to pieces and pack up, and not much to set up again," he wrote elsewhere,[468] for he had an enquiring mind and was much inclined to pick up bits of practical and useful information.

Visiting a settlement of "Bastaards, Griquas and Bushmen (…) under the Philippolis government" on the banks of the Orange River near Ramah, Backhouse found Andries van Wyk living in a hartebeest hut; "adjoining to this is another of the same structure: the rest of the inhabitants live in hemispherical mat huts, except the Bushmen, whose shelters are only semi-hemispheres".[469] The hartebeest house was a structure of poles covered with branches and mats which resembled the pitched roof of a house and was a compromise between the traditional huts and rectangular houses, but it was more usually built and inhabited by whites.

The most prominent of these Griqua settlements seems to have been that of Piet Sabba, former teacher of the LMS at Ramah, which is nowhere named.[470] "This werf consists of 12 Griqua and 17 Bechuana families," wrote Melvill in 1827,[471] adding after another of his periodic visits, "The people at this place are the most indifferent of any of the Griquas to the concerns of their souls, and it is not improbable that the contact and example of Piet Sabba, a former native preacher, has brought religion into disesteem among the people who have been living with him."[472] In 1835, however, two German missionaries arriving there one evening on their way from Philippolis to Bethanie could write,

> Many of the people had gathered together in a hut in which Saba was at that minute holding evening service. He read a chapter from the Bible and accompanied the text with a few explanations. After the prayer, "*Hy, die den Heiland nog niet heeft,/ Is dood en zonder God*" &c. was sung. Saba told us that all the people gathered together in this hut were Griquas, and how he had formerly lived in Griquatown and received instruction from the missionary Anderson.[473]

On the way from Thaba Nchu and the Modder River back to Philippolis, Smith, obviously referring to the same place, noted in his journal:

> The first village we reached consisted of about forty ill-conditioned huts, also a delapidated house built in European style which was employed as a schoolroom. It was pleasing to observe in such a situation that low and degraded as the natives appeared, they were not insensible to the advantages of education, and that they even prized it so highly as to contribute each his quota towards supporting the schoolmaster, who, though a native, was a person of much information and tact, and was once a native teacher upon the strength of the London Missionary Society.[474]

In his diary Smith refers in the same context to a spring "where about 40 families are living and where there is a considerable quantity of land covered with waving corn, where they have a Bastard residing in the capacity of a schoolmaster who is called Jan Hoyman":[475] this was Jan Goeyman, the original teacher and catechist at Philippolis, and presumably he was therefore the individual who, "though a native, was a person of much information and tact"—while he was still in the service of the

LMS the white missionaries had likewise thought highly of him.[476] Some months later, however, the German missionaries recorded after their visit to Sabba's *werf*, "Goemann, another Griqua,[477] who had moved away from them a few days before, had conducted the morning service hitherto, and he himself the evening service. Goemann had also taught reading, but as he had only had a single school book, and had taken it with him, the instruction could not be continued."[478]

The Griquas often lived together in family complexes; many were also surrounded by dependants and clients of other races, and in some cases these people seem to have been looked upon as servants. In 1873, for example, Fytje Isaac, a "Bushwoman" living in the Griquatown district, declared, "At the time of the death of David Isaac I was a servant girl of Anna Isaac (she gave me her name): I was with the wagon when we all went to see him after he was wounded."[479]

Initially the Griquas supported themselves in the traditional way by herding and hunting. Even when agriculture and sheep farming had made considerable developments among them in the 1850s, hunting continued to be a part of their way of life, and the Scottish traveller Cumming painted a vivid picture of a hunting party in the Transorange in the 1840s, described patronisingly as

> a party of ruffianly Griquas who were proceeding with a dilapidated-looking waggon, which had no sail, to hunt hartebeests and blue wildebeests in the vicinity of a small fountain to the north-east where game was reported abundant. They were accompanied by several wild-looking, naked Bushmen attendants, whom they had captured when young and domesticated. These drove their shooting-horses loose behind the waggon, grazing as they went along. I also observed a couple of milch-cows with calves among their loose oxen, a healthy luxury without which that race of people seldom proceed on a journey.[480]

In 1854, Adam Kok, attempting to secure his supply of ammunition from the British authorities, could still write, "Ammunition is in this country one of the necessaries of life. Many of the poorer of my people have to get their supply of meat by killing the game in which this country abounds, and were hunting discontinued, our *crops* as well as our pasturage would be destroyed by the game."⁴⁸¹ There is no reason to doubt the accuracy of this statement, for Hamelberg in 1856 still saw "a multitude of springbok and wildebeeste" on the road between Philippolis and Boomplaats,⁴⁸² and Ds. J. Beijer, travelling from Reddersburg to Fauresmith in 1862, noted "whole troops of spring- and blesbok, as well as pairs of wildebeest".⁴⁸³

Some degree of agriculture had already been practised by the Griquas at Griquatown, however, and in his informal census of the Philippolis Captaincy on 18 January 1831 Melvill could give the following farming statistics:

> Cattle and implements, belonging to the Griquas: 362 horses; 4550 oxen, cows and calves; 14 200 sheep and goats; 45 wagons; 15 ploughs. (…)
> Land and houses: the territory in possession of the Griqua in connection with this station, though the boundaries have not been correctly defined, comprehends about 3000 square miles, of which about 350 are capable of cultivation. At the station there are about 42 acres which are cultivated.
> State of cultivation. Sown or planted—wheat: owing to the ravages of the locusts, one half of the corn was destroyed, yet 750 bushels were harvested this last season; oats: none; barley, 60 bushels. Maize, beans, potatoes, peas, carrots, beet, onions, pumpkins have been sown and planted in abundance. Number of trees—400.⁴⁸⁴

Hunting and trading expeditions into the interior also continued in the old way, and Methuen wrote in 1844: "The Griquas are in the habit of making annual hunting expeditions in the months of June, July and August, on which they obtain ostrich feathers, carosses, ivory and hides, besides large quantities of dried eland and giraffe flesh for home consumption",⁴⁸⁵ and more specifically with regard to Daniëlskuil: "An annual expedition is made hence by the Griquas into the far interior for the purpose of collecting skins, ivory, feathers and dried flesh, a sort of arrangement being often entered into with them by the traders, to which the latter supply beads and gunpowder for a share in the spoils."⁴⁸⁶

Of all the settlements scattered throughout the Griqua territory, Philippolis alone might in European or Colonial terms be called a village, though throughout the 1830s even Philippolis seems to have remained basically what it originally was, a mission station of the LMS dominated by the church building, with the missionary and his family among its few permanent residents. "The population of the place is 20 families of Griquas and about 50 of Bechuanas," reported Melvill in January 1827,[487] and in April, "Today three or four families came from the outposts to live upon the station. (…) There are now 27 Griqua families and 3 of the Old Inhabitants and 50 Bechuanna families residing on the station. More are expected, but the small quantity of water for the cattle I am afraid will deter some from coming."[488] Four years later, however, he gave the Griqua population as six men, ten women and sixteen children,[489] and it is clear that the figures fluctuated dramatically as the inhabitants moved back and forth between their cattle posts and fountains and the incipient village: Backhouse, for example, who counted sixty mat huts on his arrival at Philippolis, noted on his return two months later that only forty remained.[490]

"There are seven clay-built houses belonging to the Old Inhabitants," wrote Melvill in 1827,

> and five of the same description unfinished. One of these houses is now used as a place of worship and school, which, with another adjoining, is claimed by Jan Goeyman. There is also a square building 20 feet in the sides which was built by the Old Inhabitants at the suggestion of Brother Clark for a place of worship, to be enlarged when convenient. For the present it is used by me as a dwelling house.[491]

By the time Andrew Smith arrived there in 1834, not much seems to have changed, and to him Philippolis had "little in its appearance calculated to denote the importance it virtually possessed, and were we to exclude from consideration the church, the schoolhouse and the dwelling of the missionary, we might describe it as consisting of a few European-shaped houses in a state little removed from ruin";[492] his travelling companion Gebel wrote more precisely, "Apart from the church we counted 13 houses, but partly uncompleted, partly dilapidated."[493] By the time of

James Backhouse's visit five years later, it had clearly not undergone much further development: "It consists," Backhouse wrote, "of a single street of cottages, a chapel, and a number of mat huts; the latter are scattered on a flat at one side of the village, on which are also the cattle kraals and the foundation of a schoolhouse." Later he noted, "The more permanent houses I may have mentioned are twelve",[494] and recorded 60 huts, remarking further, "Many of the people living in mat huts were possessed of oxen and wagons", which indicates a certain measure of westernisation. "Houses of a more substantial kind are too costly for many of the Griquas," he added, "the timber needful in building them having to be brought from the woods between Klip Plaat[495] and the Kat River, distant about 200 miles. Timber was worth from 5d to 72d per foot at Philippolis."[496]

Backhouse visited Philippolis in the winter and there was a fall of snow while he was there: "We were much occupied in writing," he recorded in his journal, "which it was difficult to effect from the cold. The houses were badly constructed for warmth, and fuel was scarce. I walked a few times, enveloped in a karros of coney fur, among the stony hills, to acquire warmth";[497] "Short wood for fuel is obtained from the neighbouring hills," he noted elsewhere.[498] He and his companion were staying, however, in the house of Theophilus and Eliza Atkinson, probably the most convenient in the village: it had been completed shortly before, apparently on the site of the present *pastorie* of the Dutch Reformed Church, which may incorporate sections of the earlier structure: "37 ft by 22," according to Atkinson, "one story, with cottage roof, and without ceiling or boarded floors".[499] Elsewhere Atkinson wrote to the Directors of the LMS in London, "The house is open to the thatch, and the floor will be of clay. The doors are all of the plainest kind, none of them being panelled. And the glazing and painting I shall do myself."[500]

None of the houses at Philippolis was, however, by any means luxurious, and in the winter of 1837 the Atkinsons, then still occupying rented accommodation, could mention that "our personal accommodations are rather more comfortable than they were last winter, and we have now a glass window, by which the cold winds are excluded, while daylight is enjoyed".[501] By the time of Backhouse's visit, Atkinson wrote gratefully concerning the new mission house, "We are now able to have a fire, which we could not before, but which is very necessary at this season of the year, when the frost is often severe."[502] According to Backhouse the church was the only stone building; "that of T. Atkinson is of brick, the rest are of clay, and all are thatched".[503]

The Kaptyn and Raad served in practice as the town council of the settlement, and among the earlier entries in the Griqua law book are *"Dorp's wetten"* for Philippolis which were to be implemented by December 1831: they refer to the obligation of occupying the houses and keeping the streets clean, damage done by cattle, and the presence of "ox wagons, hides, wood or blocks" in the streets.[504] Andrew Smith in 1834 mentioned "an order that all the houses in the village shall be repaired; such a law has long been in existence, but never acted on".[505]

Bell's painting of Philippolis in 1834 shows a number of small rectangular houses with steep thatched roofs and flaking whitewashed walls straggling along what is today Voortrekker Street towards the church.[506] The foundations of the latter building, by far the largest and most imposing in the village, were begun on 21 March 1827, according to Melvill's journal, where he wrote, "It is 56 by 18 feet, to be attached to the building that I live in",[507] and his successor Kolbe recorded that it had progressed sufficiently to be used for the first time on 1 April 1832: "It will contain 500 persons. The walls are of stone, two feet and a half thick and 12 feet high."[508] According to Bell's painting it was a T-shaped building, thatched and gabled, such as was common in the Colony at the time.[509] Inside it had a clay floor and was open to the thatch; the pulpit stood on an elevation between the two entrance doors in the facade, while the congregation sat on long benches, and a candelabrum, probably of brass, was suspended from a beam. Church buildings of this construction may still be found in Paarl and Tulbagh, and in the mission church at Kuruman, built about the same time and still in use, it is possible to get an even clearer impression of what the building at Philippolis must have been like.

It was normally only on Sundays that the little village came to life, when people flocked in from the surrounding district for the church services. Under Melvill attendance does not appear to have been good, possibly because he was personally unpopular among the Griquas as a former Government Agent, and he wrote typically of having had "a tolerably good congregation, several persons having come from the outstations".[510] Kolbe, however, seems to have been an active and popular preacher under whom there was a great improvement in church attendance, and he reported enthusiastically shortly after his arrival at Philippolis in 1831: "The congregation increased so much that the place of worship would not contain them, and they were obliged at times to erect a temporary tent to screen those that were outside from the sun."[511] This was before the new church building was completed, but in later entries he wrote, "In the evening 29 wagons arrived, all loaded with people who came to attend the services of religion",[512] and mentioned congregations of three or four hundred.

"Our chapel was filled, yea, literally crammed," reported Kolbe in 1832. "500 persons attended the various services of religion, among whom were a Dutch Colonist, three English traders, Captain Waterboer and his Council from Griqua Town, and a few persons from Bootschap",[513] and on another occasion he mentioned that a hundred people attended the customary mission prayer meeting on a Monday.[514] "A traveller who spends only two or three days on this station would run the risk of judging it unfavourably," observed the French missionary Eugène Casalis in 1835, "for most of the natives live at some distance from the establishment. But when one sees on Saturday the wagons laden with men, women and children arriving for the service, one can only bless the Lord and admire the enlightened zeal of the London Missionary Society."[515]

Services were often emotional, as was customary with the LMS and their Wesleyan colleagues: "We trust that the Spirit taught us to pray," wrote Kolbe on one occasion, "for the blessing of the Lord was evidently with us during the prayer meeting. During the morning service one person left the chapel, being overcome by his feelings";[516] and on another, "In the evening the whole congregation was melted into tears during the administration of the sacrament."[517] "On Sunday, 30 August [1834]," reported the German missionaries,

> we heard Kolbe preach on [II?] Cor.5:1–10 in his church, which can hold more than 300 people. The singing of the heavy English melodies was quite surprisingly true. The London Society has on each of its stations its own little hymnal with Dutch translations of English hymns, such as the well-known *Remember me*, the favourite hymn of Henry Martin.[518] The Hottentot tribes are in general able to sing well, much more so than the Kaffirs. (…) He has approxi-

mately 30 full members of the church, i.e. communicants, and celebrates the sacrament [*Communion*] every two months.[519]

Smith, who was also present on these occasions, found "a number of persons in attendance, many of them well dressed and orderly, and attentive throughout the service";[520] a week later he described services at two o'clock and half past six, writing, "Each time the church was pretty well attended and most of the people were respectably dressed, a few very well";[521] and on a third occasion he noted, "The children belonging to the infant school sang two verses of the Infant's Hymn and the performance was very creditable to them."[522]

The Kaptyns were at any rate nominal Christians and conscientious churchgoers, and the successive missionaries, aware of the influence this could have on the development of the Captaincy, watched anxiously over their spiritual progress or lack of it. In 1827 Adam Kok II "spoke with much feeling of his former state of backsliding, which was occasioned by his leaving the means of grace at Griqua Town and living at his cattle post. At present," added Melvill, "I have reason to think that his soul is restored, and that he really enjoys religion."[523] The death of the promising Christian Cornelius Kok III has already been described, but of his brother, Adam Kok III, Schreiner wrote in equally optimistic terms in 1840:

> There is much that is pleasing in him, and I cannot but hope that he is not far from the Kingdom of God. He feels his political situation a great hindrance to him in attending to the things which belong to his peace. If it pleased the Lord to make him a decided Christian and consistent follower of the truth, it would be a great blessing to all.[524]

Hendrickze too was nominally a Christian, and Melvill, likewise recording in 1827 a "serious conversation with Klein Hendrik, the Chief's son-in-law, about his soul", wrote concerning him:

> This man was a member of the church at Griqua Town, and can read and write. He fell into sin, and became one of the leading men of the Bergenaars. He seemed to be deeply confinced[?] of

the sinfulness of his former life, and scarcely thought it possible that there was forgiveness for him. He felt so much that he trembled exceedingly and could hardly speak. He compared himself to the dog returned to his vomit, and, believing him to be under strong convictions of conscience, I exhorted him to return unto his offended God with full purpose of heart like the Prodigal Son and throw himself into the arms of Mercy.[525]

The return to grace here described does not seem to have lasted long, but under the ministrations of Kolbe, Hendrickze underwent a similar brief conversion seven years later, so that Gebel could write in 1834: "Because of his wild life he was formerly one of the greatest scourges of the mission; for the past six months, however, says Kolbe, he has joined the lambs in the pasture of the Gospel."[526]

Officially the Captaincy declared itself a Christian polity, and one of a series of laws passed in 1833 laid down, "That in God's House prayers are to be said every Sabbath for the Captain and Raad, that they may conduct(?) themselves according to the laws in the fear of God. And it is recommended that each person shall pray in his house for the Government and the country."[527] Marriages also seem to have been recognised only when conducted in church: the annual report of the LMS for 1834 stated, "Thirteen couples have been united by legal marriage",[528] and in 1840 there were 29 marriages.[529] Monogamy, the calling of banns in the church and a church wedding were all required formally in a law which seems to have been passed in the early 1840s.[530]

As an indication of church attendance, some random figures may be quoted from the annual reports as published over the period up to the death of Peter Wright in 1843: the figures are for the Sunday services, with those for attendance at weekday services given in parentheses. According to the report published in 1828, "The usual attendance on the Lord's day is about 25, besides a few children"; in 1829 the figures given were 60 to 90 (20 to 40); in 1831, 80 to 200 on Sundays; in 1832, 160–280 (50–120); in 1833, 250–500 (80–200); and in 1836, 200–400, and as for the previous year on weekdays. In 1837 it was reported, "The attendance fluctuates, sometimes not exceeding 150, but more frequently amounts to 250 or 300", but this fluctuation would have been brought about by the unrest on the station during the brief Captaincy of Abraham Kok and the campaign against Kolbe.[531] By 1844, shortly after Wright's death, the average attendance at the services had risen rather dramatically to 700–800.[532]

The figures quoted and the descriptions of the services which have survived give the impression that the latter were looked on largely as social gatherings, and do not necessarily imply wide acceptance of or adherence to the Gospel or even formal church membership; as to the actual impact of Christianity on the people, it is not possible to form a reliable judgement. As far as church membership was concerned, as opposed to mere attendance at church, progress was slow, at any rate during the early years of the mission, and in January 1838, Atkinson reported, "The church members are 52 in number, 17 having by the blessing of God been added in the course of the year."[533] Schreiner seems to have been considerably less strict in accepting new members, and after a temporary absence from the station two years later, Atkinson wrote rather apprehensively: "In the *church* the number of members has been increased by the addition of 31, 11 previous to my leaving and 20 (Bechuanas) during my absence. Of these I know but little, and can therefore only express my *hope* that they may remain stedfast and be enabled to adorn their professions."[534] By September 1840, under Schreiner, the total had risen dramatically to 133, "34 Griquas and 55 Buchanas",[535] by December to 181,[536] and by August 1841 to 218, "almost as many Bechuanas as from the others".[537] As will be clear from the above quotations, it was mainly the Tswana refugees living in the Captaincy on whom the mission depended for its success: "The members on the side of the Bechuanas were always a cause of joy and gratitude to me, following in the footsteps of Jesus," remarked Schreiner, "but it was not so with the others."[538]

The events connected with the respective removals of Kolbe, Atkinson and Schreiner from the station show how successful the Griqua and Bergenaar elements at Philippolis were in manipulating the missionaries and playing them off against one another to their own advantage, a process in which the hand of Hendrickze may be especially detected. Specifically the dismissal of Kolbe in 1837 must be seen as the triumph of the Griqua over the Baster party and of the Captaincy over the church: in 1841 Schreiner wrote of readmitting to church membership individuals "who were scattered by the painful circumstances attending the dismissal of their beloved and worthy pastor Brother Kolbe".[539]

The above applies only to the strictly religious activities of the mission, however. From a social and cultural point of view, and with regard to the provision of rudimentary social services, it retained its importance in the Captaincy throughout its existence, and played an invaluable role among the Griqua people for more than thirty years.

The successive missionaries usually kept school at Philippolis, insofar as their itinerating duties permitted, while their wives were responsible for the infant school and for the women and girls in general. In 1838 Eliza Atkinson was helped by a young woman from Port Elizabeth, as already mentioned,[540] and Rebecca Schreiner for a time had the assistance of a daughter of Adam Kok III.[541] The school was well attended, and Melvill in 1827 noted that there were 95 children and that the schoolhouse was too small,[542] while Kolbe on one occasion gave an attendance figure of 335.[543] This was, however, on a Monday, and had obviously been brought about by a large attendance at the church services the day before.

In Atkinson's correspondence there are references to tracts, spelling books and sheet lessons for the schools, and in a letter to London he wrote:

> I am also in need of *writing paper* for the school, and as it [is] much cheaper in England than here, it would be an advantage to have a ream or two of foolscap, the *yellow wove* is preferable for school purposes to the other sort. It would be advisable to send some packing paper (2 or 3 quires) for making covers for the copybooks, or any other paper would answer the same purpose.[544]

By the end of 1832 a new schoolhouse had been commenced "and the 4 feet of stone work pointed. The building is 60 feet by 16."[545] By 1838, however, it seems still not to have been completed,[546] and further difficulties and disputes in connection with it were among the reasons adduced for the dismissal of Gottlob Schreiner in 1842; in 1840 the building used for the infant school also collapsed, and for a time Rebecca Schreiner kept school in her kitchen.[547] In spite of the setbacks of the intervening years, the annual report of the LMS for Philippolis for 1838 could still state: "In connexion with the schools there is ample encouragement. The general attendance of adults and children is from 100 to 150, infant school from 80 to 90. Sabbath Schools about the same numbers respectively."[548] The following year Schreiner wrote of an average attendance of 251, diminished for a time during an epidemic of measles and the sowing season.[549] The number of children in the school continued to fluctuate, depending on the movements of their parents and the demands of their farms and flocks, and in 1841 Schreiner reported, "though 253 have been at school, yet scarcely ever more than 50 at a time".[550] Few Griquas could afford to board their children in the village, and Schreiner likewise wrote, "it often grieves me to refuse their requests to take their children into the house".[551]

Visiting the outlying Kalkfontein in 1827, Melvill "was much gratified to find the children, about 17 in number, anxious to return to school. I heard their lessons, and after I had finished, it was pleasant to see them sit down and teach others."[552] The activities of Jan Goeyman at Piet Sabba's kraal have already been referred to.[553] During the 1830s there is evidence of a general and growing desire among the Griquas to have their children educated, and Atkinson in 1837 mentions schools at "Toom Fountain" (probably Toomfontein, north-east of modern Trompsburg) and at Uitkomst, where there was a "young woman" as teacher.[554] Schreiner four years later wrote of three schools for "Bastards", "in each of which 30–50 children are instructed daily".[555]

It is not clear what benefits the Griqua parents expected from the education they sought so eagerly for their children, and while many of course realised the advantages which literacy gave to a man like Hendrickze, opportunities for advancement were rare in the Transgariep. With regard to Griqua family life Schreiner could write in 1840, "their whole training consists of beating, and almost the only request I have ever received from parents respecting their children in the school is that I would beat them; their prejudices on this head are many and deeply rooted and cannot be expected to give way in a day (…)."[556] Moreover the medium of instruction was Dutch, taught by English or German speaking missionaries to pupils who themselves spoke a form of Afrikaans, and the outcome of the undertaking seems somewhat doubtful. Schreiner, however, wrote:

> As a reward and incentive to diligence I have introduced English for those who read Dutch fluently; some read English very cor-

rectly, but I cannot say they understand anything in that language. A prior acquisition of Dutch reading is therefore very necessary and important. I am very much in want of school materials, particularly English Testaments.[557]

Though possibly inadequate in itself, some form of education was obviously necessary to enable the Griquas to cope with the rapidly changing circumstances in which they found themselves.

Since at least the early 1830s there was an Auxiliary Mission Society at Philippolis which supported the work of the LMS with gifts in cash and in kind, and in 1834 it had 91 annual subscribers;[558] Bible classes, enquiry classes, sewing classes and a "Maternal Association" are variously mentioned,[559] but for the Griqua people as a whole the most significant development in this regard was possibly the establishment of a temperance society. The excessive consumption of strong drink, and more specifically cheap brandy or "Cape smoke", had long been a problem in Griqua society, and the Wesleyan missionary T.L. Hodgson, visiting Philippolis in 1828, wrote in his journal:

> Grieved to find Mr M[elvill] labouring under much discouragement from the state of the people amongst whom he had some time ago a prospect of seeing some good, but some brandy having of late been brought into the neighbourhood, his people at the station have been almost entirely engaged in scenes of drunkenness; and he has been obliged to discontinue his religious services, as not only the women but some of the school children have been in a state of intoxication. A canteen has lately been established on the borders of the Colony, and the people are flocking to it and exchanging their cattle for brandy, the consequence of which will be that they will drink themselves poor, and probably fall into the temptation of stealing cattle from tribes in the interior.[560]

In May 1832 Kolbe recorded in his diary, "Having preached various sermons against drunkenness, calling upon the Chief and his Council from love to their country, to their people and to their own souls, to do all in their power to prevent the bad practice which the Colonists have of bringing brandy into this country, I rejoice to hear that the Chief has prohibited the sale of spirits at the station."⁵⁶¹ In spite of this, however, the presence of brandy wagons in Griqua territory, and specifically the sale of brandy to the inhabitants of the Transgariep by Boers, which is repeatedly mentioned throughout the early decades of the nineteenth century, would remain a serious threat to the stability of the Captaincy.

Towards the end of 1832, under continued pressure from Kolbe, a public meeting was held at Philippolis in a further attempt to oppose the evil of drunkenness.

> Several persons addressed the meeting, and 83 signed as members. Joseph de Bruin (a member of the church) promised that the use of spirits should be entirely discontinued, even for medicinal purposes, for he observed that under the name of using spirits as medicine drunkenness would secretly be indulged in. This proposition was unanimously agreed to, with an amendment. A memorial was also presented to the Chief and Council, signed by all the members, requesting him to issue an order that all spirits brought from the Colony for the purpose of trafficking in this district should be considered as contraband and forfeited goods.⁵⁶²

The annual report of the LMS for 1834 could state concerning the Temperance Society, "The members have increased from 87 to 203. The opponents of this society when it first commenced have now become its staunch advocates. Drunkenness, which was lately a pest in the land, has now ceased."⁵⁶³ This account may well have been overly sanguine, and many may also have joined for social rather than idealistic reasons, but the success of the movement does seem to indicate a reasonably wide awareness of the dangers of alcohol abuse among the Griqua people. Unfortunately the Society was one of the victims of the unrest and instability of the late 1830s, but it was re-established in 1839 at a meeting held in the presence of the British Quakers James Backhouse and G.W. Walker: "two of the people spoke much to the purpose and in a very Christian spirit," reported Backhouse.

> The temperance cause formerly gained some ground here; but it afterwards fell into neglect in consequence of the unfaithfulness of some of the committee. Strong drink has made great ravages

among these people; it is still sometimes brought amongst them, notwithstanding that it is interdicted by the Government. The mischievous effects of the use of tobacco and snuff were also stated at this meeting. Even young children are suffered, if not encouraged, to smoke and take snuff!⁵⁶⁴

"An anti-tobacco society containing a little more than 301 members, most of whom were snuffers and smokers, has also been instituted among us," wrote Schreiner at the same time.⁵⁶⁵

A few months later Schreiner could report that the revived Temperance Society had 393 members, "a great many of which were some time back confirmed drunkards. With one exception all have continued steadfast. We have a monthly meeting to receive new members and to enquire into the conduct of old members, that we may not have mere names on the paper. I am happy to say that the Captain and Council have all signed, most of them previously confirmed drunkards."⁵⁶⁶ Two years later he wrote, "The abstinence cause continues to prosper; the Chief and most of its members have strictly adhered to their promise, though often solicited by traders, farmers, etc. to take a glass of brandy or wine."⁵⁶⁷ Peter Wright on settling at Philippolis in 1842 found that "the spread of intemperance among the people has operated very injuriously",⁵⁶⁸ but the increased influx of white farmers at this stage, combined with the unrest caused in the community by the stubborn and aggressive Schreiner, may well have had an unsettling effect. Schreiner for his part claimed, "During the last year of my residence at Philippolis there were several who had for three years and upwards strictly adhered to their abstinence pledge [who] resumed their evil habits of drinking, being induced to do so by one or two profligate European[s] and some farmers presenting them with brandy on hiring their places."⁵⁶⁹ The temperance movement and its advocates were, however, fighting an uphill battle, and the very last law recorded in the law book of the Philippolis Captaincy was one forbidding anyone living in the village itself to provide any Griqua citizen with liquor, including "brandy and E[a]u de Cologne, porter or all intoxicating drink";⁵⁷⁰ it was dated 8 July 1861, immediately before the departure of the Griquas from Philippolis.

Two other important functions of the missionaries in this isolated little community may finally be noted, one being the distribution of religious literature—400 tracts were provided in 1834,⁵⁷¹ for example, and five bibles, four New Testaments and 200 tracts during the following year,[572] while Schreiner wrote in 1840, "The people often come with their money in their hand for bibles, etc., and you will well conceive how much it grieves me to be obliged to refuse them the Word of God";[573] for 1841 he could report, "bibles, Testaments, hymn books and spelling book[s] I disposed of this year both in the Dutch and Sechuana languages for £35.15.6, and more bibles would I have disposed of had I had them of the new print."[574]

The other notable social function of the missionaries in the Griqua community was the provision of at least rudimentary medical services. Kolbe reported vaccinating 26 people early in 1832,[575] and Atkinson appealed in 1837 for "jalap, rhubarb, ipecacuanha, James powder, &c. &c. Also sulphate of quinine",[576] and mentioned having had "numerous applications for medicine": "Ipecacuanha powder has been one of the most useful, and my stock is nearly exhausted";[577] elsewhere he added "calomel and tatar emetic" to his list.[578] In 1838 there was an epidemic of measles at Philippolis, followed in 1840 by whooping cough, at a time when both illnesses were often fatal, and Backhouse noted, "Convulsions carry off many of the children, and pulmonary diseases are very destructive among the older people."[579]

Apart from the missionary and his family, Adam Kok II seems to have lived permanently at Philippolis, although he was likewise often away visiting his people in the district or his own outlying farms. In 1829, when the settlement was transferred temporarily to Boesmansfontein some 10 kilometres to the north-west because of the better water supply there, the first people to move were "The Chief with his son-in-law H[endrik] H[endrickze], the widow of his late son Cornelius, and his wife's mother and family",[580] and this group seems to have constituted the resident Griqua community in the village. Adam Kok III similarly lived at Philippolis, and Backhouse described his "small thatched cottage, built of clay, but far superior to the mat huts of the generality of his people".[581] Most of the permanent population of Philippolis were, however, "Old Inhabitants" or Basters who were members of the church and attached in some way to the mission: it was this group which opposed the projected move to Boesmansfontein on the grounds that they had already erected houses for themselves at Philippolis, and they were most likely responsible for the ultimate failure of the project.

Andrew Smith found a blacksmith in the village, which is understandable in view of the number of wagons in the Captaincy requiring repair; the German missionaries referred in the following year to "the smith Wiese",[582] who must have been the Andries Wiese already mentioned, for he is known to have owned and occupied a house at Philippolis.[583] There were likewise a few isolated white people living there apart from the missionary and his family, and a very early resident was Alexander Davidson, who seems to have come to South Africa as one of Moodie's Settlers in 1817;[584] Kolbe, recording his conversion in 1832, describes him as "a Scotchman who has long resided as smith at this station".[585] He subsequently became a deacon of the church, and in 1846 he appears still to have been living at Philippolis,[586] but by 1857 reference was made to his deceased estate.[587]

Most of the whites whose presence on or around the station is mentioned were traders, one of the earliest being the Englishman James Fossey, whose name occurs in this connection from the beginning of the 1830s, and who is said to have been the first trader to visit Thaba Bosiu; he subsequently farmed in Griqua territory and died there in 1859.[588] Fossey must have spent his time itinerating, however, for when Kolbe's eldest son left school, also sometime in the early 1830s, Kolbe purchased a stock of goods, intending to set him up as a shopkeeper in the village.[589]

Many of these traders tended to be renegades from the Colony and a disruptive influence in the community, such as George Mills, who settled at Philippolis and caused Schreiner much trouble: "He is not only living in the grossest immorality, but being of deistical principles, endeavours by every means to infuse poison into the heart of these poor people and to degrade the Christian religion and her ministers."[590] After his violent death in 1844, he was described in the *Graham's Town Journal* as "a slave to Bacchus, and a most desperate and determined character, he cared not with whom he fought,— he bore the reputation of being a great pugilist, and was often confined to bed for days together, from the bruises he received in his various combats."[591] In 1845 again, Buck Adams, arriving in Philippolis with the British troops, encountered "a young man about 28 years of age standing at the door of a shed on which was written *Negotie Winkle* – Retail Store".

After a few words of conversation he invited me into his house—a building 45 feet in length, 14 feet in breadth and 12 feet in height, which contained the shop, one sitting room and two bedrooms. He also had a very large piece of ground under cultivation. His name was Charles Webster. He was a native of Nottingham; he had been 12 years in the country, 5 of which in this desolate place. He traded in coffee, sugar and tobacco by barter in skins, ivory, ostrich feathers and gum, in fact anything that came his way. He had two waggons then on the road to Colesberg—the nearest European settlement—each laden with skins, wool, ostrich feathers and about half a ton of ivory. He expected their contents to realise over £100.[592]

Webster seems to have been living somewhat dubiously with two young coloured women described as "servants", whom he had taught to sing "Cherry Ripe" and "Home Sweet Home", accompanied by himself on the violin. In 1848 Edward Solomon of the LMS could note disapprovingly, "in the village there are three European shopkeepers, two of whom are decidedly immoral characters."[593]

The Transgariep was also visited by itinerant traders from the Colony, and Backhouse wrote of meeting at Skietfontein "two [waggons] of a trader, called in this country a Smous, which literally means a cheat. One of the company of the trader was an English comedian, of bad character; they all, however, accepted a few tracts."[594] Schreiner complained vehemently and incoherently of the "bad influence of the traders", mentioning specifically that "they try to make up the people against their missionaries, who, of course, for conscience sake are obliged to lead them in a better way, which if listened to injures their ungodly designs; but alas, in some instances they have prevailed [upon] some persons to try to do mischief; such indeed are of the worst class."[595]

Trade was usually carried on in the form of barter, and Backhouse mentioned horses being sold in this way, adding a note on the people "not clearly understanding the relative value of money and goods"; according to him, he paid Rds140 or 10 guineas (£10 10s) each for horses at Philippolis, while Moshweshwe was in the habit of giving six oxen for a horse.[596] This system was criticised by Schreiner, who indulged compulsively in trading activities himself, and who wrote of the Griquas:

They take goods from the traders for a large amount, and though in most cases they are able to pay off immediately with cattle, they let it stand for months and years, and which is a source of much unpleasantness here, especially when everything has long disappeared and payment shall then follow. If no alteration takes place in this respect, I apprehend it may with some other things mentioned and not mentioned effect their ruin as an independent people.[597]

In 1841, referring to the economic difficulties on the station, he added:

This has been effected also particularly by the sinking of the price of cattle fully one half from last year, and even for such a price it is difficult, almost impossible, to get money, for no-one will purchase for money, the few traders that come here take well cattle from the people,[598] but only for merchandise. I am unable to picture the real state of things, the misery caused by this. Many of the people are hardly able to keep up their decent appearance as before, and some even get careless about what they possess. It is here not as at other stations where they at all times can find a ready market for anything they may have for sale. Though there is a market at Colesberg, only two days with the wagon, but very seldom the people can bring anything from there, for the greater part of the year the river is not passable with the wagon, and though also for that is cared by means of a little boat, but the expence (£1.0.0. each way) is too great for most of them with sheep, it is, I may say, always attended with some loss. Added to this there are but few inhabitants at Colesberg, and so it happens that the farmers even must take their produce back again.[599]

As already mentioned, itinerant brandy merchants were especially common in the Captaincy and, for that matter, throughout the Transgariep, and the missionaries working in the area regularly complained about their presence. In spite of repeated laws passed by the Griqua Raad to outlaw the liquor trade, whites continued to traffic in strong drink, and in 1840 the German missionaries at Bethanie mentioned that there were two wagons at Kaffer River (modern Tierpoort River) belonging to "Basters of Philippolis" selling brandy to the Korana.[600]

As appears from some of the passages quoted above, the village of Colesberg had been established in 1830, 60 kilometres from Philippolis across the Orange River, to serve as the northernmost outpost of Colonial authority, and after this Philippolis was no longer as isolated as in the early years when its nearest point of contact with the Colonial authorities had been Graaff-Reinet. A magistrate and civil commissioner was placed here, and it soon became an important trading centre; several shops were established, while at times it also enjoyed the services of a doctor and a midwife, and Gebel wrote in 1834 of a monthly postal service between the two villages.[601] White farmers from the interior travelled to the Dutch church at Colesberg for christening, marriage and communion, and Theophilus Atkinson worked among the local coloured community for some years after his departure from Philippolis, retaining his contact with part of his former congregation in a manner not necessarily calculated to heal the divisions in mission circles, as did a later successor, C.J. van der Schalk.

Inevitably, the development of the Griqua people was affected not only by the personalities and talents of the individual missionaries themselves, but also, more unfortunately, by the unedifying and disruptive events in mission circles during the late 1830s: the scandal surrounding Kolbe, the dissension between Kolbe and Atkinson followed by that between Atkinson and Schreiner, the antagonism aroused in the community by Schreiner himself, the successive departures from the station of all three men, and finally the sudden death of Peter Wright in 1843. The increasing pressure of white farmers moving across the Orange River to settle in the Captaincy and the violence surrounding the deposition of Abraham Kok all had a further unsettling effect, and even the well-disposed Backhouse gave a somewhat dispiriting account of his observations at this time.

> There is a remarkable degree of supineness among the people of Philippolis. While living under privations in regard to the common necessaries of life such as would be very hard for English people to sustain, they seem ready to lay hold of any kind of excuse to escape exertion, or to avoid allowing their children to go from home in service that might turn to profit, except on hunting excur-

sions or a few other exciting engagements. They are also slow to make improvements. Their gardens are suffered to lie waste during the winter, the walls to be broken down, allowing cattle and goats to browze over them, to the injury and often to the destruction of their fruit-trees. Their fountain is trampled in by the cattle, and left in such a state from floods as allows much of the water wanted for irrigation to escape another way.

Want of industry indeed marks the population generally; but the better training of the children affords hope of improvement in the rising generation. Within a few days several youths have expressed a willingness to engage to lead our oxen, but their parents have invariably thrown difficulties in the way, notwithstanding some of those who would have gone were spending their time in idleness.[602]

Basically the problem was probably the clash of very different cultures. Given the inexorable progress of white farmers into the interior and the growing involvement of the Colonial authorities in the affairs of the Transgariep, it was, however, essential for the Griquas to come to terms with Western culture and to learn to assert themselves against it. Some far-seeing individuals among them seem to have been aware of the fact, and amid the unrest of this period, and in spite of the unfavourable conditions, the young and feeble Griqua polity managed to survive and gradually to establish itself.

6. The Government of the Captaincy: Officials

Apart from such laws as happen to have been entered in the Griqua law book,[603] knowledge of the government of the Philippolis Captaincy is fragmentary and must be gathered from a wide variety of sources. Concerning the Griqua form of government at Kokstad much more has been recorded, but as it seems to have undergone drastic changes after they had moved from Philippolis in 1861, this information is of doubtful relevance and will not be considered here.[604]

Nothing is known of the original form of government among the Basters of the Kok group and others similar to them in the Transorange, but it most probably followed the traditional Khoi models. In the words of Richard Elphick:

> Among the Cape Khoikhoi, as among the Namaqua, chieftainship passed from father to eldest son and remained in the tribe's dominant clan until that clan died out or was displaced by another. Very often, if the chief lived to an old age, his son took over effective leadership during the life of his father, though the latter retained his ritualistic prerogatives. (...) If there were no direct male heirs, a brother or brother's son of the dead chief could be chosen as his successor, probably by the council of the heads, as was definitely the case among the Korana.[605]

Burchell, writing on the basis of his observations at Klaarwater in 1811, remarked:

> The authority of these Chiefs (...) is of a patriarchal nature, and extends very little beyond a voluntary submission on the part of their people. It is confined principally to that of ordering out the force of the tribe to attack an enemy or to take up arms in defence of the settlement. (...) But in ordinary cases their power does not seem to be so strong as the good of their society requires.[606]

Lichtenstein for his part observed in 1805 concerning the Korana,

> Their form of government is the same as with the other Hottentot tribes: the richest person in the kraal is the Captain, or provost: he is the leader of the party and the spokesman on all occasions, without deriving from this office any judicial right over the rest. His authority is exceedingly circumscribed, and no one considers himself as wholly bound to yield obedience to him; nor does he himself ever pretend to command them.[607]

In another relevant passage, which deserves quoting at length, Elphick writes of the traditional Cape Khoikhoi:

> The chief was assisted by a council consisting of the clan captains under his jurisdiction. The council met at the chief's kraal and under his chairmanship; one of its main functions was the adjudication of interclan disputes. In most matters affecting only one clan, the captain, and not the chief, had effective authority. Individual justice was normally meted out at a gathering of all the males of a clan, though apparently some chiefs could exert influence on the outcome of the proceedings. Even in matters of tribal significance the chief was no autocrat; he could often be overruled by his council, though he was theoretically sovereign in decisions relating to war and transhumant movements.[608]

This is confirmed by a later writer on the Korana, J.A. Engelbrecht:

> A Kora hereditary chief (…), who would also be the owner of the country, not in a personal capacity but as head of the tribe, generally had a large number of kraals. Except for the one in which he himself lived, these kraals would be looked after by sub-chiefs or what might be called "field-cornets". For the latter there was no special name: they were merely referred to as the Chief's arm (…) or substitute (…). These men constituted the council which limited the Chief's authority and which could overrule most of his decisions. (…)
>
> Normally the hereditary Chief's successor was his eldest son, but the law was sometimes suspended if the heir was cowardly or

otherwise incompetent. Any Chief appointed by the council was called a "made" chief, in distinction to the "born" Chief or hereditary Chief.[609]

Elsewhere Engelbrecht uses the Afrikaans terms *"gemaakte kapteins"* and *"gebore kapteins"*.[610]

As regards Philippolis, however, much of the detail of government was transferred or copied from that instituted at Griquatown in the early nineteenth century, so that reference to the Griquatown Captaincy is necessary in this regard as in others.

After the missionaries had settled among the Basters on the Orange River, Lichtenstein wrote in 1805 that "[their] regulations as a community, and [their habits and customs] exhibit a curious intermediary state between savage and civilised life. They have only recently begun, under the conduct of some shrewd and understanding missionaries, to unite in one general and firm bond of union."[611] According to him, William Anderson "divided the whole population into six parts, who were distributed in the like number of villages (...). Here the persons of most distinction among the Bastard Hottentots were appointed as magistrates[612] to inspect and take care of the rest. Anderson, with Kramer, performed the office of pastors," he added,[613] and elsewhere referred more expressly to "the Hottentot republic which has been formed under the patriarchal government of the missionaries".[614] It is not clear what the functions of these "magistrates" were or what their position was in regard to the two Provisie Kaptyns who acted on behalf of Cornelius Kok: it is possible that the latter were regarded as two of their number ex officio, although they may have possessed relatively greater authority in the community or greater independence of the missionaries. Burchell referred in 1812 to "an order from the Klaarwater Captain appointing [Hendrik Abrahams] to the duty of superintendent, or, as they call it, corporal, of one of the outposts",[615] without explaining the implications of the action or the duties of the office referred to.

The origins of more formally organised government at Klaarwater may be found in the discussions held there on 7 August 1813, during the historic visit of John Campbell, when according to Campbell's account, "We had a meeting with all the male inhabitants of the settlement who were in the town, to consider various points, especially about regulations for the protection of lives and property of the community."⁶¹⁶ At this meeting, which was addressed by the two Provisie Kaptyns, Cornelius Kok I and Barend Barends, Campbell, John Read, who was a member of his party, and the local missionaries William Anderson and Lammert Jansz, the following "general laws", stated to have been drawn up by Campbell, were adopted. They are basic regulations covering the matters which were obviously of the greatest importance in the daily lives of the small Griqua community of the Transorange: murder, housebreaking, cattle theft, damages to gardens and cornfields, and raiding expeditions.

I. That wilful murder be in every case punished by the death of the murderer. The execution to be always public, either by hanging or shooting.

II. That housebreaking be punished by public whipping—for the second offence, whipping and hard labour during a term which the judges may consider proper, or which may be afterwards agreed to.

III. Stealing a bull, ox, cow, horse, sheep or goat to be punished by restoring double or more, as shall be decided by the court—for a second similar offence, whipping and restoring double—for a third similar offence, a term of labour to be added to the former punishment.

IV. For stealing from a garden, either whipping or a term of labour for the person in whose garden the robbery was committed.

V. For robbing from a field in autumn, double restoration.

VI. For allowing cattle to feed near growing corn, if they go into that field and eat or destroy the grain, the proprietor of the cattle to pay double the loss that may have been sustained.

VII. If a Bushman, Coranna or any stranger be murdered, the murderer shall receive the same punishment as for murdering a Griqua.

VIII. Going upon a commando for plunder to be punished by a term of labour, and the property taken to be restored to its owners.

IX. If a Bushman, Coranna or other stranger commits murder, theft or any other crime within the limits of the Griqua country, the punishment to be the same as if he had been a Griqua.

X. That no person shall take it upon him to punish another, whatever injury he may have received from him, but must bring his charge against that person and prove it by witnesses before the court, which shall determine what is fit to be done.

XI. That no person who is to be a judge in any cause is to receive a present, directly or indirectly, from any of the parties whose cause is to be tried before him.

XII. In order to evade rule eleventh, should a person promise to give at a future time a present to any of the judges who are to try his cause, that person shall be fined, and if unable to pay the fine shall be adjudged to give a term of labour in proportion to the value of the fine.

XIII. That all persons flying from justice in the Colony in consequence of some crime they have committed, and coming among them, shall be delivered up to such persons as may be sent in pursuit of them.

XIV. That every person who shall endeavour to prevent the execution of the laws shall be punished as the court shall judge proper.

They likewise resolved that nine magistrates should be chosen to act as judges at Griqua Town, and one at each of the two principal outposts, who is to judge in smaller cases, but others are to be remitted to the judges at Griqua Town.

That the two Captains, Bern and Kok, with Messrs Anderson and Janz, be a court of appeal.

That the limits of the country be marked out in the course of one month, and the magistrates chosen.[617]

Some months later the missionary Jansz could report that nine magistrates had duly been elected in September, although they had difficulty in establishing or exercising their authority. The names he listed included those of several individuals prominent in the affairs of Griquatown and Philippolis: Jan Hendriks, Piet Pienaar, Willem Fortuyn, Petrus Davids, Klaas Barends and Moses Adam Renoster.[618] "The laws and regulations were written from time to time, and commenced as far back as 1822," declared Kaptyn Nicolaas Waterboer of Griquatown and his Councillors half a century later,[619] and this may be connected with a further development in the government of the Captaincy described by Melvill in his report: "In the beginning of January 1823 a union of the three Chiefs was effected, and at a meeting held for the purpose a plan was adopted for the government of the country, and some useful regulations were made, which were adopted by His Excellency the Governor."[620] The latter reference is, of course, to the time after the division of authority in the Transorange between Waterboer, Adam Kok II and Barend Barends.

More detailed information about the workings of the Griquatown Captaincy is no doubt to be found in documents in the Cape Town Archives Repository and the contemporary letters and journals of the LMS missionaries, and would also cast light on later developments at Philippolis, but for the present outline no further research has been undertaken in this regard. It is noteworthy, however, that the missionaries played an active role in the affairs of Griquatown from the days of Anderson's "Hottentot republic" and the establishment of Klaarwater, partly by the direct assertion of their authority over the settlement itself, which remained essentially a mission station, and partly by interference in the internal affairs of the Griquas, as illustrated by the election of Waterboer in 1820. Their special role was acknowledged and tacitly approved by the Cape Government in its instructions to Melvill, who was informed: "It is fortunate for the inhabitants of Griqua Town that the London Missionary Society has established a resident missionary there to communicate to them religious instruction. It will be a most essential part of your duty to encourage the attendance of the people to the instruction so charitably and zealously proffered to them, and you will be pleased to keep His Excellency apprised of the progress made in the introduction of Christianity among the Griquas and adjoining tribes."[621]

Waterboer's lively awareness of his debt to the missionaries,[622] and more specifically, as from 1826, his dependence on the guidance and advice of the forceful Peter Wright, strengthened the influence of the LMS in the affairs of Griquatown, and this was the pattern which Philip was consciously or unconsciously trying to imitate when he helped bring the Philippolis Captaincy into being, although the Koks and their followers were to prove considerably less pliable than Andries Waterboer and the Christian congregation at Griquatown.

As far as the government of the Philippolis Captaincy was concerned, when Adam Kok II was elected Kaptyn by the Griquas, Bergenaars and Korana of the Transgariep in October 1825, their first step was to obtain the approval of the Colonial authorities for the election. The Griquas, having moved into the Transorange from the Colony with the permission of these authorities and under the leadership of Kaptyns officially acknowledged by them, were always regarded as Colonial subjects, and when John Melvill in 1822 became the Government Agent at Griquatown, his appointment was stated explicitly to be "to tribes who have invariably been considered as dependent on this Colony". At the same time, however, the semi-autonomy of the Griquatown Captaincy was acknowledged in the statements: "It is His Excellency's[623] desire to interfere as little as possible with the customs which the Griquas have established among themselves, and by which they at present regulate themselves, as it is his desire to introduce order gradually, and more by recommendation than enactment"; and, "Assuming that the limits of the Griqua country and possessions are regularly defined, there remains no doubt but that all tribes residing within them should be considered subject to the laws of the Griquas, whether they be Boshuannas, Corrannas or others; and that any excesses, particularly murders, should be forthwith punished, under the Authority of the Heemraden, according to their own regulations."[624]

Melvill himself emphasised this situation in his lengthy report from Griquatown in December 1824:

> It may be well to premise that the Griquas have always been considered by the Colonial Government as dependent upon the Colony. The two old Chiefs, Adam Kok and Barend Barends, were appointed by Lord Caledon; and although these Chiefs were tolerated in their patriarchal or peculiar form of government, and not brought under the Colonial laws, the Colonial Government nevertheless took cognizance of their affairs, and on two different occasions, when disturbances rose among them, Captain Stockenstroom, the Landdrost of Graaff Reynet, was sent to endeavour to re-establish order.[625]

Philip made great play of Adam Kok's dependence on the Cape Government in his letter to Wade in 1834, writing, "The whole of the peaceable and industrious people of this district [*Philippolis*] would consider anything done against their Chief as done against the Colonial Government, while he retains the insignia of office conferred upon him by the Government; and it is on this principle that they have hitherto borne their condition, and the sufferings they have had to bear from the weakness of their Chief, and the influence of the Berghannas over him"; at the same time he made an energetic attempt to strengthen his own position with the assertion: "The Government appointed all the Chiefs on the recommendation of the missionaries."[626] It was in this context that Philip advised the Government to cut arbitrarily across the existing system by the appointment of new Kaptyns.[627]

In instituting and developing a form of government for his Captaincy within this framework, Adam Kok's precedents were the traditional Khoi system as retained or remembered by his own people, the customs and expectations of the Korana element among his followers, the government of Griquatown as it had developed formally over the preceding quarter of a century, and finally the Griquas' own knowledge and experience of the government of the Cape Colony, a system originally introduced by the Dutch, which was to survive well into the nineteenth century, and which comprised a Governor and Council assisted on a local level by landdrosts, *heemraden*, field-cornets, *wijkmeesters* and commandants. Colonial examples continued to be followed, and during the session of the Philippolis Raad which Andrew Smith attended in 1834, he found Hendrickze instructing the Councillors "as to what would be done in the '*Colonie*', while doubts were often expressed whether certain decisions were in keeping with the Colonial laws".[628]

The head of the polity was the Kaptyn, and the office seems to some extent to have partaken of what Elphick calls "the flexible nature of the Khoi captaincy"[629] already described above.[630] Andries Stockenstrom, who had close dealings with both Griquatown and Philippolis during the 1820s, declared before the Aborigines Committee that all the Kaptyns he had known were hereditary except for Waterboer, "a man that had worked himself up; he has been elected by the people", and that Adam Kok "was the son of old Cornelius Cock, who was the Chief, and that would make him a Chief", but at the same time he added concerning the latter, "I cannot recollect at this moment that I ever heard of his being appointed by any authority except that of the natives themselves."[631] This reflects the somewhat obscure nature of the succession, for among the Griquas the elective element seems to have become stronger than it had traditionally been, possibly as a result of missionary influence: this led most notably to the election of the outsider Waterboer at Griquatown in 1820, though when he died, he was in turn succeeded by his son Nicolaas Waterboer in the traditional manner. References to a Kaptyn appointing a successor may well have meant in fact that he gave an indication of his preference and that this was subsequently put to the vote.

On occasion the Kaptyn's place was taken by a deputy known as a Provisie Kaptyn (in later years—more correctly—Provisonele Kaptyn), who seems to have been appointed by the Kaptyn himself from among his Councillors. Andries Waterboer declared that Cornelius Kok I, while still living in Namaqualand, had appointed "deputies" over his people along the Orange River,[632] and in the same way he was claimed to have appointed Cornelius Kok II as Provisie Kaptyn at Campbell in 1824;[633] Barend Lucas who acted briefly after the departure of Abraham Kok from Philippolis in 1838 was presumably appointed by the Raad or elected by the people. In 1849, Jan Pienaar was described as "a person who usually acts in the absence of the Chief"[634] and in 1854 as "*onder kaptyn*",[635] while Ross refers to the "almost institutionalized installation" of Adam Eta Kok in the same capacity later in the 1850s.[636] This implies that the Provisie Kaptyn may have been a permanent official,[637] which could also well have been an survival of a traditional Khoi custom, for Elphick writes,

> In the western Cape it was very common for a chief to have a second-in-command (often his "brother" or a "brother-in-law") who was always present at parleys with the Dutch. For example, in 1707 a traveller among the Chainouqua and Hessequa listed two leaders for almost every kraal he encountered.[638]

In describing the events of 1825, Waterboer later stated, "When A. Kok arrived at the Mountains,[639] he made Counsellors and field cornets to assist in the proper government of the people."[640] This was the origin of the Philippolis Raad, but the historical development of this body is not clear.

During the meeting at Griquatown in 1813, it was determined, as already described, that laws be made "and judges or magistrates chosen to put them in execution", nine being elected for Griquatown and one each for Campbell and Hardcastle; the two Kaptyns and the two Griquatown missionaries were to serve as court of appeal,[641] which implies that the Kaptyns had by that time already acquired some form of authority over the magistrates originally instituted by the missionaries to administer the Baster settlements in the Transorange. The basic unit of Griqua government, the two Kaptyns and the eleven officials called "magistrates" or "*heemraden*" in contemporary documents, together approximated the Colonial landdrost and *heemraden*. Andrew Smith, however, visiting Griquatown some years after the event, noted on the basis of the information he received there: "Upon the elevation of Waterboer into power, something like a regular form of government was introduced. A council was elected to assist him, consisting of six of the most respectable inhabitants of his district, and with their advice he enacted laws, tried offenders, and punished crime (…)."[642] Following this information, one may therefore perhaps venture the opinion that the body comprising Kaptyns and "magistrates" had in practice assumed a shape approximating more closely to the traditional Khoi "council of the clan captains under his jurisdiction" described by Elphick, and that this transformation, formally recognised under Waterboer, was the origin of the Griqua Raad as it was henceforth to exist both at Griquatown and Philippolis.

In 1827 Cobus Pienaar was described by the missionaries as a *heemraad* of the Philippolis Captaincy,[643] but this term is not found elsewhere, nor does the term "magistrate" seem ever to have been used in this sense as far as Philippolis is concerned. The body governing the Captaincy was consistently known as the Raad (later also *Wetgevende Raad*), while a member was called a *Raad*, *Raadsman* or *Raadslid*; in English texts "Legislative Council" and "Councillor" were mostly used.

Apart from the stray reference to Pienaar mentioned above, the existence of the Philippolis Raad as a body appears for the first time in the memorial to Sir Lowry Cole dated 23 January 1829, which was signed by Kok and nine Councillors.[644] A similar document drawn up in October 1829 gives the names of ten Councillors,[645] after the elections in 1832 the Council appointed, according to Captain Armstrong, consisted of "three Griquas and three Bastards, Adam Kok President",[646] and the session of the Raad at which Andrew Smith was present in 1834 was attended by "eight members (…), in addition to the Secretary who was also a Councillor".[647] The full number would appear to have been ten, although twelve are mentioned in a law apparently dating from the 1850s.[648]

Something of the structure and workings of the early Captaincy may be learned by examining more closely the first identifiable members, those who signed the two memorials of 1829, although identifications must inevitably be tentative because of similarities of names and surnames.

Besides Hendrickze, a former member of the church at Griquatown, ex-Bergenaar and son-in-law to Adam Kok II, the signatories in January comprised: Willem Kok, who may have been either the uncle or the brother of Adam Kok; Gert Kok, who was killed on the expedition against Mzilikazi in 1831, and who was possibly a brother of Adam Kok, although the latter had a son of the same name who was a member of the Raad during the 1830s;[649] Jacobus or Cobus Pienaar (also known as "Kowis"), who was a member of the Raad by 1828;[650] Klaas Pienaar, baptised at Griquatown in 1808 and elected magistrate in 1813;[651] Jager Boer, brother-in-law to Kort Adam Kok (who is known to have been the brother of Cornelius Kok I and was therefore the uncle of Adam Kok II), who settled at Campbell in 1811 and signed the petition in favour of Adam Kok in 1825;[652] Goliat Jagers, whose name occurs on a collection list for the LMS at Campbell in 1820;[653] Piet Sabba, the former assistant of the LMS at Ramah, who has already been mentioned; and Arnoldus Constabel, who may be the same person as the "Brother Arnoldus of Grace Hill" (that is, the Bushman mission at Toornberg) who was paid by James Read in 1817 for transporting corn to Lattakoo— Jan Goeyman complained in 1825 of the raiding activities of members of the Constabel family settled at Philippolis.[654] Bearing in mind the fact that Adam Kok's wife was a member of the Pienaar family, as already mentioned, six of the nine are therefore known to have been related to the Kaptyn, and seven in all were connected in some way with the Kok group and the old Griquatown Captaincy; at least two seem to have had links with what may be called the "Bergenaar" element. Six of them are known to have been baptised or been supporters of the mission, but only two directly represented the "Baster" group and the mission connection.

Nine months later the names of Gert Kok and Andries Constabel had disappeared, and there were three new signatures to the memorial of September 1829, those of Cupido Dirks and David Jansen, of whom nothing more is known, and Lodewyk de Bruin. The latter was another of the original Baster settlers at Philippolis, who is still mentioned as Councillor and magistrate in the 1830s,[655] and the family seems to have been prominent members of the Baster group, for Joseph de Bruin was active in church affairs and recommended by Philip in 1832 as a replacement for Adam Kok.[656]

While the earliest members of the Raad may have been appointed by Kok himself, as claimed by Waterboer, there is a reference in 1831 to "the Counsellors last chosen",[657] and the Griqua treaties of 1837 and 1838 both stipulate, "The Chiefs shall have the power of appointing all the officers of the Government except the Legislative Council, which shall be elected by the people".[658]

The office of Secretary to the Raad is mentioned for the first time, albeit in an ambivalent way, in a surviving extract from a letter written by G.A. Kolbe of Philippolis to Dr Philip in August 1834 in which, discussing Griqua affairs, he adds, "I am of your opinion that it would be well if Hendriks were appointed as clerk to the Chief."[659] Andrew Smith, arriving at Philippolis in the same month, called Hendrickze "the secretary to Kok",[660] although the passage quoted earlier[661] might also imply that he was Secretary to the Raad, and Charles Bell described him as "Secretary to Government of Griqualand".[662] It was in 1834 too that Hendrickze is first known to have signed an official paper as "*Secretarij*", on behalf of Kok,[663] and the following year, during the interregnum after Kok's death, the document granting the land at Bethanie to the Berlin Missionary Society was signed by eight "Raden van Philippolis" who included "Hendrick Hendrickze, Secretaris".[664] Under Adam Kok III, Hendrickze regularly countersigned official letters and other documents with the Kaptyn, and the impression is given that he may originally have been both Councillor by virtue of his appointment or election and *de facto* personal secretary to the Kaptyn by virtue of his literacy and natural gifts, and that by his energy and talents he managed to combine these offices, making himself in practice Government Secretary of the Captaincy. In the formal Government notice concerning his dismissal in 1850, his office was stated to be "Secretary to the Griqua Government".[665]

Early directions for the proceedings of the Raad are given among the seven clauses of a somewhat rambling act in the Griqua law book dated 28 March 1821, a date which is written out in full, but is nonetheless obviously incorrect and must probably be read as 1831. It was to meet every other Monday, all deliberations were to be held with open doors, three members were to form a quorum, and differences of opinion were to be decided by a simple majority.[666] Its powers and duties, as set forth in a law dated 18 November 1833 were to call burghers to arms and try civil cases, but it also served as a court of appeal and as a village council for Philippolis.[667]

The only known account of sessions of the Raad was given by Andrew Smith, who attended those of 1 September and 22 December 1834, or rather forced himself upon the Councillors in the high-handed way of white observers.

> I proposed to Mr K[olbe] to request that I might be present. Upon the demand being made to the Captain, he evinced considerable reluctance as far as could be inferred from silence and look. I however persevered, and offered to assist with my advice, provided they would consider and discuss matters connected with themselves and the Colony. At last they agreed, and we entered upon the consideration of what would be the best understanding that should exist between them and the Colonial Government.
>
> From the first they all evinced a great suspicion of me, and from seeing that so evident, I could not refrain from requesting Mr Kolbe to inform them that I observed it. The Captain replied that I was a stranger to them, and that they did not know me; he neither said they were suspicious nor that they were not. It appeared to me that he comprehended the tendency of the suggestions I offered more thoroughly than the others, but he was less ready with remarks than the others. Hendrick Hendricks was the most pertinent in making sensible remarks, and the most clear in stating objections. The others occasionally offered very fair arguments against measures I suggested, and I was struck with the great caution they displayed in their various observations.[668]

On the second occasion Smith described the session as taking place "in the principal chamber in the dwelling house of the Chief. (...) The Chief himself appeared as president, and the other members were seated in chairs around a table on which was placed several documents that bore reference to the subjects which were to engage their attention."⁶⁶⁹

Summing up with reference to this latter session, Smith wrote that "no stranger could have been present without feeling that all that was required to make the Griqua nation an orderly and flourishing community was simply a little more strength in the executive government and a systematic mode of levying an adequate revenue to meet its expenses";⁶⁷⁰ but in his description of the proceedings he remarked at the same time that

> enough transpired to convince us of the weakness and inefficiency of the government. The want of a prescribed order of proceeding, such as existed in the magistrate's court,⁶⁷¹ exhibited the many deficiencies under which the nation laboured. Here opinions required to be formed according to existing circumstances, and many collateral subjects were of necessity brought forward, the importance of which were [*sic*] to be judged by the knowledge and discernment of the members before any determination could be arrived at relative to what ought to be the course of proceeding in the case.⁶⁷²

It was not until the 1850s, when laws were written down more conscientiously, that there is any fuller description of the duties of the Raad. Here an undated law which occurs in the sequence between acts of 1852 and 1858 referred to twelve members, apart from the *Provisie Raden* or deputies, who were to receive ten shillings per day during sessions and to meet twelve times a year on the first Monday of each month in the council chamber (*"bij de zitkamer des Raads"*); provision was made for keeping written minutes, and for a clerk or *"schrijver"*—apparently a distinct functionary from the Secretary—to take down evidence given before it. The business of the Council was clearly defined as:

> determining laws and necessary measures and institutions, hearing and investigating criminal cases as well as those of a civil nature in which the magistrate's office is not competent to judge, and for cases of appeals against the judgements and decisions, should there be reason thereto, of the magistrate's office.⁶⁷³

A magistrate or *magistraat*, in the sense of an official administering justice and resembling the Colonial magistrate or landdrost, had his seat at Philippolis, though seldom referred to, and the office survived until the last days of the Captaincy. In 1834, Smith identified the magistrate at Philippolis as "Cornelius ...";[674] this may possibly have been Cornelius Niels who had been deposed as Councillor in the Griqua *"coup d'état"* of 1832. In 1842, Gottlob Schreiner was accused "of having refused to appear before the magistrate of this place, or even the Chief and his Council",[675] and during the 1850s Jan Pienaar was mentioned as magistrate or acting magistrate (*"prov[isie] magistraat van Philippolis"*).[676]

The session of the magistrate's court attended by Smith took place on the morning of Monday, 22 December 1834, before the meeting of the Raad.

> When the time for these assemblies arrived, considerable bustle was observed in the village and a number of strangers poured to it from all directions. We repaired to the court of justice, which was held in a small building chiefly appropriated for legal proceedings. The judge we found to be a respectable looking Bastard, genteelly dressed in black clothes and seated before a large table well loaded with papers and record books. At a little distance from him the clerk of the court was actively preparing the various documents necessary for the proceedings that were about to commence. In the doorway stood the messenger of the court maintaining order and quiet without, and obstinately refusing entrance to anyone until the proper time of admission. On our arrival the magistrate rose from his seat, bowed respectfully, and made some remark to the clerk which was followed by the latter offering us seats. The preliminary arrangements were then resumed and, when completed, orders were given to admit the populace and to call on the first case, the particulars of which were read aloud.[677]

The session of the court were described in some detail by Smith, who concludes: "The order and regularity with which the various proceedings were conducted amply justify us in considering that, as far as regards details, the Griquas possess efficient materials for dispensing justice among themselves if they had but an executive government armed with sufficient confidence and furnished with adequate means to meet the necessary expenses should such a measure prove expedient for their general interest."[678]

Judging by the examples which have survived, Griqua justice was initially as rough as elsewhere on the South African frontier in the early nineteenth century. According to Waterboer, three Korana convicted of cattle stealing at Griquatown in the 1820s received 150 lashes each, "and then their liberty was given them. Two of them afterwards died in consequence of the severe cold on their wounds."[679] At Philippolis in 1827, Bushman cattle-thieves received 125 lashes each, "and the boys 8 or 10".[680] By 1859, however, the *Friend* of Bloemfontein could complain that three white men who had robbed the store of James Murray & Co. at Philippolis had received too lenient sentences: fines of £10 and £15, and one year's hard labour with 30 lashes.[681]

According to the law book, manslaughter was punishable with "*onthalzing*" (literally "beheading") and poisoning was "punished with the sword",[682] which may be reminiscences of eighteenth-century Dutch law, but robbery was to be punished "with the cord unto death",[683] and the normal punishments at Philippolis were lashes or hanging.

The law tentatively dated 1831 referred to disobedience to the orders of "the Kaptyn and Council, commandant, fieldcornet or any [other] official",[684] and Adam Kok II in 1834 appointed his son Abraham "Commandant of the country",[685] but this does not appear to have been a permanent post. Griquas took part in the battles of Swartkoppies (1845) and Boomplaats (1848) and in various of Major Warden's ill-advised campaigns under the Orange River Sovereignty, but this was probably on the informal basis common among the whites as well, and it is not known under whose leadership they stood, if any.

There are regular references to field-cornets in the Captaincy, who represented the authority of the Kaptyn on a local level, though their exact number is not known; in 1850 the names of six individuals were mentioned in a document, and this may well have been the total.[686] When Frederik Krotz was appointed field-cornet for Ramah in 1858, his salary was stated to be Rds50 a year, which was equivalent to £3 15s.[687] The document appointing Jan David as field-cornet of the ward of Riet River in 1852 concentrated on describing his duties in his judicial capacity as "*onder magistraats persoon*", which may be connected with the fact that this area had a sizeable white population and asserting the authority of the Kaptyn must have caused particular problems. It was the field-cornets who were most often involved directly in the squabbling and violence caused by the intrusion of white farmers who refused to acknowledge the authority of the Kaptyn.

While at Philippolis, Smith referred to "the Wyk master Vice",[688] who was probably the Andries Wiese already mentioned,[689] but this is the only known reference to this office in the Captaincy. The office was originally confined to Cape Town, where the official concerned was responsible for local matters such as licenses and the registration of strangers, but was extended to Stellenbosch in 1818 and Graaff-Reinet in 1821, and it will be remembered that Wiese came from the latter district.

A lesser-known functionary of the Captaincy was the *opziener van de zoutpan*, the keeper of the salt pan situated between Ramah and modern Douglas. The field-cornet Jan David was appointed to this office in 1852 and received detailed instructions as to his duties, including the stipulation that Rds1.5.2. be charged for every muid of salt removed; in the instructions his salary has, however, been left blank.[690] This too cannot have been a sinecure, for in 1834 already Andrew Smith noted that salt "has furnished a fertile source of dissension between the Griquas and the Colonists",[691] and elsewhere illustrated this statement with the description of an encounter with two white farmers from Zevenfontein (later Beersheba, near modern Smithfield):

> The object of their visit (…) was neither more nor less than to ascertain from me if I had given the Griquas orders to prevent the Christians—as the whites of South Africa designate themselves in contradistinction to the blacks—from gathering salt at the pans in the district of Philippolis. The answer was readily given, of course, in the negative, I at the same time informing them that I had no such powers entrusted to me. The elder of the two then stated that he had sent a waggon to bring some salt for himself and his companions, but that it had returned empty in consequence of the drivers having been ordered away by a party of Griquas, who stated that the Commission (as the farmers called our party) had given instructions that none of the Boers were in the future to obtain salt without buying it. "Now," continued he, "as that ap-

pears not to be the case, I shall send again and insist upon the supply required, or even secure it by force."[692]

In August 1852 the Griqua Government formally took possession of the salt pan and appointed David as *opziener*.[693]

In a survey of the government of the Captaincy, mention must finally be made of the church council, not only because it was a notable source of authority in the small community, but also because in practice it represented mainly the Baster party, and as such may almost be regarded as a political body, public meetings on church affairs largely serving to ventilate general grievances. The council was instituted in 1832, and consisted then of two elders and two deacons;[694] Prosper Lemue mentioned six members at a church service in 1855,[695] and seven signed the letter sent to the LMS when the congregation became independent of the missionary society in the same year.[696] While the subsequent independence of the church meant greater authority for the church council, this was, however, largely negated by the fact that they were deprived of the moral and practical support of the LMS both in the Cape Colony and England.

By the treaties between the Philippolis and Griquatown Captaincies in 1837 and 1838 a further element was added to Griqua government in the shape of a *Vereenigde Raad* or *Algemeene Raad*: this consisted apparently of the Kaptyns and Councillors of the two Captaincies, and was to be held alternately in each of the two capitals at least once a year, the Kaptyns alternating as chairman. In February 1848 the joint session was to have been held at Ramah, situated conveniently between the two capitals,[697] and in 1850 a supplement to the original treaty formally stipulated "that the annual meeting shall take place at Ramah (…) in the month of September; the half-yearly meeting shall take place according as circumstances shall require".[698]

Descriptions of the workings of the Vereenigde Raad are limited to its judicial functions, which attracted the attention of the outside world more readily than its legislative deliberations. According to the 1838 treaty it would act as a court of appeal for cases involving Rds200 or more, and was to confirm all death sentences;[699] in 1850 it was stipulated that six members, three from each Raad, plus the two Kaptyns, would constitute a quorum for this purpose.[700]

In 1871, Jan Pienaar, then living at Griquatown, declared, "so long as I was in the country, the Combined Court had two Bushmen hung at

Ramah and one at Griqua Town. The Bushman [sic] hung at Ramah had shot a Boer, but what offence the one at Griqua Town had done I don't know."[701] The trial at Ramah in 1848 received some publicity in the Colonial press, as already noted,[702] and the subsequent execution of sentence was described at length in the *Cape of Good Hope Observer*.

> (…) on the following day, the 22nd December, about 4 p.m., the criminals were led to the scaffold, accompanied by about 200 spectators. Before the sentence was carried into execution, Mr Frederick Kotzee [*Krotz*], a native local preacher in connection with the London Missionary Society, offered up prayers. The criminals were hanged after that, to wit, Jacob and Vigiland. Zwartbooy was beaten under the gallows with a hundred and fifty lashes.
>
> After all this, Capt. Waterboer made a speech to the spectators, to the effect that it was his duty and consistent with his office and situation to have performed this painful duty, how unpleasant so ever it may have been to him, and remarked that had it been Griquas who were guilty of such a crime, he would have performed that duty with redoubled vigour &c. &c.
>
> The Chief Kok likewise addressed the spectators, showing that evil begins with little things and proceeds from little to great. That it begins with the stealing of a knife, yet gets to stealing cattle, horses, &c., and what is worse, theft ends with murder, as is the case of the late individuals, who robbed other people's cattle, and eventually murdered the owners, and that he was obliged, consistent with his own laws, to punish by death those who designedly and deliberately deprive their fellow-creatures of life, and that unexceptionably, Griqua and Bushmen as well as any of his other subjects.[703]

In 1852, the *Friend* reported that "some cases of importance" were due to be heard by the Vereenigde Raad in a session at Philippolis.[704]

7. The Government of the Captaincy: Laws and customs

The boundaries of the territory regarded by Adam Kok II and his successors as falling under their jurisdiction were established in a gradual and erratic fashion, and initially there was no great need for them to be clearly defined.

In the agreement signed by Adam Kok II and the French missionary Jean-Pierre Pellissier of Bethulie in 1835, the boundary between the Captaincy and the "institution of the Caledon", as it was then called, was said to be Bossiespruit,[705] and in the treaty of 1837 with Waterboer, Abraham Kok's boundary was partially described as "Ramah on the west, and running eastward along the boundary line of the Colony [*i.e., the Orange River*] to Cornet's Spruit. The northern boundary line remains unfixed."[706] Two years later, however, Backhouse explicitly mentioned the "Mankey River", six miles (some 10 kilometres) to the west of Ramah, as the boundary between the Philippolis and Griquatown Captaincies.[707]

In the definition of the area of white settlement issued by the Kaptyn and Raad to the party of M.A. Oberholster in 1840, the northern boundary of Griqua authority would seem to be defined by implication as the Riet River from David's Graf eastward to Renosterspruit "and upwards in a direct line to Caffre River [*Tierpoort River*] where the wagon road crosses for Nieuwland;[708] and further in a direct line to the high country of Caffre River".[709] The Maitland treaty of 1846 defined only the southern portion of the Captaincy, in which ground was to be regarded as "unleasable" to whites, accepting David's Graf and Ramah as boundaries to the west and Bossiespruit to the east.[710]

The territory described in this book as the "Philippolis Captaincy" also did not have a definite name for the first few decades of its existence. The term "Griqualand" occurs in John Campbell's first travel journal, published in 1815,[711] as an indication of the Klaarwater or Griquatown Captaincy. After the establishment of Adam Kok at Philippolis it appears to have been used loosely for the entire area of Griqua occupancy in the Transorange, in much the same way as "Bushmanland" or "Korannaland"; it seems to be in this sense that Andrew Smith wrote in 1834, for example, of Hendrickze being "a person not at all desirable for Griqualand".[712] The treaty between Adam Kok III and Waterboer in 1838 confirmed this comprehensive usage officially in its declaration: "The country belonging to the two Chiefs and their people shall be called Griqualand and shall be governed by the presently known Chiefs, viz., Andries Waterboer of Griquatown and Adam Kok of Philippolis."[713] "Basterland", a term frequently used in Dutch, had the same general descriptive value, referring either to Griquatown or to Philippolis or both: so Frans Lion Cachet could write in 1882, "Among the Boers [Griqualand West] is still called 'Bastardland'."[714]

The Philippolis Captaincy seems at first to have been referred to more specifically as a "district" or else—both in Dutch and English texts—as a "*wijk*", clearly distinguished in this sense from the *wyk* falling under a field-cornet. One of the earliest recorded Griqua laws, tentatively dated 1831, already uses the term "no burgher of this district",[715] while Peter Wright in 1838 commented that Adam Kok, with his election, "took upon himself to care for the honour and interests of the district"[716] and the Dutch inscription on Wright's tombstone speaks of his own labours *"in het district van Philippolis"*. Gottlob Schreiner in 1840 referred to "the [white] farmers who live within this district", but in the same letter proposed leaving Atkinson in charge of the station and himself acting "as an itinerant missionary in the *Wijk*" and stated, "To attend to this *Wijk* as it ought to be, two or three missionaries besides a number of native agents and schoolmasters are required"[717]—examples such as these could be multiplied.

When local government was instituted for the Orange River Sovereignty in 1849, one of the magistrates' districts in the area of white occupancy was defined as "The district of Griqua Land, of which Bloem Fontein and 'the Queen's Fort' is the seat of magistracy";[718] the name soon seems to have been appropriated by the Philippolis Captaincy specifically for its own territory, however, and the declaration by which the "*Lands Raad*" or Land Council was established in 1850 held it responsible for "the beacons and all farms within the territory of Griqualand".[719] By the end of the decade the term had been generally accepted in the latter sense, and it was freely used both by Adam Kok and the Free State authorities when the purchase of the Philippolis territory was being negotiated.[720]

The Captaincy had no coat of arms, flag or anthem, and obviously felt no need for these trappings, but it is interesting to note that printed land grant forms known to have been issued by Adam Kok III *"te Nieuw Griqua-land, Mount Currie"* (the later Kokstad) in 1867 bear at the head the image of a lion.[721] This is a realistic, non-heraldic image which seems obviously to have been derived from a cliché in the standard stock of a local printer, but its use indicates that the need for some form of national emblem had by that time come to be felt.

The inhabitants of the Captaincy were referred to indiscriminately as "Griquas" and "Basters", and infrequently also as "Hottentots". A clear sense of self-awareness on the part of the Griquas themselves, or at least of their leaders, may be found by at least 1843 in Hendrik Hendrickze's reference to the fact "that we (…) are a people this day" and his statement "We are a Christian nation."[722] By 1852 the Kaptyn and Raad could acknowledge Nicolaas Waterboer's succession to the Griquatown Captaincy on behalf of "the Griqua nation",[723] and in 1860 Adam Kok III expressed his wish for peace "between the Griqua nation and the Government of the Orange Free State".[724]

By a law of 1833 every citizen (*"een ieder burger"*) of the Captaincy was obliged to fight for and defend the country (*"het land"*) when called upon to do so by the Kaptyn and Raad,[725] but citizenship was not formally defined until 1858, when a law was made stating "That all youths [*"jongelingen"*] as soon as he [*sic*] attains the age of 20 years shall be regarded as a burgher, and then the Government will require military duties [*"burgerdienst"*] from such person or persons through the field-cornet under whom he falls."[726]

The Sotho refugees in Griqua territory Kok regarded as "subject to my laws only as long as they reside in my country",[727] and this would also have been the attitude of the Griquas to the white Colonists living in the territory. While the British authorities at the Cape, by means of the Cape of Good Hope Punishment Act of 1836,[728] extended their authority over Colonial subjects as far as the 25th degree of south latitude, Andries Stockenstrom at the time of his meeting with Abraham Kok on the Orange River in the following year informed the whites of the region explicitly and officially "that any Colonist entering the territory which the Griquas occupy must submit to the laws and authorities which may be there established',[729] and this was subsequently confirmed by a letter from

Stockenstrom's secretary to the Civil Commissioner of Colesberg:

> It is in the mean time necessary that you be made aware that His Majesty's Government claims no jurisdiction of any kind over the said Griquas, that they are consequently to be considered as independant [sic] people, and that those who go amongst them must submit to their laws and regulations.[730]

This principle was repeated at intervals until 1848, when Sir Harry Smith abandoned all pretext of supporting the Griquas against the whites, but the white Colonists themselves consistently refused to acknowledge Griqua authority, and by the statement of policy issued in 1840 the Kaptyn and Raad were obliged to permit "the governing members of the Colonists' community" to appoint and instruct their own field-cornets.[731] At the same time the whites for their part clearly stated: "Although the emigrant farmers acknowledge the Government of Philippolis as proprietors and owners as far as our country exists, (…) yet we declare that the Colonists in this country retain their own Colonial laws according to their customs and can at all times act accordingly without molestation."[732]

As appears from various documents already quoted, the Kaptyn was elected and, on occasion, deposed at public meetings, and these were also called for the election of Councillors or to debate any development of general concern, such as the projected treaties with Waterboer and the Cape Colony. Concerning the proposals of Sir George Clerk in 1853–54 that sale of land in the Unleasable Territory be permitted, Adam Kok III wrote, for example, "I summoned a meeting of my people, but they immediately rejected the proposal, and decided that they would not leave the country, but that they are ready and prepared if the circumstances should make it necessary even to lay down their lives should circumstances render it necessary to retain their country and freedom."[733] At Griquatown, at any rate, the Kaptyn would seem to have been responsible to the Raad and the people, for Andries Waterboer declared, with reference to the events of the early 1820s: "The Captains Barends and Adam [Kok II] were several times brought before the Council and people, and spoken to respecting their neglect of duty, and at the same time warned of the uproar they were causing in the country through this neglect and unfaithfulness in duty."[734]

Although it is nowhere expressly stated, only the male members of the community had these privileges and responsibilities, as was customary at the time, both in the Cape Colony and in indigenous African societies.

As far as land ownership is concerned, Nicolaas Waterboer and his Councillors declared in 1872 with regard to the customs of Griquatown: "Private owners could sell and buy among themselves, i.e., one Griqua subject to another; but the consent of the Chief in Council was necessary to render the transaction lawful. No foreigner could obtain lawful right to land. These occupiers had no right to sell." In addition, however, they pointed out, "there are other members of the Griqua community who occupied 'kraals' or stations with common rights, such as are generally observed by the aboriginal inhabitants of Africa."[735]

Adam Kok III later mentioned to Dr Philip "a law against selling any of the lands" which was made in 1830,[736] and while this is not recorded in the law book of the Philippolis Captaincy, a law "Concerning the transportation or sale of farms" passed in 1838 clearly stipulates that in such a transaction "the farm mentioned can in no way be sold to any Colonist or burgher or anyone else except legal subjects of Kaptyn Adam Kok or his successors".[737] In 1845, Kok wrote to the Colonial Secretary:

> Individual right of property is recognized by our laws, but no lands can be hired or sold among my own people without my consent, and it is contrary to our laws to sell land to any person not being a Grikwa subject.
>
> I should not be able to alienate any portion of my territory without the consent of all my people, as such an act would require the change of one of our fundamental laws.[738]

J.J. Freeman of the LMS, when questioned in 1851 by a Select Committee of the British Parliament on land ownership in what had by then become the "leasable" portion of the Captaincy, explained that Griqua farmers might not necessarily occupy the land they owned: "they might not be living upon the spot, but it had been distinctly recognized as theirs, as much as in the case of any English gentleman here having three or four estates, and not living upon the whole of them. The land was marked out; each Griqua was recognized as having a right to his particular farm. There he may take his cattle in the dry season if there is a fountain there, or he may reside there himself." He likewise noted the ownership of the Griquas as regards the fountains: "The Griqua may have been living 20 miles from it, but the fountain has been recognised as his. He goes there occasionally; in the rainy season he may send his cattle there to obtain fresh grass, and so on."[739]

As an example of the granting of land to Griquas by the Kaptyn and Raad, the following request which has been preserved in the Free State Archives Repository may be quoted. It is dated 13 September 1842, and is a renewal of an original request of 1833 involving an unnamed farm (translated literally).

> Herewith the request is renewed as the old request has been lost (of 1833) issued by the old late Kaptyn Adam Kok Senior at the request of the burgher Jan Kraalshoek,[740] as lawful property of him and his heir, according to the laws of the country now in force, on condition that the burgher Jan Kraalshoek shall on no account sell this farm to any burgher or Colonist, and if such sale should take place, that such farm is to be hired out [to another?].[741] Confirmed by his successors, viz. Kaptyn Adam Kok who now rules as Kaptyn with his Council.[742]

The agreement between the Kaptyn and the missionary J.P. Pellissier of Bethulie in 1835 concerning "the limits between Philippolis and the institution" would seem to be an implicit acknowledgement of the independence of Bethulie, but the Paris Missionary Society had settled there with the encouragement of Dr Philip, and the conditions on which they did so were never stated clearly.[743] As the local Chief, Lephoi, succeeded in gaining control of the station, the Griquas attempted several times during the 1840s and 1850s to assert their own authority over him and thus over Bethulie as well, and in 1859 Adam Kok III went so far as to depose Lephoi in favour of his son Kgora. His authority to do so was not, however, acknowledged by any of the parties involved, and in the same year Lephoi sold the station to the Free State Republic, over the protests of both Kok and Pellissier.[744]

In 1834 Bethanie near the Riet River was granted to the German missionaries intending to work among the Korana of Piet Witvoet as "legal property of the [Berlin] Missionary Society in accordance with the laws of the country now in force", and the proviso was added "on the condition that the said place Bethanie and (?) the school fall under the territory of Philippolis";[745] according to Andrew Smith, who was present when the matter was discussed by the Raad, "it was determined that the recently formed establishment should be considered as a branch of the mission at Phillipolis [*sic*], its inhabitants to be ruled by the Griqua Government".[746] Smith stated that the Raad

> seemed to consider that [the German missionaries] were too distant from Philippolis or else too near it; they seemed to fear that their residence amongst them would be followed by division in the country; that an independent party would rise up with them and endeavour to establish an independent Chief. From the state of the country and the characters of the people I am not disinclined to adopt the same opinion.[747]

The Maitland Treaty of 1846, however, stipulated that "the lands heretofore enjoyed by the Korannas under Chief Goliat[748] and by the missionary station at Bethany shall be considered as excepted, which lands shall be preserved inviolate for the said Chief and station."[749] By 1854, Bethanie was governed by its own "local laws", and among the ten men who declared themselves unwilling to submit to this were members of the Buffelboud family and other Korana,[750] together with "Bahrend Philipp" who had signed the petition requesting the appointment of Adam Kok II as Kaptyn in 1825, whose arrival on the station the missionaries had reported in 1835,[751] and who had been a member of the local Raad in 1850.[752] What occurred here was the opposite of what happened at Bethulie, for the German missionaries managed to wrest from the Korana whatever control they had ever possessed, although Goliat Ysterbek tried vigorously to re-assert his authority during the 1850s, and as late as 1867 had still not abandoned the attempt.[753]

The French missionaries had been established at Bethulie by Dr Philip in his usual high-handed way, while permission for the establishment of Bethanie was somewhat grudgingly granted by the Raad. In 1839, when it was suggested that the problems between Atkinson and Schreiner be solved by the establishment of a second station for the LMS within the Captaincy, the Kaptyn and Raad procrastinated, and on one occasion are said to have written informing Schreiner "that they did not any longer intend to have another station established, being fearful of a division among the people".[754]

At Griquatown the "general laws" of 1813 must have been written down, and after the Council of the three Kaptyns in 1823, "a paper containing the regulations" made by them was sent to the Bergenaars for their information,[755] while the Waterboer treaty of 1837 stipulated of the two Griqua Kaptyns that they "shall govern according to the written and known laws".[756] The existing law book of the Philippolis Captaincy, now in the Cape Town Archives Repository, is a large bound volume obviously much used and containing laws made both at Philippolis and subsequently at Kokstad.[757] The earliest is dated 1821, which, as already stated, seems to be an obvious error and indicate 1831; the earliest law which can be dated from internal evidence must have been passed in the latter year. The first law entered in the book, however, is one enacted on 11 March 1838, which may be presumed to be the year when entries in the book were begun, and these become notably fuller and more regular after 1852, when Conrad Windvogel was appointed Secretary. Earlier laws would have been entered retrospectively as there was time and opportunity or as they occurred to those concerned, but the law book is by no means complete. Writing to Philip in 1842, for example, Adam Kok III stated, "We have a law against selling any of the lands, that was made in 1830, in my father's time",[758] and in a diary entry for 23 May 1832, Kolbe mentioned "that the Chief has prohibited the sale of spirits at the station",[759] but neither of these enactments is recorded in the law book.

As in the case of the early regulations for Griquatown, the laws entered here illustrate the matters which were in one way or another of practical importance to the people of the Captaincy; these were robbery, theft, murder, malicious injury to "cattle, horses, dogs &c.", libel, marriage, the transfer of land, trading in liquor, the salt pan, the duties of the Raad and of field-cornets, and the rights and duties of citizenship, including military duties. A number of the laws, however, such as those affecting land ownership, the absconding of Bushmen in the service of Boers and others, and assaults on officials, were probably occasioned mainly by the presence of white farmers in Griqua territory and the friction to which this gave rise.

Apart from the law book which has thus survived, the Philippolis Government also had other records, and on his departure for Nomansland in 1861 Adam Kok left his "Government books" in the hands of the former Griqua Secretary, W.J. Crossley.[760] These would seem to have disappeared, although fragments may well be scattered among the extensive records of the Griqualand West Land Court now in the Cape Archives Repository; the official records of the Kokstad Captaincy have, however, survived, and are likewise in the Archives Repository.[761]

As already mentioned, the Griqua law book also contains among its earlier entries municipal regulations for Philippolis, and it was with specific reference to these that Andrew Smith felt called upon to comment on the innate weakness of Griqua authority. "Mr Kolbe once was upbraiding the Chief for not punishing certain offences," he wrote, "and was telling him it would never do if things were to go on so. At last the old man got a little vexed and replied, 'If I begin to punish, I must first punish myself ten times as severely, for I have equally broken the regulations'."[762] Elsewhere Smith reported that at one of the sessions of the Raad he attended, "some desultory conversation took place during which allusions were made to the inefficacy of several of the enactments that had lately been made, and to the inadequacy of the present executive to maintain the existing laws, or even to carry on with success the general affairs of the tribe";[763] in his diary he commented, "Many of the irregularities which occur in this country are passed without punishment, not because they are considered not meriting punishment, but because the Government of this country are afraid of the offenders. Till some more efficient system of Government be introduced, good order will never be established."[764] By the late 1840s and 1850s, when both the government and the economy improved and a sense of national identity began to develop among the Griqua people, the LMS was, however, no longer able to provide effective support, and the authority of the Kaptyn and Raad was increasingly and systematically defied by the white settlers in the area with the tacit support of the British authorities and later the active encouragement of the Orange Free State. In fact the Philippolis Captaincy never had the opportunity to prove itself.

On the whole, the missionaries at Philippolis were inclined to adopt an autocratic manner, as when Schreiner—admittedly an extreme case—reported on his having "insisted on the Chief's ordering [a 'profligate European'] from the place".[765] The missionaries were also much inclined to refer to all Griquas, and to all non-whites in general, indiscriminately by their first names, regardless of status, and this included the Kaptyn himself on occasion. As far as the missionaries are concerned, there was, however, constant friction of some sort, but although the Griquas had in 1826 settled on an established mission station, James Clark's authority over them as mere mission artisan was not strong, and the fact of his having made the station over to the Griqua formally placed them firmly in control from the beginning. "The Old Inhabitants of Philippolis have become subject to Adam Kok," wrote Clark to Stockenstrom, apparently early in 1827, only a few months after the arrival of the Griquas, "as it is impossible for the missionary to act as Captein and Adam Kok also",[766] and this seems to have been the attitude of Clark's successors as well, even though they may have been better educated and possessed more self-confidence than he.

For all practical purposes, Philippolis was governed as a Griqua village, and it does not appear that the missionaries interfered unduly in its affairs, as they were only too ready to do in similar situations at Griquatown and elsewhere. Dr Philip's regular assertion of the dependence of the Kaptyns on the LMS also does not seem to have had any noticeable practical effect on the government of the Captaincy. The Kaptyn and his Raad realised the importance of Philip's influence with the Colonial authorities, and were to some degree dependent on the individual missionaries for assistance in drawing up documents and for advice; but the Griqua party demonstrated its independence quite clearly during Philip's visit to Philippolis in 1832, and in the regular clashes on the stations the missionaries were invariably worsted and compelled to retreat.

With regard to the neighbouring polities, there appears to have been constant contact between Philippolis and Griquatown, which was formalised by the treaties of 1837 and 1838 and the institution of the Joint Council already described.[767] As regards the Captaincy of Cornelius Kok II at Campbell, there seems likewise to have been good relations and regular contact, and some of the correspondence between Campbell and Philippolis has also survived;[768] Cornelius was present at Philippolis during the visit of A.B. Armstrong in October 1833 and that of Andrew Smith in September of the following year. Armstrong described him simply as "Capt[ai]n of Campbell",[769], while according to Smith he was "a provisional chief under 'Dam Kok"[770] and "his deputy in that part of the country"—an impression possibly fostered by Adam.[771] On the other hand, Smith also gave an account of discussions some months later between Adam Kok and his brother, here described as "the Chief of Campbell", at which the two seem to have met on an equal footing.[772]

After his ill-advised support of his nephew, Kaptyn Abraham Kok, during the Griqua civil war of 1838, Cornelius's position became even more anomalous, and the situation is further obscured by various prejudiced statements later made on the matter, especially at the time of the Diamond Fields dispute, but in practice he seems to have continued acting as Kaptyn at Campbell without interference. In 1840, only two years after his deposition, a "general assembly" was held at Philippolis to settle the differences between him and Waterboer,[773] while in the same year he and the Kora leader Jan Bloem Jr issued an independent statement acknowledging the rights of the white settlers in their territory similar to that issued by the Philippolis Captaincy.[774] In 1848, in spite of Philip's opposition, Cornelius was formally recognised as Kaptyn by the Cape authorities.[775] He resigned in 1857, in favour of Adam Kok III, who appointed as his Provisie Kaptyn John Bartlett, son of the former missionary artisan of the same name,[776] Bartlett being succeeded in 1861 by Dirk Kok.[777] After the sale of the Philippolis lands to the Free State Government, Adam Kok III denied that he had, "as heir to Cornelius Kok", disposed of Cornelius's rights and claims to "both on the near and the far side of the Vaal River".[778]

Concerning the relationship between the Philippolis Captaincy and the various other tribal leaders in the Transgariep less is known, although it would appear to have been good, and it was moreover increasingly necessary for them to make common cause against the encroachments of the whites moving into their respective territories. So Kok could, for example, be requested to act as Chief of the independent Springbok Korana in the temporary absence of Jan Bloem,[779] and he later consulted "my friends Moshesh, Waterboer and Letsea"[780] on his difficulties with the Free State.[781]

As far as the Cape Colony is concerned, the dependence of the Captaincy on the Colonial Government for ammunition and for recognition of the authority of its Kaptyns has been mentioned already, and this was never denied by the more law-abiding section of the Griquas. As early as January 1834, Adam Kok II in his interview with Henry Somerset requested that the British authorities place a Resident in or near the Transorange, and by the middle of the year a treaty with the Cape Colony had already been mooted, a possibility earnestly pursued by means of Kok's visit to Cape Town in the winter of 1834 and Abraham Kok's interview with Stockenstrom in January 1837. The eventual result of the sustained endeavours of the Griquas was the successive treaties with Sir George Napier in 1843, Sir Peregrine Maitland in 1846 and Sir Harry Smith in 1848,[782] in which their rights were established but at the same time progressively eroded in favour of the white settlers in their territory and the protection afforded them by Great Britain steadily diminished. During the 1850s the possibility of a treaty with the Free State Republic was raised by the latter, but the Griquas, still preferring to ally themselves with the British and, hoping for British support, managed to postpone it indefinitely, in spite of the pressure exerted on them by the Free State;[783] it may be said finally to have been concluded in the form of the deed of sale by which "the lands in Griqualand still belonging to the [Griqua] Government" were sold to the Free State Government on 26 December 1861.[784]

8. The Captaincy in the 1840s (1843–1851)

After the unexpected death of Peter Wright in 1843, his family continued to live at Philippolis, and his son John temporarily took charge of the station.

An interesting occurrence in the church life of the community during this period was that the women of the congregation some time after Wright's death wrote formally to their sisters at Griquatown. This letter has unfortunately not been traced, and the only record of it is the reply they received, an English translation of which is to be found in the archives of the LMS. Though only indirectly concerned with Philippolis, this document is so remarkable a record, especially as regards the women of the Griqua community, that it deserves full quotation. It is dated Griquatown, 29 May 1843.

> Beloved Sisters in our Lord Jesus Christ—We have received your mournful letter, for which we heartily thank you; we read it at our meeting Thursday morning before all the sisters of the church in Griqua Town. We have learnt of your painful situation through the loss of our beloved Pastor, that you are now in distressing circumstances, without a guide, without a shepherd and without a leader, and all this when the church is in a very weak state.
>
> You request our sympathy with you and our prayers that the Lord will be merciful to you and not altogether leave you alone. Beloved sisters, Jesus said: I will in no wise leave you, I will come to you and I will give you my Holy Spirit to teach you and lead you unto all truth, and to be your Comforter in the time of persecution and trials; and this Comforter will remain with you and shall not be taken from you for ever.
>
> Beloved sisters, this is a very trying time for us all, but especially for you who are now deprived of the privilege of a teacher. We feel with you: the tears which you shed are *our* tears also, your interests are *our* interests, the welfare of the cause of Christ among

you is *our* welfare. We hope that we have all one aim, one endeavour, one cause alone worthy of our tears when it is in adversity and our joy when it is prosperous, and that is the Kingdom of Christ on earth and the glory of his name. Thus, beloved sisters, we cannot but feel with you, and we hope that we shall never forget you in our weak prayer at the throne of grace to which the Apostle urges us to come with confidence through Our Lord Jesus Christ who is our mediator with the Father and who can sympathize with all our sorrow and our necessities. There we can together as one church pour out our wants before the Lord, and He sits on a throne of grace and waits to be gracious to every one who takes refuge in Him.

Beloved sisters, the Lord has called his Church here and at Philippolis with a loud voice: "Awake ye that sleep and Christ shall give you light." The Lord has seen it needful to call us thus. He knows the state of each heart in the Church. He knows when his Church is wakeful and zealous in his service, and he knows also when it is in a slumbering state, and each one should earnestly ask "has this voice come o my heart?" He has stretched out his hand to us and taken away one who was dear to us, in whom we had the greatest interest; yes, we loved him, because he has done much for our souls' welfare; he was with us in much suffering and made many sacrifices for the good of the cause amongst us; in prosperity and adversity he had at heart the welfare of us Griquas and Bechuanas; his company among us was for many years the comfort and stirring up of our hearts; he was indeed our spiritual father, our friend, our brother and our counsellor whenever we met with difficulties in the narrow way; he was always ready to give us instruction and encouragement where it was needful. Who among us will not be thankful after his death for all the love he showed us? He spent his life among us in doing good.

Such a friend have we lost; the loss is great and discouraging, but we rejoice even here that what has happened is with the permission of our Heavenly Father who has all things in his hand and does all for good to those that fear Him. His cause is dear to him as the apple of his eye, and no hair of our heads can fall without his holy will. Death has no power to rob us of any one dear to us without an order from the throne of God; but the time which God had appointed him to strive for the Gospel was ended, he must lay down his weapon and rest from his labours.

We have right then to mourn over our loss as the children of Israel mourned the loss of their leader; but we have no right to murmur; we dare not find fault or say, Lord, why hast Thou done this? But may this be the language of each one's heart:

> *Submissive to the will, O God!*
>   *We all to Thee resign,*
> *Bowing beneath thy chastening rod,*
>   *We mourn but not repine.*
> *It is the Lord should we distrust*
>   *Or contradict his will,*
> *Who cannot do but what is just,*
>   *And must be righteous still.*

We rejoice much over what we have heard from time to time and also from your letter respecting the prosperity of the work of the Lord among you. It appears that the last work of his servant has been followed by his blessing; we hope and trust that he will pour out more of his blessing on us; if we but earnestly pray and seek the Lord, He will not leave us without a blessing, and we hope that you will also pray for us that we may be stirred up to new zeal. Our hearts, dear sisters, are much inclined to grow cold in what is good, and if we do not watch and pray for one another and stir one another up, we shall become quite careless in what respects our salvation. Thus, dear sisters, we must work the work of him who sent us as it is called the day, for the night cometh wherein no man can see to work. "All that your hand findeth to do, do it with all your might."

We have resolved to hold our prayer meeting on the Thursday at the same time with yourselves, and we hope that the Lord will bow down his ear to our unworthy prayers for his Son's sake.

We greet you all with one heart and one voice, and remain, your affectionate sisters in the Lord, G. Fortuin,[785] in the name of all the sisters of the Church in Griqua Town.[786]

After Wright's death, the members of the Philippolis congregation tried energetically to obtain the services of James Read Sr of Kat River, a well-known champion of the Khoikhoi, or failing him, James Read Jr, his son by his Khoi wife. From Cape Town, however, Dr Philip wrote to the missionary James Kitchingman of Bethelsdorp:

> For the present necessity I have informed them that I am going to send Mr Thomson to their assistance. Mr Thomson has been five years in my family; he is a very acceptable preacher in the Dutch language; he is well acquainted with business and will be able to assist them greatly in their correspondence with Government, and from his [*word illegible*] and his general information he will be of great use to them for a time. Mr Thomson will leave this on Monday by the steamer, so that you may expect him soon after you receive this letter.[787]

W.Y. Thomson arrived at Philippolis in the course of 1843, was ordained there in February 1844, on which occasion sixty to seventy wagons were noted in the village,[788] and was married in the same year to Agnes Wright, a daughter of the late missionary. Her mother, the widow Margery Wright, who was a strong personality and an extremely difficult person, not only remained at Philippolis, where she continued to occupy the mission house, but her brother, John Wright, farmed at Boomplaats nearby. This may well have had its drawbacks, but it gave Thomson the advantage of being connected to a missionary family with great status among the Griquas and possessed of considerable influence in local affairs, as well as enjoying their immediate presence and support. He seems to have defended the interests of the Griquas with some vigour during a difficult period which included the unrest which culminated in the defeat of the Republican Boers by British forces at Swartkoppies in Griqua territory in 1845, the subsequent negotiations at Touwfontein and the Maitland Treaty. William Porter, who met him at this time, described him as "a well-looking and intelligent young man" and "a smart young man not unconscious of his smartness, and, from temper and position, a good deal of a partizan", and suspected him of being in touch with Dr Philip's son-in-law John Fairbairn, the editor of the *South African Commercial Advertiser* in Cape Town, which had adopted pro-Griqua views.[789]

Porter, an Irishman with a somewhat caustic tongue, gave an extremely negative description of Philippolis when he accompanied Sir Peregrine Maitland to the negotiations at Touwfontein in June 1845.

> The first impression as you enter Philippolis is not imposing. (...) There are a few houses of brick and a few more of clay, but without any appearance of cleanliness or comfort about either, while the greater majority of the wretched population live in wigwams made of matting, into which they creep on all fours, and which have no outlet for the smoke except the opening which admits their occupants. The church, which stands across the main street, is broken backed, partly unroofed and in a state of general decay. Gardens (or plots of ground apparently meant for gardens) are attached to some of the houses, but though there are means of irrigation, I saw no marks indicating that anything had ever been sown or planted. In the town and neighbourhood there was not to be found a drop of milk, a bit of butter, a potato or any other sort of vegetable. (...)
>
> The Dragoons, who are encamped about a quarter of a mile up the stream of water that supplies the town, made a dam to deepen it. This might have been imitated lower down, but such is not the manner of the Griquas. When the oxen, horses &c. go to drink, the inhabitants resort with scoops and other utensils to lift out of the mud the water for the evening. The Griqua ladies were the naiads of this fountain, and when I chanced to pass were congregated in great numbers. There were cutty sarks[790] enough among them that, had Tam O'Shanter been looking on, would have made him think his "een enriched". They were an antidote to every amorous emotion. But while employed in the primitive employment of drawing water, a dispute arose between two nymphs, who instantly, like Irishmen, began to box most furiously. And then such a vociferous cawing commenced among the other fair as was never heard out of a rookery. I could make neither head nor tail of it, and the General,[791] who was also looking on, was equally at fault. The good man is always charitable. "They are very animated in their play," said he. I said I had never seen a better imitation of serious boxing, and proceeded to the spot, to which Mrs Thomson, the missionary's

wife, came up at the same time, by whose exertions the fray was brought to a conclusion. In their smoked carosses, dirty skins, half human features and wild gestures they were like so many devils.

(…) We walked round the wigwams, and I saw much misery. Huddled round some embers in the middle of the mat edifice (a thing in general 6 or 7 feet in diameter and from 3 to 4 feet high) might be seen families consisting of ten or twelve, the man in filthy tatters, the woman skinny and emaciated, with her disgusting dugs hanging down flabbily on her knees, the elder children naked except for the scanty sheepskin over the shoulders, the younger children naked wholly. The town and the people were both, on the whole, in a much lower state than I had expected. If the Griquas have much advanced, their original condition must have been low indeed. In such of the people as we saluted in Dutch I did not discover much courtesy of manner, but at the same time no incivility whatever.[792]

A similarly negative description was provided by Private Buck Adams of the 7th Dragoon Guards, who accompanied the troops across the Orange River at this time.

At length we arrived at Philippolis—Griqua Town[793]—and a few hours after I took a bit of a ramble to have a look at the place, which I found consisted of one long street. Women and children were lying about on the ground, and their only occupation, as far as I could see, was the searching of each other's heads for vermin. Their habitations were long sheds, and did not appear to contain any kind of partition, bedding or furniture whatever. Their clothing was made of buckskin. The hair of the women long and matted, and by their filthy appearance I should say they never had any connection with soap and water for cleansing purposes.

And these were our allies! The people we had come all this distance to fight for against the Dutch Boors, who had made several raids and plundered them of great numbers of cattle, sheep and goats! Such was their report, but I believe they were too lazy to look after their cattle. The stench of the place was horrible, and I was glad when I got to the end of the "town".

I walked a short distance to get a little fresh air before attempting to go through it again. The country around it as far as the eye could reach appeared a vast plain—no grass, but a kind of stubble weed of reddish colour which was very fattening for cattle.[794]

Neither of these descriptions, and more particularly Porter's series of caricatures, makes allowances for the existence of cultures other than the Northern European, or for the fact that it was winter on the Highveld, that it was wartime, or that the Griqua community in general and Philippolis in particular had suffered for some years from disturbances among the missionaries and the insecurity caused by the influx of aggressive whites, both loyalist and republican, into the Transgariep. As Adam Kok stated in his report to the Colonial Secretary shortly after the war, "during the last three years very serious loss has been occasioned by the presence of the armed assemblies which the Boers have been in the habit of calling together within my territory. On such occasions my people have been forced to draw together for mutual protection, and thus to abandon their crops of grain to their serious injury; and they have sustained great loss in cattle from the want of pasture when driven from their farms to seek safety near the station."[795]

This was similarly pointed out in the report of the Cape Town Auxiliary of the LMS for 1845 which was most likely compiled by Thomson.

> The trying circumstances to which the people of Philippolis have been exposed during the past year have not occurred without exercising influence on their affairs in some respect prejudicial. The greater part of the men were compelled to defend themselves and their families against the attacks of the farmers, and most of the women and children to leave their farms and take refuge within the village.
>
> Such circumstances are by no means favourable to the growth of religion or the promotion of civilization, and we regret to say that not only has the improvement of the village been retarded, but in many instances war and its accompaniments have excited feelings far from congenial with the spirit of the Gospel. The church members have, however, been mercifully preserved from falling under the influence of this temptation.

The contest commenced in the beginning of the winter, which added much to the sufferings of the people, and the appearance of a number of people hurried away from their farms and crowded together in a village which did not afford accommodation for the half of them would naturally convey to persons not accustomed to such sights an unfavourable impression.

A little consideration will, however, convince anyone that neither the families of the village which was thus filled nor those who had hastily been compelled to leave their homes and many of their conveniences were in a situation to exhibit much the appearance of comfort and cleanliness, especially if we take into account the anxiety all must have felt respecting their relations who were still exposed to danger from the enemy.

The loss of property sustained by them has been very heavy, and a severe drought which ensued immediately after the termination of hostilities reduced many to a state of distress bordering on starvation, which has in some measure been relieved by the late rains.

Happily for them peace had been restored through the intervention of the Colonial Government, and new regulations have been entered into which, it is hoped, will preserve the tranquillity of the country. The people have returned to their farms, and the residents on the station have recommenced their improvements and are all busily employed either in erecting new houses, enclosing their gardens with stone walls or repairing the damage sustained during the war. (...) Public worship is now held in the new school house till such time as the old place of worship is enlarged and repaired.[796]

The same source published an extract from a letter dated 2 February 1846, after normal conditions had been restored, by "a lady on a visit at Philippolis", who is most likely to have been a member of a missionary family and possibly in her turn prejudiced in favour of the Griquas rather than against them. Her report at any rate proves that it was also possible to give a positive account of the village and the Captaincy.

I had intended writing before, but I waited till I had seen more of the station, and I must confess I am agreeably surprised at what I have witnessed. I expected to see the people dressed in skins, living in mud huts, &c.; on the contrary, they are decently clothed and reside in cottages, of which I have counted 30 well built, their foundations being stonework, finished with brick walls, neatly thatched, and some with glass windows. The Chief is building a house I should have no objection to reside in when finished. I have visited several of their cottages, which consist generally of three good rooms with detached cooking places; some are furnished with tables, chairs and proper utensils for different uses; and on the side of the street where irrigation is possible there are large gardens, walled in and planted with useful vegetables.

Yesterday was the ordinance;[797] I suppose there were at least 900 assembled; about 300 communicants. I must do them justice to say that I have seldom seen a more attentive congregation. There were four different services held at the same time in the morning; 20 members were received into the church, three baptismal services, and preaching in the evening. When night came, Mr Thomson was worn out; indeed I fear his constitution will fall a sacrifice to the continued exertion he is obliged to make. Mr Wright[798] and he have been trying to get a collection for the new church. The people are willing, but the difficulties they have laboured under, together with the great drought that has partly destroyed their crops, so that they have nothing for sale, prevents them from doing what they otherwise would. May I petition a little for them? Do you think some of the good people of Cape Town would come forward in their cause? Perhaps their losses might induce the kind-hearted to assist them.[799]

Well before the disruption of the war, however, there had been indications of systematic attempts at improvement on the part of the Griquas, possibly encouraged by the promise of stability implicit in the appointment of the experienced missionary Peter Wright. Reporting in October 1842, soon after his arrival at Philippolis, Wright, after describing the neglect he had found there, could declare,

All the brandy shops have been broken up, and we are at present pretty quiet on that scene. A good number of people have removed to the station. The day school contains 80 children, and an infant school has been commenced by my elder daughter with 60 little ones. We have commenced Sabbath schools on the station with a crowded attendance, and the people seem to pay attention to the word spoken. The water of the fountain has been recovered and is now streaming through the village by a month's labour of 30 men, a considerable number of gardens have already been fenced and planted, a goodly number are engaged in making brick for new houses, and four new cattle-folds have just been completed with stone walls 5 feet high, 3 feet thick and 100 yards square.[800]

With regard to the Captaincy in general, Thomson, after taking over from Wright the following year, reported, "Large quantities of grain have been sown by the people at all the available fountains, and many respectable houses of stone and bricks have been built."[801] Adam Kok III, writing to the Colonial Secretary after the war in reply to a questionnaire dated April 1845, declared: "My people were formerly wholly a pastoral people, but they at present also cultivate the ground. They sow wheat, barley and other grain, and also plant vegetables and fruit trees; but I am not able to say to what amount. Last year many thousands of muids of wheat and barley were reaped by my people. We have also commenced the breeding of wool sheep."[802]

A particularly attractive account of Philippolis shortly before the outbreak of the hostilities leading to Swartkoppies, and one less obviously partisan than any of the above, was given by the Scottish traveller R. Gordon Cumming, who passed through on his way to the interior early in 1845. Describing the inhabitants of the Philippolis Captaincy incorrectly as "Bastards" as distinct from "Griquas", he proceeded:

> Their country is bounded on the south by the Great Orange River, and is about the most desirable district in Southern Africa for farming purposes, there being abundance of fountains throughout its whole extent capable of being led out to irrigate the land, without which no gardens can be formed nor wheat grown in that country. Rich pasture is abundant. Cattle and sheep thrive well; goats also, an animal especially valuable to the South African settler, but for

which only certain districts are suitable, are here very prolific. (…)

One of the chief recommendations of the Bastards' country is its admirable suitableness for breeding horses. Large herds of these may be seen throughout their country pasturing high on the mountain sides or scattered in troops over its grassy plains. The deadly distemper so prevalent along the frontiers of the Colony is here of comparatively rare occurrence. (…)

The Chiefs of the Griquas and Bastards are in close alliance with the English Government, which protects them from the attacks of the rebel Dutch Boers. These, well aware of the excellent qualities of the Bastards' country, are possessed with a strong desire to appropriate it. The language spoken by both these tribes is Dutch. They have in general embraced the Christian religion, and several worthy missionaries have for several years past devoted their lives to the improvement of their temporal and eternal condition.

The dress worn by the men consists of home-made leathern jacket, waistcoat and trousers, feldtschoens, or home-made shoes, a Malay handkerchief tied round the head, and on Sundays and other great occasions a shirt and neckcloth. The females wear a close-fitting corset reaching to the small of the waist, below which they sport a petticoat like the women of other countries. These petticoats are sometimes made of stuffs of British manufacture, and at other times of soft leather prepared by themselves. Their headdress consists of two handkerchiefs, one of black silk, the other of a striped red and green colour, usually termed Malay handkerchiefs. They are very fond of beads of every size and colour, which they hang in large necklaces round their necks. They have one description of bead peculiar to themselves and to the tribes extending along the banks of the Great Orange River to its junction with the sea. This bead is formed of the root of a bush found near the mouth of the Orange River, and possesses a sweet and peculiar perfume. Every Griqua girl wears at least one of these; and no traveller who has once learnt to prize this perfume can inhale it again without its inadvertently recalling to his memory the fine dark eyes and fair forms of the semi-civilized nymphs frequenting the northern bank of the Orange stream.[803]

This corresponds well enough, on the whole, to the account of the Griquas given by the equally well-born Englishman Methuen, a future minister of the church, on passing through the village of Campbell the previous year:

> The women have a peculiar appearance, clad in their leathern gowns, which resemble chamois leather, and are formed of sheep-skins tanned by a method of their own, and coloured with yellow ochre. Their complexions are not darker than those of the Gipsy race, and a rosy blush may be generally discerned setting off their tawny cheeks: some of them are very pretty, with beautiful figures, good eyes and features, and small feet.[804]

The striking contrast between the "fine dark eyes and fair forms" of Cumming's "semi-civilized nymphs" and Porter's "so many devils" described as "an antidote to every amorous emotion" probably reveals as much about the temperamental differences between the two men as about their actual experiences among the Griquas.

Under the guidance of Peter Wright, during the brief time he worked at Philippolis, and subsequently that of Thomson, who was to spend a relatively long term of five years there and enjoy some success in his work as missionary, religious life developed steadily. The Cape Town Auxiliary, for example, reporting Wright's death in 1843, could already declare:

> On the station, four services are held every Sabbath, two for the Griquas and two for the Bechuanas. The number of members amount to 258, of whom 53 have been added during the past year. The number of children under instruction on the station varies from 100 to 300, according to the season of the year, but many are taught by their parents residing at a distance from the station, whose numbers are not known. About one fourth of the children under instruction can read, write and cypher. Fifty girls and young women attend the sewing school, and 60 children are in the infant school. Both these schools are under the care of Mrs and Miss Wright.[805]

Besides the capital, Adam Kok in his report in 1845, identified Ramah and Kalkfontein as the chief settlements or *werfs* in the Captaincy, "each containing about two hundred inhabitants living in reed huts".[806]

As far as the former is concerned, G.W. Walker, visiting the "old mission station of Ramah" with Backhouse in 1839, gave the impression that it was at that time a centre for local religious activity rather than a fixed community.

> The Field Cornet succeeded in collecting between thirty and forty of the people, principally females, to whom we first read a chapter out of the Dutch Bible, and then addressed a few remarks, to which they gave serious attention. Though the outward circumstances of the poor people were of a nature to give the impression that their condition in every respect was low, there was a considerable feeling of solemnity as we sat together in the Field Cornet's hut.[807]

In the winter of 1844, Henry Methuen could write of it, "This has been a missionary station, but is now abandoned, the ruins of a square building alone indicating its site. At present the only dwellings are beehive-shaped huts, constructed with rush mats, supported upon light poles."[808] Gottlob Schreiner mentioned visiting Ramah in the course of his itinerating journeys, however,[809] and at the time Methuen stopped there, its revival as an out-station of Philippolis was already being planned, so that on his return journey in December he "observed the number of huts to be considerably increased".[810] In its survey of 1844 the report of the Cape Town Auxiliary could give an extremely positive, if possibly somewhat overenthusiastic account of this development:

> A few months ago there was nothing but drinking and dancing; the people were scattered about, and their miserable huts would have disgraced the meanest Bushmen. Since the native teacher has begun his labors, they have assembled in the station to the number of 300 or 400, have erected several neat hartebeest houses, have sown corn, and are talking of building a church at their own expense. A great many Bushmen are collected here, and all their children attend, for the parents are so desirous of their instruction that

they send none of them to herd cattle, a practice which is the common drawback to the education of the young. This state of things is a source of great encouragement, as Ramah was the nest of all the bad characters in the district.[811]

There were at this stage 150 children and adults in the school, the teacher being Piet Zaarel, described by Thomson as "a venerable and patriarchal old man" who had settled there with "a number of friends and countrymen". By 1847, however, the church at Philippolis had appointed "a pious and suitable man named Frederick Krotz" to succeed him:[812] J.J. Freeman, who called him "Kotze", described him as "an excellent native teacher".[813] "The change consequent on the labours of Frederick Krotz in the appearance and deportment of the people of Ramah has been very striking," wrote Thomson.[814]

It is typical of the violently contrasting reactions encountered in visitors to the interior of South Africa, and more specifically to Griqua territory, that the English traveller Alfred Dolman, crossing the Orange River at Soutpansdrif early in 1849 and travelling onwards through Ramah to the interior, should write disparagingly as follows:

> The opposite bank was reached in safety and we emerged dripping. A crowd of Korrannas immediately surrounded us and began to beg for brandy; they, however, got nothing, else we never should have been quit of them. One or two of these people were in native costume, the others generally wore old coats and trousers of leather, greasy and dirty from constant use. They were anxious to obtain European clothing, though nothing was refused by them. (…)
>
> *Sunday, 20th [May]*. The weather is considerably warmer. Many Korrannas and Totties[815] visit the camp, begging for all sorts of things, none of which they obtained. While dressing in the tent this morning, a deputation of native ladies waited on me to beg for sugar. I pretended not to understand, and accordingly they got none. Much amusement and laughter was excited at seeing me comb my hair, such a process being incomprehensible to them. They jabbered away, clicking like frogs, and occasionally bursting into fits of laughter. These ladies were not the most prepossessing

in the world, and the ancient odours that appertained to them, spread around a delightful fragrance. They were generally smeared on both cheeks with fat and red ochre, and wore necklaces of old bones, buttons, etc. (…)

Monday, 21st. (…) Leaving the Zout Pan's Drift, we proceeded on to Ramah, a wretched Griqua village, composed of a few rush-thatched houses of mud and soap bowl huts of Korrannas. A missionary formerly resided at this place, but the station is now given up, and a native schoolmaster now instructs the young idea how to shoot. Several Griquas came out to inspect the wagon and beg for tea. (…)

Tuesday, 22nd. A few Griquas bring us milk for sale; handkerchiefs, bullets, etc., are the mediums of exchange. Korrannas also ride past on oxback, an unpleasant mode of travelling for the European, but the plan usually adopted by the natives. (…) Today I purchased from the Griquas two fat oxen and a stout shooting horse; the oxen cost £5 10s and the horse £10. Coats, trousers and shoes and other articles of dress were sadly wanted; but I had none to spare, a waggon-load of slops[816] would be a good speculation here.[817]

There were, however, other centres in the Griqua territory besides Ramah where church activity was expanding, although it is possibly not unjust to suspect that the reasons for this may have been of a social as much as of a religious nature. Travelling onwards to the Vaal River, Backhouse and Walker also halted at an unnamed settlement where Dirk Kok was employed as teacher and conducted a service "some miles up the river" at a place "where the meeting for worship is usually held". "My dear companion had the chief service," wrote Walker,

> and it was very pleasing to observe so many attentive listeners with their Bibles in their hands, occasionally turning to the passages which he had himself to refer to in a Bible to assist him in the expression of his exercise on their behalf; at least thirty persons, principally females, made use of the Bible in the way described. The assembly might number about 200, most of whom were decently clad in European garments and presented a very tidy appearance, highly

gratifying to witness, the more so as it was unlooked for in a situation so remote from the missionary settlement. We had numerous applications for books of a religious kind, and several of the parties walked to the wagon in order to obtain some; but our stock of Dutch books being very limited, it was not in our power fully to supply the demand.[818]

It would be pedantic to divide contemporary accounts of the Griqua people according to the nominal boundaries of the respective Captaincies, but it is most likely that this attractive account refers to the settlement at Ganganup or Gangenaup near the confluence of the Vaal and Orange Rivers where the LMS in 1845 established the mission station of Backhouse (the modern Douglas),[819] and this, strictly speaking, fell under Griquatown.

The Auxiliary report for Philippolis for 1844 already quoted mentioned that a second out-station (possibly Sterkfontein) had been established besides Ramah, and added, "Besides these out-stations there are also 5 minor schools, in which upwards of 150 children are taught."[820]

All this was, of course, before the brief war which culminated in the battle of Swartkoppies on 29 April 1845, but the progress at Ramah was continued, and the survey for the year 1847 noted the erection there of "a neat and substantial chapel (…) to contain about 200 people, as their present place of worship is much dilapidated, and too small for the congregation assembling there".[821]

By the Maitland Treaty, the terms of which were settled at Touwfontein in the winter of 1845, Griqua territory was to be divided into two parts, generally known as the "alienable" or "reserved" and "inalienable" territory respectively, although the Griquas themselves more correctly used the terms "*huurbaar*" and "*onhuurbaar*" ("leasable" and "unleasable"). In the first mentioned, which was situated in the north-eastern portion of the Captaincy, Griqua farm owners would be permitted to lease their land to whites for a maximum of forty years, while in the latter this was not permitted. The boundaries of the unleasable territory were stated to be the Riet River, Kromelmboogspruit, Vanzylspruit to its source between the Pramberge, from there to Breipaal, and then along Bossiespruit, the existing boundary with the Bethulie lands, to the Orange River.[822] In practice this ruling merely legalised the existing state of affairs, untenable though it had become, but at least it brought an element of stability into the uncertain situation, as had the decisive defeat of the rebellious Boers at Swartkoppies.

The Maitland Treaty also made provision for a British Resident to be placed in the Transgariep

> to exercise constant vigilance in regard to the state and condition of the Griqua territory, so as to secure the tranquillity thereof, to represent her Majesty's Government upon the spot, to enforce order amongst all British subjects resident in any part of the Griqua territory, to prevent and punish all crimes or injuries meditated or committed by any such subjects, and generally to enquire into and determine all disputes which may arise between emigrants and Griquas, so as thereby to maintain peace and remove all occasion of mutual apprehension and distrust.[823]

At first the Civil Commissioner of Colesberg, Fleetwood Rawstorne, was stationed temporarily at Philippolis with a small garrison of men of the 45th Regiment (the "Cape Corps", a Coloured body) under Captain H.D. Warden, but in December Captain William Sutton of the same regiment took over officially as "British Resident among the tribes living beyond the Frontier to the North-East".[824] He was an Englishman by birth, a veteran of several Frontier Wars, who was known as a hunter and had accompanied William Cornwallis Harris to the interior in 1836–37 and visited Mzilikazi, passing through Philippolis on his way back.[825] By the missionary James Read Sr he had initially been praised during the Frontier Wars as "an active judicious officer and he is very friendly", though he soon became "a worldly and wicked man" and was stated to be "timid", "irritable" and "turbulent".[826] However, Sutton very quickly resigned, to be followed by Captain Warden, an Englishman of obscurely aristocratic antecedents who was to exercise his office with no great distinction for six years.[827]

The duties of the Resident extended well beyond the Griqua Captaincy, and in Sutton's original instructions he had been ordered to establish himself "so as to be centrally and conveniently situated for the tribes with which treaties shall be made".[828] Warden's choice fell for this purpose on the farm Bloemfontein, which he described as, "within a few miles, halfway between Philippolis and Thaba Bossiou",[829] and he removed from Philippolis with his little garrison at the end of March 1846. After this Philippolis was no longer an outpost of semi-European settlement to the north, but a stage on the route to the Residency at Bloemfontein;[830] at the same time the Captaincy lost the advantages which the brief presence of the Resident and the troops had afforded it. Warden was characterised by Sir Harry Smith as "very easily managed, but, like all weak men, very soon affronted",[831] and, coming under the influence of the Wesleyan missionaries working in the Caledon River valley, he allowed himself to be drawn increasingly into the tangled conflicts between the various black tribes in the area, most notably the Basotho of Moshweshwe and the Batlokwa of Sekonyela. Little time or energy remained for the problems of the Griquas, although they were on occasion called up to support the Resident on expeditions against the Basotho, with whom they themselves had no quarrel.

Very soon after the appointment of the Resident, however, affairs took a dramatic turn for the worse for the Captaincy, for at the end of 1847 Sir Harry Smith became High Commissioner and Governor of the Cape, and early the following year he travelled north to settle the affairs of the Transgariep.

Smith was a self-willed, impetuous and unbalanced man much given to histrionic gestures, and his experience as an officer on the Eastern Frontier during the 1830s had produced in him the completely erroneous conviction that he understood the problems of South Africa. In the Transgariep, however, where he saw fit to concentrate mainly on the grievances of the white settlers, he proved himself quite unaware of the distinction between the loyalist farmers from the Colony, represented most notably by the Oberholster party in the Riet River area, and the growing number of Republican-minded Trekkers mostly established beyond the Vet River in the north; the latter's numbers were swollen by the malcontents who had been leaving Natal ever since its annexation by the British in 1843, and they were to constitute increasingly formidable adversaries.

Interpreting the loyalist wish for official protection as the unanimous desire of the whites in the Transgariep, and largely ignoring the claims and needs of all other population groups, Smith on 3 February 1848 proclaimed the sovereignty of Her Majesty the Queen of England over the territories north of the Great Orange River, including the countries of Moshesh, Moroko, Molitsani, Sinkonyala, Adam Kok, Gert Taaybosch and other minor Chiefs,[832] so far north as the Vaal River, and east to the Drakensberg or Quathlamba Mountains; with no desire or inclination whatever on the part of Her Majesty to extend or increase her dominions, or to deprive the Chiefs and their people of the hereditary rights, acknowledged and recognized by all civilized nations of the world as appertaining to the nomadic races of the earth; but, on the contrary, with the sole view of establishing an amicable relationship with these Chiefs, of upholding them in their hereditary rights and protecting them from any future aggression or location of Her Majesty's subjects, as well as of providing for their rule, and the maintenance of good order and obedience to Her Majesty's laws and commands on the part of those of the Queen's subjects who, having abandoned the land of their fathers, have located themselves within the territories aforesaid; and I hereby proclaim that all the Chiefs of the territories aforesaid are under the sovereignty of Her Majesty as the paramount and exclusive authority in all international disputes as to territory or in any case whatever tending to interrupt the general peace and harmony of South Africa; but that their authority over their own tribes shall be maintained, as well as their own laws, according to their customs and usages.[833]

Though this proclamation may well have seemed promising on paper, by the time it was issued, Adam Kok and his Councillors had already learned how much support and protection it would afford them in the course of an interview they had had with Smith at Bloemfontein on 24 January 1848.

The fullest account of what transpired there is probably that provided in a detailed memorandum in the archives of the LMS, according to which Smith used a typical mixture of bluster and threats to force his will on Kok.

(…) Upon this His Excellency exclaimed in a passion, Treaty is nonsense. Damn the treaty. And taking off his glasses, he dashed them on the table. Southey,[834] His Excellency cried, tell him I am Governor General, I shall hang the black fellow on this beam—tell him, Southey, to leave the room immediately. And calling Capt. Warden, he said, Look after this fellow in the treaty—keep him by the treaty, and I will look after you. I shall exclude him from the general union. Do they think I am come here to intrigue, I who have settled affairs in India, Caffreland and other countries, and brought them under my feet? Go out of the room. Kok and his men precipitately left the room.[835]

This also was basically the version given by Philip in a letter to his son-in-law, John Fairbairn, at the end of 1848, of which only a modern précis has survived: "Griquas did not sign until Sir H. intimidated them by threatening to hang Adam upon a beam of the house, by abusing them, and by driving them out of the house because they appealed to the treaty of Sir H. [sic] Maitland."[836] Likewise it was the version given by the Griquas themselves to J.J. Freeman of the LMS when he visited Philippolis at the end of 1849, and repeated by him in his evidence before the Select Committee on the Kafir Tribes two years later.

After a good deal of disputation in the matter, the Governor, certainly in a passion, told them that unless they signed that treaty by five o'clock in the afternoon, he would "hang them at that beam". I have reason to believe that he said so, but he said it in a moment of passion. I asked the men if they sincerely believed that Sir Harry Smith intended to do it, I thought that they could not as honest and reasonable men suppose it, and their reply was very simple and just: "We took Sir Harry Smith for a sort of madman, and we believed he would do it, though we knew he had no right to do it." I said, "Did you sign that treaty under that intimidation?" "We certainly did," said they; "we did not know what he might do, and we felt compelled to do it."[837]

Though apologists for Smith have been at some pains to explain that his words, his gestures and his actions on this occasion were misunderstood by the Griquas and their supporters, they correspond well enough to what is known from other sources of his emotional and erratic behaviour. His official biographer also gave much the same account in a book published in 1901: "At first the Chief gave himself great airs, and Sir Harry, losing his temper, threatened to have him tied up to a beam in the room in which they were sitting unless he acted reasonably."[838] No source is given for the information, but it is noteworthy that it is presented as a statement of fact and not deemed to require any comment or explanation.[839] "We had every reason to be satisfied with his behaviour towards us," wrote the German missionary Schultheiss, who was also received by the Governor at Bloemfontein with his colleagues from Bethanie.

> So too the Boers; he promised to give them the farms they had up to now hired from the Griquas as their property (more correctly on quitrent tenure) if they would once more become true subjects of the Queen and not think about making war on the English any more. (...) The Griquas, however, led by their Captain Adam Kok, were unwilling to accept these changes, and insisted that the Governor keep to the existing treaty. The Governor twice chased them from the room. In the end, however, he forced on them a clause which was attached to the treaty.[840]

By the new "treaty" concluded at Bloemfontein, after these preliminaries, on 28 January 1848, the Griquas basically agreed to the payment of a sum of £300 a year in perpetuity for the farms in the leasable territory previously leased for forty years only, which meant in practice that this part of the Captaincy now passed permanently from Griqua control. Of the compensation to be paid, £200 was to be for the Kaptyn and £100 to be divided among the people, and the latter sum was still a factor of some importance to the Griquas at Kokstad in the 1870s. "That treaty created a grievance which was never forgotten," wrote their then minister, William Dower. "Every old resident in Kokstad is familiar with the ceaseless growl about the '*Ve[e]rtig jaar's geld*'".[841]

To Adam Kok the cavalier treatment he had received from the Governor at Bloemfontein remained deeply offensive, and writing to the British Assistant Commissioners Hogge and Owen four years later he referred to "the indignation I felt and still feel at the manner in which I was on that occasion treated by Sir H. Smith".[842] Nor was he slow to protest against the emendation to the Maitland Treaty which had been forced on him, and on 22 February he sent to the Governor the first of a series of memorials in which he remonstrated volubly and vigorously against it, albeit without the least visible effect.[843] "Against this act of injustice we have protested again and again for the last nine years," he wrote to the then Governor, Sir George Grey, in 1857. "We have written letters to Sir H. Smith himself, to the Assistant Commissioners Hogge and Owen, Sir George Cathcart and Sir G. Clerk, and to Your Excellency; but up to the present time we have received no address."[844]

Within months of the proclamation of sovereignty, however, the Boer leader Andries Pretorius led a group of his disaffected followers to Bloemfontein, where they forced the Resident to withdraw with his garrison. Once more the Transgariep was in a state of war, as described by C.F. Wuras, the missionary at Bethanie, who with the inhabitants of his station fled southward before the Boer advance.

> On Saturday, 29 July we arrived near Philippolis. Here too there was great distress. All the Griquas and Bastards had removed to Philippolis, where their cattle would have died from hunger for lack of grass. Our people from Bethanie therefore planned to move on to the mountains near the Orange River. On Sunday I conducted a service at Philippolis, as the missionary there had already left.[845] It was now my intention to take my children to Colesberg and to leave them there in the care of my servants, while I myself returned to my people. On Wednesday, 2 August, I arrived at Colesberg, where I hired a room. (…)
>
> In the meantime, however, the rebellious Boers had advanced as far as the Orange River and taken possession of it, so that no-one could cross. I was therefore prevented from going across and am at present (19 August) still at Colesberg. Captain Adam Kok from Philippolis and his Councillors have fled to the English camp, where I spoke to them a week ago. I heard that the people from Bethanie have also gone in to Philippolis, as they did not feel safe from the Boers where they were. As I heard later, however, Adam Kok had only come to obtain help from the Governor, as he considered himself too weak to oppose the might of the Boers. This is a sad state of affairs![846]

Hurrying northward to meet this threat, Sir Harry Smith, at the head of a military force which included a Griqua contingent, defeated the Boers at Boomplaats on 28 August 1848 and re-proclaimed British sovereignty over the Transgariep, but though order had been restored, the Captaincy had for the second time in three years been the scene of a disruptive war. Moreover the people had at this critical point also been left in the lurch by their missionary, of whose guidance and advice they were in their present situation in greater need than ever. Towards the end of 1847, W.Y. Thomson had gone to Port Elizabeth for the confinement of his wife, and while there he heard of the new agreement into which Adam Kok had been forced by Sir Harry Smith, apparently without realising the manner in which this had happened. In these circumstances he felt that further exertions on behalf of the Griquas would be pointless, and he decided not to return to Philippolis but take up work in Grahamstown instead.

The official reports of the LMS merely stated, "The mission at this place has suffered from the removal of the Rev. W. Thomson, their late missionary, to Graham's Town"[847] and "From the early part of 1848, when Mr Thomson removed to Graham's Town, until the close of last year [*1849*], this station was without a settled pastor,"[848] and refrained from any attempt at explanations, as was their wont, apparently without exciting the curiosity of their supporters. The Dutchman C.J. van der Schalk, who was sent to Philippolis as assistant missionary to take over the work, described Thomson more bluntly some time later as "a fickle-minded man, who (…), for experiencing some disappointments, leaves in a very hasty (to say the least) manner a church and a congregation who did generally love and esteem him."[849]

By the end of 1849 Thomson was already corresponding with J.J. Freeman of the LMS concerning the possibility of returning, but among other observations in the detailed reply he wrote during his visit to Philippolis, Freeman remarked significantly,

> that the change you alluded to as essential to your comfort and the improvement of the place could *not* be secured as the condition of your coming. H[endrik] H[endrickze] retains his place, if not his full influence, and his energy and tact in trying to carry his measures. The influence he exercises and the party with him may be checked for good and a change superinduced by a missionary here

who succeeds in obtaining the confidence and support of the people; but all that must come *in*directly and as the result of previous measures, and not by any direct and obvious arrangement.[850]

From Freeman's very guarded references to "the same inconvenience to which we both alluded in mutual confidence", it would further seem that the continued presence at Philippolis of Thomson's mother-in-law, Margery Wright, also constituted a problem as far as Thomson was concerned.

In April 1850, van der Schalk informed Philip that Thomson was not acceptable to Adam Kok, whom he quoted as saying: "he is not the man for this station; the two first years he was among us he was zealous, but afterwards not; we have always showed him goodwill, but he has answered us with ingratitude, it will never go with Mr Thomson, and you, Mr van der Schalk, will not only have to do with Mr Thomson, but also with his wife, his mother-in-law, and the family at Boomplaats, (and addressing my wife:) Mam, you will be unhappy."[851] Kok himself, however, writing directly to Freeman a month later, could state his desire for Thomson's return, declaring, "Our present condition is such that it is essential that we have a minister who is more or less acquainted with our needs and with the particular circumstances in which we are placed. Accordingly the congregation, the people, as well as I myself, once more desire most earnestly that our request be granted. Mr Thomson is an extremely able man, and in many respects well acquainted with our circumstances."[852] It is perhaps well to remember that this last letter was written immediately before Hendrickze's dismissal as Government Secretary, when a reaction to his influence had already set in.

After the departure of Thomson, his brother-in-law John Wright of Boomplaats returned to Philippolis, where he kept school and conducted services on a temporary basis; according to Isaac Hughes he was effectively in charge of the station since December 1847, when Thomson left, and Hughes (who was soon to become Wright's father-in-law) and his colleague Edward Solomon came over from Griquatown from time to time to administer the sacraments. "He seems to be a little bashful," Van der Schalk later remarked concerning John Wright. "Since I am here he has preached three times, but always during the time that I had Bechuana service. Mrs v.d.S. tells me that he preached very well, affectionately and full[y] the Gospel."[853] "Mr Wright reports that the usual attendance on the means of grace varies from 300 to 400," stated the Cape Town Auxiliary for 1848, "and on some special occasions as many as 700 or 800 meet together for public worship. Three sermons are delivered on Sundays, and there is an early prayer meeting conducted by the elders."[854]

While it was obviously urgently necessary to replace Thomson, the special problems of the station and the difficult situation of the Captaincy demanded much of a successor, and given the fact that every missionary stationed there over the twenty-three years of its history had been forced out by the local community except Peter Wright, it is understandable that no one was particularly eager to undertake the work. Eventually, however, Philip's son-in-law George Christie was persuaded to assume the responsibility. He was a Scot who had been stationed in South Africa as a missionary briefly during the 1830s and had since been working in England as a minister; returning to South Africa now with his family, he arrived at Philippolis at the end of December 1849, where van der Schalk wrote of him, "he takes up all very easy and quiet"[855] and described him as "a *very* quiet man".[856] According to van der Schalk, Kok declared: "Mr Christie is a good man, the best man for the station; he speaks not much, but he is a wise man, we love him."[857]

About George Christie's sojourn in the Transgariep little is known, but writing in March 1851, he reported to the LMS in London: "Philippolis has evidently suffered much from the wars and changes of recent years, and it will take some time at least before it can recover."[858] He had not brought his family with him to the Transgariep, however, and possibly he was merely biding his time and coming to his own conclusions, for when his daughter died suddenly in Cape Town he abandoned Philippolis without further ado in April 1850, never to return, and was subsequently stationed at Hankey in the Eastern Cape. In the letter to Freeman already quoted, Adam Kok subsequently wrote, "it would give us the greatest pleasure and satisfaction to acquire the services of Mr Christie, for whom we still feel the highest regard and the greatest confidence",[859] so that Christie would seem to have made a favourable impression on the Griqua community during his brief stay, and the reservations must have been on his side.

In the meanwhile C.J. van der Schalk, who had been appointed assistant missionary at Philippolis after Thomson's departure, had arrived there in August 1849. He was a Dutchman close on fifty years of age, [860] and James Cameron of the LMS in Cape Town, who seems to have known him personally, wrote uncompromisingly, "The first thirty years of his life were spent in sin."[861] After he had undergone conversion and married an English-speaking Baptist, he established himself in Cape Town, and there he occupied himself with pastoral visiting, preaching and teaching, largely among the coloured population, as well as writing and publishing, until he was accepted by the LMS for service north of the Orange River, his obvious recommendation for the work being the fact that he was Dutch speaking. Later he described his engagement as "entered into perhaps too hastily (...), but my financial circumstances were then such that I could not only not refuse, but it became my imperative duty to accept for the sake of a beloved wife".[862]

At Philippolis, van der Schalk stated that he and his wife had been received with noticeable reserve by the Wright family, who were still firmly ensconced in the mission house, "and a comfortable house it is": "I have oftentimes within myself coveted one of the spare rooms at least for Mrs v.d.S.," he wrote three months after their arrival.[863] As far as the congregation was concerned, he reported in the same letter: "The first time that I rose in the Sunday school, endeavouring to give explanations over what they were reading, they mocked openly with me; and I had it 3 times, going along the streets with Mrs v.d.S., that they were hissing and hawling [*sic*] behind us, not children, but grown-up people."[864] The Wrights still possessed considerable influence and authority in the congregation, and it is possible that van der Schalk was resented as the successor to Thomson, who formed part of the family complex; on the other hand the feeling manifested against him may equally well have emanated from the anti-mission party who had been responsible for Thomson's abrupt departure. The situation at Philippolis was by no means simple, as many of van der Schalk's predecessors had discovered to their cost.

John Wright soon withdrew from the station for reasons of health, but there were constant difficulties with the formidable Margery Wright, who continued to occupy the mission house while the van der Schalks lived in a rented cottage, making her presence felt in the community and causing much dissension, as described by van der Schalk himself in various of his letters.

During the eleven months we have been here, Mrs v.d.S. has had a fixed place in the chapel, and little Elizabeth Wright too. After Mrs Wr.'s return from Vaal River, she *forced* Mrs v.d.S. to give up that place. She will have it for her daughter Elizabeth, and threatens if she do it not, that she will ask to her Griqua friends for a place, and that she is sure she will get it. In the presence of full congregations she flings away my wife's seat, and places there her daughter's; this is only a small example.[865]

It was not until 1850 that Mrs Wright was formally requested by the LMS to leave the station.

After the brief sojourn of George Christie at Philippolis no suitable replacement could be found for some time, although the possible return of Thomson was discussed. Van der Schalk therefore continued there alone with his wife, coping with the problems of the station as best he could, but in the course of half a century the LMS had never been fortunate in its Dutch missionaries, and the cantankerous van der Schalk was no exception. By July 1850 there seems to have been decided dissatisfaction among the congregation, and Adam Kok wrote in a studiedly evasive and non-committal tone to Freeman in a letter accompanied by an English translation made by van der Schalk himself,

I have nothing against Mr van der Schalk, he is my friend, I hope when the people have got to know him they will be satisfied with him. Furthermore he is a minister who has set out to preach the Word of God among the people, therefore I am satisfied with Mr van der Schalk, it would be of no use if the people are not satisfied with Mr van der Schalk; but as far as I have investigated there is no cause or reason what they would not want Mr van der Schalk as minister, nevertheless I shall try through my influence to make peace between the congregation and Mr van der Schalk.[866]

In 1851 Edward Solomon of Griquatown was finally placed in charge of Philippolis, and some tranquillity was established in the unsettled congregation. Van der Schalk, however, continued to experience or cause difficulties. By September 1852 he had retreated to Colesberg, where the local LMS missionary S.N. de Kock complained about his "machinations",⁸⁶⁷ and the Directors of the LMS had decided to terminate his connection with the Society. Early the following year he was in Cape Town on his way to England, where he intended stating his case in person, and the files of the LMS contain an extensive correspondence on the subject. His departure brought to an end the constant succession of quarrels, divisions and upheavals which had characterised the Philippolis congregation since the precipitate departure of Jan Goeyman in 1825, causing untold harm to its development and that of the Captaincy itself over a period of twenty-eight years.

9. The Captaincy in the 1850s (1851–1861)

C.J. van der Schalk, writing to a colleague in Cape Town in September 1851, after three months at Philippolis, gave a predominantly negative description of the community from the missionary point of view. Within its obvious limitations, it may, however, serve as a useful overview of the village as it appeared at the beginning of the 1850s.

Having briefly described the achievements of the late Peter Wright and lamented his premature death, van der Schalk proceeded:

> Ph[ilippolis] is now retrograde, and if there is not soon done somewhat, it will retrograde still more; the Chief Adam Kok is a man without energy. The fountain which has supplied the place with water is in a miserable condition, and in a short time, if nothing be done to it, Philippolis will be lost. The water will be lost for this place. Last year they have not been able to irrigate even not the missionary garden, though that garden is the first to be watered. I have narrowly inspected the garden, and I fully believe that if Captain A.K. would give twenty of the inhabitants we could in four weeks make the fountain in the best condition and supply Ph. with abundance of water. But I dare not to do any thing which would seem to go farther than my engagement as a secondary missionary.[868]

Much of the negative quality of this description, and of the further details provided by van der Schalk, can probably be ascribed to a finicky and querulous temperament, and this supposition is strengthened when one compares his account with that which his colleague Isaac Hughes of Griquatown gave after his visit to Philippolis at the end of May 1848, shortly after Thomson's departure. On the other hand it must also be borne in mind that van der Schalk came to Philippolis from Cape Town, while Hughes lived in a largely similar community at Griquatown, so that their respective standards of comparison were very different. Finally,

Hughes' daughter Mary at this very time married John Wright, who was related to both the previous missionaries and had himself for some time been in charge of the station. Hughes' positive description of the station may therefore not be quite objective, a striking reminder of the built-in bias which distorts almost all the surviving information on this subject.

By Hughes the church was described as

> a large substantial stone building, just rebuilt, and enlarged so as to contain an area of 2000 square feet. It is covered in with good thatch and now only awaits the carpenter to make doors, windows, pulpit and benches or seats, to be in weekly use. Large as it is, the congregation on sacramental occasions will scarcely find sufficient room in it. This building has been brought so far without any expense to the Society, but the funds are now exhausted, at least till the people recover themselves from the damages of the resent [*sic*] Boor war, and so I fear that if help come not from the Society, it will be some time before the carpenter can be employed to finish the doors &c.[869]

By Van der Schalk, newly arrived from Cape Town, the same church was described as follows:

> A very large place (…). The building can hold 700 people; it has a miserable look; no taste whatever, James Watt's place[870] is a palace in comparison. No doors (only bad temporary ones) neither windows in it, the people seem too lazy and indifferent to care about it. You can not make an idea of the cold they suffer during the services; they ought to be stirred up to do something for the house of God. (…) If you saw what is called the pulpit you would have to laugh a week long; except seven forms, there is nothing for the people to sit on; some bring their wretched chairs with them, and others some benches. The building is at the end of the village in the midst of the street, not pleasant and very insignificant in appearance; the largeness is not in the front but in the back building,[871] and it has a mean appearance; nobody would believe it to be the house of God.[872]

The school, according to Hughes, stood next to the church, and was described by him as "60ft by 20 inside measure—a new, good building of burnt brick, plastered outside with lime, and covered with thatch". To Van der Schalk it was "a good large airy room, but very badly provided with school furniture, or no school furniture at all; the forms must be fetched from the chapel, which they call church. No place to write on. A few books in a wretched condition. (…) The children are very disorderly (of clothing I will not speak, the most are dressed in a skin). Tell nothing of what I write concerning the school to the Doctor [*Philip*]; it would grieve him."[873]

Hughes stated that he inspected the writing of the pupils "on slate and paper, and I feel confident that the children are making progress in a very satisfactory degree"; but he added, "I had only to regret the want of better apparatus for the school, such as large maps, globes, Dutch and English dictionaries, &c." Here he may well have been proceeding cautiously in view of the fact that his son-in-law had been acting as schoolmaster. Van der Schalk mentioned more specifically with regard to the school, "there are 17[?] who read very well; but the rest know nearly nothing, and reading is the zenith of their knowledge of the R's", though he said in extenuation, "John Wright tells me that he found the school in that state", adding that "Mr Wr. as a pro tempore missionary has not had any influence to make any alteration".

"On looking round the buildings of the village," wrote Hughes in 1848, "I saw brick houses of the European cottage style"; Van der Schalk, commenting a year later on the same village, could only remark disparagingly, "From my house door I see half a score of houses wholly in ruin, and not a house in building (there is one in building). The most of the inhabitants here live still in their most miserable mat huts." Margery Wright and her family were at this time still installed in the mission house, and the van der Schalks' views of Philippolis must inevitably have been coloured by the fact that they themselves were initially obliged to live in a house she had prepared for them, which he described as "a most wretched one, no windows; therein was some thing called a chimney; but instead of the smoke going through the same, it had no other passage than the door. Ten days we have lived in that so called house, but I did not know that I have ever suffered so much from cold and smoke as there; and my poor wife! the tears did often run from her cheeks." After this they managed to hire what seems to have been a rather comfortable house "consisting of a hall, a front room, a bedroom and a kitchen. We have hired it for two months at £25 per month, an exceedingly high price, and notwithstanding I had to pay the rent of two months in advance; an example of the haughty independency of the people."[874]

"There are 350 church members on the books," wrote van der Schalk. "The population is 5000 in all the land of Adam Kok; count the half to be children, then there are 2500 adults, that is 7 church members for every 50 adult inhabitants. This seems rather a very large number, and I believe a too large number, but in that I am for the moment an incompetent judge." Hughes for his part noted that 260 church members attended the communion service conducted by him ("It was to me a very exciting scene, and I endeavoured to make it edifying to all"), but he added, "Of the above members in attendance, about 1/3 will have been Bechuanas."

As regards the local population, van der Schalk's experiences were, for a variety of reasons, not destined to be very fortunate, and it is particularly necessary to bear this fact in mind when reading his extensive account of "The people of town and country":

> And first you must know them, they are an independent people. Some of them are rich, a few very rich, but even the man with a few cows and sheep feels himself as independent as the best; now generally that independency makes them unbearably haughty and proud, and by [to] that add laziness and filth and dirt. I speak generally, for there are honorable exceptions and that not a few, who are very industrious and behave very honorably. Secondly, they are generally, and that very generally (only a very few exceptions, if it may be called exceptions) not at all thankful for what the LMS has done for them; and many would not care a straw if all were removed, only they like to have a political missionary. I have heard that they had a scheme to propose to Mr Freeman[875] to have their own missionary, to pay him themselves, and that they will have the control over him. I hope Mr Freeman will not fall in that trap. Thirdly, they are cunning and sly. If you had to talk to them for the first time, and that they were dressed decently, you would not look on them as half civilized; they look to be reasoning men, and I was

highly wondered to find in this part of the world people that can talk so much, and with an air of reason, but it is rather very superficial, notwithstanding they have a way by questioning and coming in different groups to pull [*draw*] from the missionary those things which they wish to know. They do not show much tenderness generally speaking; for the least service they will be highly paid: witness the rent of the house wherein I live, a house which has not cost £75 in building, and it stood empty, but the owner was not to be moved to give it for less than £25 per month. In the first days we were here we have had several applications for coffee, sugar, rice, tea, &c., but they themselves will nothing do for the missionary. Mrs Wright Sr has never received even as a widow so much as a farthing worth of any of them.[876]

Once again it is to be regretted that there is no similar account by a Griqua observer of the national characteristics and failings of the English and Dutch missionaries working among them.

As already stated, much of what was wrong here must obviously be ascribed to the unrest caused by the Boers in the Captaincy, and much also to the inadequacies of Thomson, the limitations of John Wright and the lack of more active support and encouragement from the LMS, for in this regard the village and the Captaincy both remained to a large extent dependent on the mission. With the arrival of van der Schalk as resident missionary assistant, however, the power of the mission to constitute an active force in Griqua life immediately became apparent again.

"The congregations since I have been here has been on the Sundays between 200 and 300," he wrote, "but by reason of the drought and other reasons there are hundreds that remain away; there could be and have been congregations of 700." As regards the school, less directly and obviously linked to the mission and religion, he could report even more positively:

The school had been neglected; when I took the school there were 75 children, which have now increased to 125 (this increase seems rather in five weeks exorbitant, but so it is), and though the children are checked in all their disorderly conduct, they seem to love to come now to school. The parents seem exceedingly pleased, and begin to leave their children in the village when they return to their farms (…). We have succeeded already to establish comparative order; the children, especially the elder ones, are not stupid, and I believe that they like to be taught. I have the greatest hope that if God spare us the school will soon be in another state. I have begun school in the afternoon for 25 of the most sagacious to impart general knowledge and to stir them up to zeal and the use of their thinking powers.

"Now the fourth part of the number 125 are no young children" he added, however, "but young men and young women from 12 to 20 years, and have been for years in the school."[877]

During the 1820s and 1830s the Philippolis Captaincy had struggled to maintain its authority against the Bergenaar and Kora raiders of the area, and during the 1840s constant unrest had been caused by the immigrant Boers, culminating in the battles of Swartkoppies and Boomplaats. Under the protection of British sovereignty, however, a period of tranquillity began in which the Captaincy could begin to prosper, and most of the accounts of its affairs during the 1850s give evidence of remarkable progress.

As has already been stated, the dismissal of Hendrik Hendrickze in 1850 seems to have removed another notable source of unrest and dissension, and the event is of sufficient importance in Griqua affairs for contemporary references to it to be cited here. Whatever ulterior motives there may have been for his removal, the immediate cause was his role as a member of the committee appointed for the appraisement of the farms affected by the new treaty with Sir Harry Smith in January 1848. "H. Hendriks has not behaved too well," van der Schalk reported in this respect on 14 May 1850, adding, "Unhappy Hendriks could not resist the glass of liquor offered by the boors [*Boers*], and the Captain thinks he took advantage of that."[878] On 18 June he wrote to the LMS in London: "Captain Kok begs you to disregard any letters which may be written to you by that bad man, H. Hendriks, he is no more Secretary, all confidence in him is gone; he betrays his people and their cause, and tries to do all injury possible. (…) last week he was summoned, and he told the Griqua's Council that he would have nothing more to do with them."[879]

On 9 July Kok himself wrote to J.J. Freeman more fully:

> Our old friend H. Hendrikse is now going around selling the land to the Boers within this Griqua Line, he is also trying to bring around the Griquas to his point of view; there are only a few people on his side. He is also trying to make the people rebellious against the Government; he is trying his best to cause trouble at this time. At this moment I have received a letter in which he gives a Boer authority to draw a farm within this Line. He is not to be trusted at all in the affairs of the country; I cannot use him at all.[880]

On 12 July an official Griqua Government notice announced "that Hendrik Hendrickse has ceased to be Secretary to the Griqua Government, and that Mr Conrad Windvogel has been appointed provisionally to that office",[881] and four days later Van der Schalk reported that the Kaptyn and Raad had set out that morning with an escort to arrest Hendrickze.[882] His name occurs somewhat unexpectedly among those present at a meeting of the native chiefs summoned by the British Resident at Viervoet in Sotho territory on 29 June 1851, where he was described as "late Secretary to Captain Adam Kok" and "gave his opinion at length"; it may be significant, however, that he did not arrive there with Kok's party.[883] After this he disappeared from the local scene completely; the only subsequent record of him which has been traced is a long statement on Griqua affairs which he made before the landdrost of Fauresmith in 1863.[884]

The removal of this last representative of the old, anarchic Bergenaar element from local affairs seems to have been of general benefit, and instead of the former factions, Griqua society after this would appear to have been quite clearly divided into two economic groups, an emerging bourgeoisie of prosperous farmers, who were coming increasingly to be identified with the church at Philippolis, and an improvident section who soon proved unable to maintain themselves in the altered conditions. This is reflected in the following account of Griqua society, in slightly different terms, given by Edward Solomon in 1853, even though it may be a somewhat opportunistic oversimplification in favour of the mission, intended to prove the beneficial influence of the latter.

> The population of this district may be divided into three great classes, the old Griqua party, the Bastards and the Becuanas. The majority of the former I regret to say are a wreck. They have given themselves over to strong drink and seem to be callous to every appeal made to them. They are spiritless with regard to their temporal interests, and many of them I regret to say are indifferent about their eternal concerns. (...) The Bastards (and with them may be associated the late apprentices[885]) form a very interesting and now the most influential portion of our community. They are decidedly progressing. They are working vigorously to improve their farms and increase their stock, and they seem alive to the importance of seeking for themselves and children religious knowledge. Among this class we have much encouragement.[886]

For the early part of the 1850s there are a number of other reports on the village of Philippolis from visitors passing through on their way to Bloemfontein, and the first of these was J.J. Freeman of the LMS, who spent some time there in November 1849. He described it as follows in the published account of his travels in South Africa, naturally concentrating on the affairs of the mission.

> I took up my temporary abode with Mr and Mrs Vanderchalk [*sic*] in their hired cottage, and soon began to find, from the conversation of the Chief and the people who called on me, that my time and my thoughts would have full occupation during my visit.
>
> The mission chapel here holds about 700 people. It is in a very imperfect state, and indicates, I fear, some want of earnestness and liberality on the part of the congregation. There are no pews, and but a few regular benches. The hearers bring their own seats with them—chairs and stools of all possible variety and of the rudest description—a plan extremely inconvenient and undignified, though just a little *above* squatting on the ground.[887] And yet this absence of comfort does not originate in the poverty of the people. Many of the Griquas possess considerable property. I counted not less than from forty to forty-five wagons belonging to the people who had come from the country to attend the services at Philippolis on the Sunday. Great numbers of the people

also came on horseback. They are rich in wagons, horses and oxen.

The attendance at the chapel is usually large and encouraging. It has occasionally been six hundred or seven hundred, and sometimes only half the number. Many Bechuanas live in the neighbourhood and attend the chapel. Services for them are held in their own language, the Sichuana, once in the school room and once in the chapel. I think they are sufficiently numerous and intelligent to have a missionary specially for and wholly devoted to their interests.

The state of education is not very satisfactory. The attendance in the school at Philippolis varies from thirty-five to seventy. At the out-station of Ramah there is about the same number. The fewness of scholars, amidst a large population, does not arise wholly from indifference on the part of the parents to the instruction of their children, but to the circumstances in which they are placed. But few families live at the town itself. The people reside on their farms or cattle-posts, where pasture and fountains can be obtained, and the distances are too great to permit the attendance of the children at any central station; besides which the actual services of the children are in many cases required to assist in tending the flocks and herds.

It is an extremely desirable measure that the Griquas should devote themselves more extensively to *agricultural pursuits* as a means of advancing them in the scale of civilization beyond the condition of the pastoral life, and still more as a means of weaning them from their fondness for *hunting excursions* in distant parts of the country, and in which they sometimes engage for months together, to the neglect of all domestic and civil institutions. Their agricultural pursuits require the services of the youthful members of their families, and hence the absence of the children from the mission schools may be accounted for without imputing it to wilful neglect on the part of the parents. But even in these cases their elementary education is not wholly forgotten. A few *Griquas have united to pay the salary of a schoolmaster*, who resides at their farms and instructs their families on the spot. This indicates a very laudable desire of improvement. I wish it were more general.

The Griquas might have improved more than they have done.

They certainly have not fully availed themselves of all their advantages. Philippolis itself is a poor town. Very few of the people have constructed good houses. They are not indeed addicted to the use of ardent spirits, but their fondness for tea, coffee and tobacco amounts almost to a fever, and which, unhappily, never becomes intermittent.[888]

Some six months after this, Philippolis was visited by the Anglican Bishop of Cape Town, Robert Gray, in the course of an epic journey which took him over the Highveld and across the Drakensberg to Natal: "The Bishop of Cape Town is quietly sleeping in one of the rooms among sacs [sic] of corn," wrote Van der Schalk on 30 April 1850. "He seems to be a nice gentleman, and we have spent a very agreeable evening with him." Sympathetic to the mission though he may have been in principle, Gray had no connection whatsoever with the LMS, and his account of his brief sojourn is probably less biased than those of the missionaries quoted above.

[30 April 1850]. (…) Slept at Philipolis [sic], the capital of Adam Kok's territory. Mr and Mrs van der Scholk [sic] (of the London Missionary Society) received me very kindly.

In the evening I called on Captain Adam Kok, who is the Chief of a portion of the Griquas.[889] He is a very common-place looking man—a Christian and, as I believe, a sincere one. He does not appear to have much authority over his people. His country forms part of the Sovereignty, but he governs it under British protection. Any Europeans, however, that may be living in his territory are under British rule, and he has no authority over them. At this present time I understand that he and other Chiefs are much dissatisfied with the Government regulations respecting land. Several Dutch Boers hold farms under him upon lease, the payment, I imagine, being nearly nominal. At the expiration of the leases, Government requires the Griquas to pay the tenants for the improvements made upon the farms by the erection of buildings &c., or to lose the land altogether. This they feel to be oppressive, and assert, with I know not what truth, that nothing was said about such payment in the original agreements.

Philippolis is a tolerable-sized village, and has its chapel and school. The missionary speaks with much interest of his work, and says that very many of the people are sincere Christians. He has received upwards of £100 from them this year as their contribution towards the London Missionary Society. He thinks also that the Griquas are advancing in civilization and industry. Some with whom I conversed on this subject at Colesberg think differently.

The country is fertile, with abundance of springs. The farms (if you may call them so) appear very poor and miserable. I did not see a single patch of ground under cultivation, though I am told there is a great deal. (…)[890]

A fuller albeit equally patronising picture, with more human detail, was provided by Gray's colleague, Archdeacon N.J. Merriman, who visited Philippolis at the end of the same year in the course of a long journey from Grahamstown to Bloemfontein which he made, characteristically, on foot.

Philippolis is a very respectable-looking European village, with a good church, a prison, and Adam Kok's residence, a good-sized, substantial cottage with trees round it (trees are rare things in the Sovereignty). The buildings, I learnt, were mostly erected by the natives. Adam Kok was absent, but I saw one of his brothers, a substantial-looking Boer. I was pleased to learn that some of the Griqua farmers in the neighbourhood drove in a wagon and good span of horses to church on Sunday; that one or two were breeding woolled sheep;[891] that Adam himself was a respectable and shrewd man, not always on good terms with his resident missionary, but a punisher of crime when detected, and one that would not wink at offenders.

This is the best side of the picture, and it is, under any phase, a pleasing sight to view even a single tribe of these natives so far Christianized and civilized as to be living as they do at Philippolis, and I cannot but think it a great honour to the London Missionary Society to have been instrumental in such a work, and a great thing to be thankful for that our Government has dealt so indulgently and with such a paternal spirit towards these its feeble children. (…)

One token I could not but observe at Philippolis, the same which I remarked on at the Kat River settlement, of the incapacity of the natives, though they may build decent houses and even manage farms, to cope or keep pace with the civilized man. Not a native of Philippolis or (as I learnt) at Griqua Town, not even a Bastard among them, could keep a shop; not from any deficiency of arithmetical talent or inability to keep their books, but from the impossibility which they find in preventing their countrymen from getting into their debt, or making them pay their debts when they have contracted them. In fact, there is a universal prevalence of social dishonesty among them, and almost as universal a prevalence of the questionable quality of a "good nature", so called, that cannot say "no" to a begging idler of a fellow-countryman.[892]

At all events, Adam Kok and his tribe have at present a splendid country, well watered and with plenty of grass;[893] how long they will keep it, foster them as we may, it is hard to say. Many people think they will one day trek in a body to the interior, to occupy other vacant land or to plunder some defenceless tribes. This probability I cannot assent to, for I think their Christianity, though it be of a feeble stamp, has been sufficient to leaven the lump and prevent such a result as this.[894]

The last extensive description of Philippolis as a Griqua town dates from a few years later, and comes from the Dutch advocate H.A.L. Hamelberg, newly arrived in South Africa and on his way to Bloemfontein, where he was to establish a practice and for several years play a prominent role in the affairs of the Free State Republic. Hamelberg had as many preconceptions as his compatriot van der Schalk, and judging by his journal clearly found it extremely difficult to accept the fact that South Africa did not resemble the Netherlands more closely.

4 August [1856]. (...) The country is hilly; the road is good, apart from a considerable number of dips.

Arrival in Philippolis, capital and sole town in the state, at 6 hours, 40 min. The country is somewhat less arid than on the far side of the river.

The head of state is Adam Kok; he is called Captain. I am told that he has 600 or 700 horses at his disposal and owns much landed property.

The schoolteacher receives £100, which sum is collected for him by various inhabitants. He has a place for grazing his cattle, and a house is being built for him.

The missionary Salomon[895] receives £150. We[896] betook ourselves to the latter for information. He was so good as to take us to a shop where we could buy fodder for the horses. Each of us carried two sheaves of oats, in addition to which I also had a bucket of millet, through the streets to the place at the edge of the town where our carts were waiting, accompanied for a part of the way by the missionary. We resembled two dragoons foraging under supervision of a sergeant.

There are a large number of dogs in the streets which do a great deal of barking.

We were invited in by Mr James Ainsworth,[897] in front of whose house our carts were standing, obtained stabling across the street from him, and were given a bed on the floor.

5 August. Philippolis, I am told, has about 150 inhabitants in all. The Griquas are Bastard Hottentots. In the shop where I went to buy fodder for the horses a brown woman asked me for tobacco, which she smelt and appraised very carefully.

The houses are situated largely in a single street, all standing detached from one another. They have one storey; most of them are brick, a few of clay or stone. The doors and windows are painted. Some of the houses are plastered. They have no gardens, and the erven are not divided by walls. Here and there are houses formed from branches of trees bent over each other diagonally and planted in the ground at both ends. They resemble round needlework baskets turned upside down. The branches are covered with mats.

Some of the inhabitants are clothed in the European fashion, partly in any case, whereas others, men as well as women, wear sheepskins. I saw a woman who had drawn a broad line with a brownish substance under her nose close to her ears, which gave her an extremely ugly appearance.

Before my departure I went with Foreest to the Captain, who

lives in a pretty good house with two windows on either side of the door.

"Is the Captain at home?" I asked.

"Yes," replied the man at the door, dressed in a drab coat and trousers, with a muffler and a hat with a grey silk scarf around it, whom I took to be the Captain's coachman.

"May I speak to him?"

"Yes, you may speak to me," said the same man.

"Are you the Captain?"

"Yes!"

We thereupon entered the house, but we got no further than the apartment communicating directly with the front door,[898] in which, apart from the Captain, who kept his hat on,[899] while we took off ours, four men were also seated and two women were squatting at the fire below the chimney.

I conveyed to the Captain the greetings of Mr de Wit of Beaufort[900] and gave him some news of this gentleman, to whom he now undertook to write, which he had not been able to do lately, as he knew the latter had moved but not where he was at present living. Mr Foreest remarked that Philippolis is a fine town. This is by no means the case; however, the Captain agreed, adding only that there is very little water. Mr Foreest also asked whether we were not four hours away from the border of the state. "No," said the Captain, "two days still; the state extends as far as Bethanie." Actually it extends no further than the river at Boomplaats; that is the boundary.[901]

Behind or next to the main street there are also some houses. In one of these, constructed of branches and mats in the manner already described, a brown woman was preparing food. She had a shawl tied around her, and a child in it on her back.

Left Philippolis at 9 hours 15 minutes.[902]

As appears from Hamelberg's account, Philippolis had once more acquired a resident missionary, for in March 1851, Edward Solomon had been transferred there from Griquatown. Solomon belonged to a family of Jewish origin, several members of whom were to become prominent in South African affairs, and had studied under Dr Philip in Cape Town.

His wife Jessie was moreover Mrs Philip's niece, and apart from the fact that he obviously occupied a favoured place in the local LMS hierarchy, he was especially suited for the work at Philippolis by the fact that he had been involved in Griqua affairs at Griquatown since 1843, had often visited Philippolis in later years, and was fluent in Dutch, at any rate by missionary standards. He was an active champion of the Griquas during the difficult period they experienced in the early 1850s.

From about the middle of the century, however, it would increasingly be the various black tribes of Southern Africa who came to enjoy the attention of statesmen and politicians and the interest and support of the LMS. In 1851, moreover, Dr Philip died, followed the next year by James Read Sr, and the Griquas thus lost their two most redoubtable champions in missionary circles.

Almost simultaneously came another heavy blow to Griqua independence, for after having struggled for some years to gain control over the Transgariep and its turbulent population, Britain precipitately abandoned it in 1854. By the Bloemfontein Convention, signed with local Boer leaders on 23 February of that year, the area of white occupancy became the independent Republic of the Orange Free State, while the peoples of Adam Kok, Moshweshwe and other indigenous leaders were left to arrange their affairs with this new state as best as possible. As far as the Griquas were concerned, not only were Kok's efforts to negotiate their future with the British Special Commissioner, Sir George Clerk, completely unsuccessful, but in his attempts to be rid of the Sovereignty as quickly as possible Clerk also entered into a secret agreement with the Free State by which, among other things, it was agreed "That whenever any Griqua lands shall be sold to any person of European descent, such land falls at once under the Orange River Government", and that the Free State Government held authority over the leasable territory.[903] In this manner the Griquas were abandoned by their sole ally.

Shortly afterwards, in 1855, the LMS withdrew from the work at Philippolis and the congregation there became independent, a step which formed part of the general policy of the Society, but occurred at a particularly awkward time. It says much for Solomon's guidance, and for the stability of the local community, that the change was accomplished successfully.

Edward Solomon left Philippolis in 1857, according to his fellow missionary David Livingstone, because "his wife's health was *not good*",[904] although the rather odd underlining may indicate more than meets the eye. His successor was W.B. Philip, a son of the Doctor, who was in later years praised by the Revd William Dower of Kokstad as "a man of gentle and amiable disposition, held deservedly in high affection and esteem by the body of the people" and "one of the saintliest and wisest of men",[905] presumably on the basis of his reputation among the Griquas. It is notable that all the missionaries who served at Philippolis from 1843— Wright, Thomson, Christie, Solomon and W.B. Philip— had close connections with John Philip. Even more notable, however, is the fact that the station had no fewer than nine missionaries and missionary assistants over the 26 years between 1825 and 1851, all of whom (apart from Wright, who died within a year of his arrival) left amid much quarrelling and recrimination; against this there were only two over the next ten years, whose terms of office seem moreover to have been relatively tranquil. Various explanations may be given, but as has already been indicated, it is probably not without significance that that prominent source of dissension, Hendrik Hendrickze, was dismissed in 1850.

Travellers on their way to Bloemfontein, the Transvaal, Griquatown or Kuruman almost invariably passed through Philippolis and recorded their impressions of the village. There are relatively few descriptions of the remainder of the Captaincy for the 1850s, however, although Hamelberg did describe his journey from Philippolis to Bethanie and Bloemfontein.

> [*5 August 1856*]. (…) The road was good, apart from some dips. There are virtually no stones. There was some wind. The country is arid, hilly at first, subsequently a large plain surrounded by hills.
> Arrived at Kalkgat, to the left of the road, at 11 hours 15 minutes. It has two miserable little stone houses.[906] In a kraal a man, a woman and some children were squatting down. The man wore a short jacket and trousers and was sawing on a violin. The woman wore only a sheepskin and a head scarf. In the little house near the kraal a clothed woman[907] was sitting beside a fire burning in the middle of the floor.
> Left Kalkgat at 12 hours 45 minutes.
> The road was good.

Passed Vogelfontein, to the right of the road, at 2 o'clock. The farm is situated so far from the road that it took twenty minutes to walk there and back in order to enquire about the distance to the next farm. A woman at Vogelfontein, who was smoking a pipe and spitting from time to time like a man, asked for tobacco, and Mr Foreest took her to his cart and gave her some.

Arrived at Vissershoek, to the right and left of the road, at 2 hours 30 minutes. Here there were seven Kaffir houses made of branches and mats as already described. Attached to each house there was a small enclosure made of branches, The children were running about naked or wore sheepskins or in some cases a small skin for the sake of decency. The men and women were wearing sheepskins, some of the men wore trousers and shoes. Apart from them, an English shoemaker was living here in a linen tent with his family.

Left this place at 3 hours 15 minutes.

The road was very good. We saw a multitude of springbok and wildebeeste. The country is hilly and arid.

Passed Touwfontein, to the right of the road, at 5 hours 15 minutes. The road was very good.

Arrived at Boomplaats, the farm of Mr Rabi[e], to the left of the road, at 6 hours 30 minutes. (...)[908]

A livelier and less querulous account of a journey through the Captaincy and a sojourn at Philippolis is provided by the French missionary Prosper Lemue, stationed at Carmel, between Bethulie and the new village of Smithfield, who attended a mission anniversary meeting in the village in 1855, only a year before Hamelberg's visit.

In crossing the eastern part of the lovely country of the Griquas, occupied for a great part by freed slaves,[909] we were struck on finding there establishments which yielded in nothing to those of the most industrious Dutch farmers. Among those on our route I shall mention particularly that of Slammert,[910] a member of the Church at Philippolis. This man established himself in the country with his family seven years ago; today one sees on his farm six buildings consisting of a dwelling house, barn, stables, mill and a chapel where his neighbours come together with him; stone kraals for the cattle, a large cultivated piece of enclosed ground, fruit trees, ox and horse wagons, and 700 merino sheep. His house is open to all visitors, whom he receives with liberal hospitality, for these good people consider it a great honour to receive the visit of a European.

As we approached the capital, we frequently encountered the local people making their way to the church. Some transported their families in ox wagons, the majority owned lighter wagons drawn by eight horses, all of the same colour. Some were resting on a verdant couch in the shadow of a rock, others milking their cows for the evening meal.

It was twenty-five years ago that I had seen Philippolis for the first time[911] and fourteen since the second: I might therefore expect to find it much changed. In fact the Griquas, following the example of the Dutch, have built small European houses for themselves there in order to have shelter when they come to take part in divine service with their families; but few of them really live there, for the greater part cultivate their farms in the neighbourhood. The place has the disadvantage of a lack of water for irrigating the gardens; the torrents have worn out such a deep bed at the fountain that in spite of repeated labours it has not been possible to lead out more than a weak quantity of water to the village; this is why it presents such a desolate appearance. The chapel is a solid building which can contain 700 people: the mission house is built with taste.

On Saturday evening we climbed a little hill, from which we counted 100 wagons. At daybreak on Sunday there was a prayer meeting conducted by the deacons to implore the blessing from on high on the exercises of the day. At ten o'clock the church was filled with people; six deacons surrounded the communion table (…).

On Monday at ten o'clock everyone assembled again in the church to take part in the annual mission meeting. Adam Kock [*sic*], the son of the old Chief of this name whom we met at Philippolis in 1830, took the chair. He is a man of very simple tastes, but has given his subjects a good example of industry, temperance and piety. In his opening address he urged the assembly to be generous to the Mother Society. After him the deacons spoke, placing great emphasis on this idea: The time had come, they said, for the Church to undertake all its own expenses, such as the construction and upkeep of public buildings, the support of its pastor, etc.[912] (...)

The zeal, the activity and the talents of the missionary at Philippolis[913] are equal to the difficulties of his situation. Many of the old Griquas have given way to the temptation of selling their property; others have fallen into intemperance by the abuse of the strong drink with which their country has been flooded; but nonetheless good work is being done there which aroused our gratitude towards the Lord. It was with these feelings that we took leave of our friend and his family to return home.[914]

Edward Solomon, in a lecture given in Cape Town in the same year, presented a similarly optimistic picture of the Philippolis Captaincy which, while naturally biased in favour of the people in his charge, cannot have been entirely without foundation.

Taken as a whole, the Griqua tribe will now amount to from 8000 to 10 000 souls, and it is decidedly the furthest advanced in civilization of all those connected with the Hottentot race. The country occupied by those under the Chief Adam Kok is one of the finest in the whole of South Africa—not, indeed, presenting such rich and varied scenery as some parts of the Colony or Kafirland,[915] but its value for agricultural and pastoral purposes is very great; and either for the raising of grain or the rearing of all kinds of stock may be advantageously compared to any portion of this promontory. (...) The territory has been found especially favourable to the growth and improvement of woolled sheep, and from that quarter a large and constantly increasing quantity of wool is brought into the Colony. And I am sure you will be glad to hear that many of the Griquas, seeing the advantage resulting from the possession of such flocks, are endeavouring to obtain them, and for this purpose are devoting all the money they can raise. Some of them have now flocks varying from 500 tot 1500, and many of the people are anxious to increase the number and improve the breed of their sheep. This is one proof of the position we have advanced, that the Griquas are the most civilized portion of the Hottentot race. (…)

The more respectable and advanced of the Griquas occupy European houses, wear European clothing, and live upon food similar to that consumed by Europeans. They are engaged in agricultural as well as pastoral pursuits, many of them having fine farms, their own personal property, admirably adopted for the purpose. They possess a considerable number of good Colonial-made wagons. The last Saturday I spent at Philippolis prior to my visit to this city, one hundred ox and horse wagons arrived at the station, bringing a large number of people to join in the religious services of the following Sabbath. Altogether the Griquas must have about three hundred wagons in their possession, worth at a very low valuation at least £15 000 sterling. As an instance of incipient enterprise I may mention that the Griqua Chief, Adam Kok, has lately expended above £400 in erecting a very superior water-mill, which is now, I believe, in full operation.

They have an increasing desire for knowledge, and are anxious that their children should receive a higher education than any with which they have been privileged; and to meet this desire I have a week ago sent down from this city a young man, a native of this place, but whose education has been completed in Europe, who is well known here as an active and successful teacher, and who has now been engaged to educate the Griqua children, their parents being willing to allow him a respectable salary.[916]

All these are encouraging signs of advancement in civilization, and though much injury has been done to that people by the policy of the British Government, though much has occurred calculated to depress their minds and to throw them back into barbarism, disgusted with the injustice of civilized and professedly Christian men and nations, and though sad havoc has been caused among them of late by the immense quantity of brandy brought into the country—yet we have every reason to believe that should peace be maintained between these people and their neighbours of the Orange Free State, or should strong national antipathies or deep-rooted prejudices be so far overcome as to allow of their amalgamation with their more powerful European friends, they will in a very short time form a highly respectable, intelligent and wealthy community. Already are several placed beyond the reach of want and have accumulated property to a pretty considerable amount, and in point of shrewdness and intelligence will bear a favourable comparison with those Europeans who are living near them.[917]

The same positive account is to be found in the reminiscences of the LMS missionary James Mackenzie, who travelled through the Transorange in the late 1850s on his way to Kuruman.

> Both in Griqua Town district and Philippolis we found some of the people in possession of houses, waggons and clothing quite equal to that of many Dutch farmers. For several years they had had good central schools, while rudimentary instruction was given in the villages by schoolmasters who were usually office-bearers of the Church. (...)
> When I first visited Philippolis in 1859 I was surprised at the intelligence and apparent respectability of many of the people. Even from a local or caste standpoint, their only fault was their features. Some showed considerable enterprise in farming and in rearing sheep. It was here I first saw a flour-mill driven by water in possession of a native. The Chief, Adam Kok, who succeeded his father of the same name, enjoyed the confidence of Mr Philip, the missionary, as a Christian man, and showed considerable ability in conducting public affairs. At the same time they supported their own minister and also paid a good salary to a schoolmaster.[918]

These highly favourable accounts from missionary sources are, however, confirmed from a quarter less likely to be partial to the Griquas, for the *Friend* of Bloemfontein, reporting a visit by President J.N. Boshof to Fauresmith and Philippolis in 1857, wrote:

> We understand that His Honor was well satisfied with his reception at the different places he visited, as well as gratified at the striking indications of prosperity and progress both among the

Griqua and white inhabitants. Not having been at Philippolis for many years, he expressed his surprise and pleasure at the substantial and almost genteel dwellings of certain of the principal Griquas, and at the liberal provision made for education by subscriptions among themselves.[919]

Further illustrations of the prosperity arising from the more settled conditions of the 1850s, and founded mainly on agriculture, may be found in Solomon's report to the LMS in England. "Our people are also busy building more respectable houses in the village," he wrote in April 1856, shortly before the visit of the unenthusiastic Hamelberg,

> nine are in the course of erection, four of which are nearly completed, and others will soon be commenced. All these are built of stone and burnt brick, and will greatly improve the appearance of the village.
>
> Our school committee are also preparing materials for building a house for the schoolmaster—they have borrowed £200 of our people, for which they will have to pay 4 or 5 per cent per annum interest, and with this money they will be able to build a comfortable house for the schoolmaster, and the interest will be considerably less than the rent they now pay for a small and very inconvenient house in which he now lives.
>
> Our people have had a remarkably good harvest of wheat this year, and their clip of wool is better than they have ever had before. One of our members has realized £180 for his clip this year, and several individuals will realize from £50 to above £100 each, and this tho' the wool is selling at a lower rate this year than usual. All these are elements of prosperity in which we rejoice, and we trust that God will abundantly bless us in all our interests.[920]

Early in 1857 Solomon reported in a similar vein:

> Fifteen new houses have been erected during the past year, all of them built of stone and burnt brick, and some of them very excellent houses. One in particular is an excellent comfortable dwelling containing parlour, dining room, three bed rooms, kitchen,

pantry and store room. All the timber in the house is good European deal, and the house has cost the proprietor about £300. This is the best and largest house, but two others will almost compete with it, and it is a cheering proof of the progress of civilization when individuals are willing at such an expense to raise comfortable houses. There are at present two houses in the course of erection, and several of our people are preparing bricks preparatory to building, so that I think, should no disturbances occur, we shall have as many new houses built this year as we had last.

Our people have prospered with their wo[o]llen sheep. I cannot at present form any estimate of what amount of wool our people will send to market, as the clip for this year is not yet finished, but one of the Griquas took this year 21 bales of wool to market and realized by its sale £293. This is a sure sign of progress in civilization and wealth.[921]

In his published report for 1856 Solomon could write, "At least 200 bales of wool have been produced this year from the flocks of our people, and has realized to them in the market about £2000 sterling."[922] A Cape Government report stated of Adam Kok many years later that his interests in the former Philippolis Captaincy had "amounted to some £90 000",[923] and while Kok had always been a wealthy man and was well placed to promote his own interests, there is every reason to believe that a considerable section of his subjects prospered in proportion.

A striking illustration of the general prosperity at Philippolis and the generosity of individual church members is provided by two lists of contributions to the work of the LMS published in the annual reports of the Cape Town Auxiliary Mission Society,[924] which in 1853 amounted to £85 13s 9d, and over the first nine months of the following year to £62 6s 6d. In 1854 there were 52 individual contributions, husbands and wives being named and listed together: one contributor was apparently a European and two were Batswana, but the remainder were Griquas. Adam Kok, Hans Bezuidenhout and Hendrik Zwaart gave £3 each, and Piet Draai, Jan Pienaar (Gamja) and "Bella Wiesie" £2,[925] while further donations were for lesser amounts, those under 7s 6d not being listed individually. A detail worth noting is the number of economically independent single women, presumably widows, listed—seven in all.

An extremely important development for the Philippolis congregation during this period, and in its way for the Captaincy as well, was the fact that in 1855 the LMS withdrew from the work in which it had been engaged for more than thirty years, upon which the mission at Philippolis became an independent Congregational church with its own minister. While this was in keeping with the general trend in LMS policy, it occurred at a particularly delicate point in local affairs, only a year after the withdrawal of British sovereignty and the establishment of the Free State Republic; but in spite of some initial doubts, the Griquas proved well able to manage their own church affairs and also to provide for their own financial support. At the end of 1856 Solomon could report to the Auxiliary Mission Society in Cape Town that over the past fourteen months the voluntary contributions of the people amounted to £371, "thus averaging £26 10s per month, a sum considerably more than double what was ever before raised in one year at this station, and nearly *four times* as much as the average sum raised annually for the last ten years."[926]

While the evidence cited here is naturally partial, it would seem to confirm the impression that the old "Church party" at Philippolis had by this time become representative of, and to a large extent even synonymous with, the developing Griqua bourgeoisie of the Captaincy.

Further illustrations of local activity and prosperity are also to be found in the above report, in which Solomon continued:

> Besides paying the whole salary of pastor, and part of the salary of schoolmaster (a part is being paid out of the allowance of £50 per annum made by the Colonial Government in aid of the school of Philippolis), our people have this year had some unusual expenses. They engaged to pay the expenses of Mr Crossley's journey from Cape Town; these were heavy, amounting to £80; towards this you kindly consented to leave £20 belonging to the London Missionary Society in our hands; the balance (£60) was paid by the people. They have also built for Mr Crossley a comfortable and respectable house at a cost of £250.
>
> In addition to these expenses, our people propose building at once two class-rooms as wings to our school, which is altogether insufficient for the accommodation of the children who attend, and they contemplate as soon as possible enlarging our present

place of worship or building a new one. Our chapel now, though capable of seating 750 persons, is frequently so full that many are unable to gain admittance.[927]

In the report to the Auxiliary Society for 1853 schools were still mentioned at Ramah and Sterkfontein, in addition to unspecified "other schools [which] have been closed during a part of the year owing to the dispersed state of the people", and contributions of £22 10s recorded for the teacher at Sterkfontein.[928] It is interesting also to note that when the 77-year-old W.F. Corner petitioned the Free State Volksraad for financial support in 1866, he declared "That he had formerly always been catechist and teacher in the time when the Griquas were still living in this district",[929] although it is not known where he taught. Corner is a particularly interesting figure, for he was a black man, a Demeraran from the West Indies, who had been educated in Scotland; he came to South Africa in 1811 in the service of the LMS and was dismissed for alleged immorality eight years later. He had married a sister of Jan Goeyman, the first teacher at Philippolis, and was presumably the father of the Griqua official W.O. Corner.[930]

The article "The Griquas and their exodus" which appeared in the *Cape Monthly Magazine* in 1872, the author of which was obviously well acquainted with the Captaincy and it affairs,[931] writes in much the same strain when describing the Griquas' decision to remove to Nomansland in 1861:

> About the time this movement was necessitated, the people were in a prosperous state; they had their titles to their farms, on which they had built substantial cottages and out-buildings; orchards well stocked with good fruit trees, garden grounds and lands for cultivation were in many cases enclosed with stone walls; good stone kraals and one or two dams were to be found on most farms; troops of from twenty to one hundred horses, about the same number of cattle, and hundreds of well-bred woolled sheep were running on these farms, and many a man brought his ten, twenty and twenty-five bales of wool at once for sale; while the shopkeepers found them as good customers for clothing, groceries, guns, saddlery, carts and furniture as any of the Boers. Of course

there were many poor people, whose poverty was brought on by their own laziness, pride and drunkenness.

They voluntarily contributed from £500 to £600 per annum for the support of religion and education amongst themselves, paying their own minister and head schoolmaster in Philippolis and schoolmasters in the country.[932]

An unexpected source of information on the village, the Captaincy and the people is the little monthly newspaper called *De Dagster*, which was published and edited by the enterprising missionary W.B. Philp.[933] Only three issues seem to have appeared in all, and the only copy known to have survived is of the first of these, dated May 1859.[934] "Do not despise it because it is so small," wrote the editor in somewhat shaky Dutch; "we are making it as cheap as we can, but in order to pay the cost, many hundreds must be sold." The contents were mainly of an edifying nature, and great satisfaction was expressed at the reaction of the Philippolis magistrate to the discovery of a pipe of wine and a pipe of brandy in private hands, "which were immediately brought in his office and there poured out into a deep ditch. The guilty party was also fined £15 sterling."

Some incidental detail of life in the village may be obtained from the supplement to the *Dagster*, which contained advertisements for the storekeeper J. Vaughan, the tailor J. Muller, "lately from Cape Town", and M.C. Viret, also "lately from Cape Town", who advertised as "tin smith, copper smith, pump maker, bell hanger &c., &c., &c.", while the contractors for the postal service between Fauresmith and Colesberg announced that they were "always prepared to take one or two passengers in their strong spring postcart".

In 1860 there were references elsewhere to the firm James Murray & Co.,[935] and towards the end of the next year, on the eve of the departure of the Griquas for Nomansland, there were said to be six shops in the village.[936] In 1859 mention is made of the presence at Philippolis of the wagon-maker J.G. Flooks, who had been declared insolvent in Bloemfontein,[937] in the following year Charles Loding opened an "accommodation house" called The Traveller's Rest in Church Street—"Good accommodation for horses, and forage supplied on a liberal and economical scale"[938]—and in 1861 W.H.A. Bowden advertised as "chemist, druggist, &c.".⁹³⁹ All these men seem to have been English speaking. The account of "Piet Pienaar, Griqua" (probably the Griqua Councillor, a prominent member of the local community) which has been preserved by chance is not with any of these firms, however, but with W.A. Dickson at Fauresmith, from whom he bought an overcoat, a hat, a field cape, a martingale,⁹⁴⁰ sugar and "2 [bags?] sulphur" on 26 May 1860 for Rds266.2.4.⁹⁴¹

Further information on the workings of the Captaincy and on life there is to be found in a surprising number of official, semi-official and personal documents of the late 1840s and the 1850s which confirm the fact that conditions in the Captaincy had by this time become more stable, that government had improved and that literacy was more common. Their preservation was not, however, a matter of chance, for they were carefully collected in the early 1870s with a view to proving the Griqua case before the Griqualand West Land Court at the time of the Diamond Fields dispute: Piet Pienaar's account referred to above is among them. ⁹⁴²

From the *Friend* of Bloemfontein it is possible to obtain an description of the execution of justice at Philippolis in 1852, after one Cornelius Kok was sentenced to death for shooting his brother-in-law in a drunken quarrel: the newspaper report states that he was tried by the Combined Court, but refers at the same time to "the jury impanelled to try the case".

> Monday the 25th [October 1852] being the day appointed for his execution, at 10 a.m. he was conveyed from prison in a cart to the gallows, surrounded by a guard of 150 armed men on horseback and 50 on foot, and followed by a large number of people; he mounted the gallows with an unfaltering step, spoke calmly and clearly a very few words to the people, warning them to take example by his fate. Prayer was then offered up by the missionary— at the request of the unfortunate man, the people sung the Dutch version of Cowper's beautiful hymn,
>
> *There is a fountain filled with blood,*
> *Drawn from Immanuel's veins,*
> *And sinners plunged beneath the flood*
> *Lose all their guilty stains.*

At the close of the singing the signal was given by the magistrate—the drop fell, and after a few struggles life was extinct.

Immediately afterwards another prisoner, a Griqua named Cotje Cloete, was brought forward to receive his punishment. This man had also been tried on a charge of murder, but had been found guilty of culpable homicide, and had been sentenced to receive 60 lashes by the hangman under the gallows, and then to be imprisoned with hard labour for one year. He was accordingly tied up and flogged, and afterwards removed to the prison to undergo the other portion of his sentence.

The spectators behaved with the greatest decorum, and it is to be hoped that the awful example will prove beneficial to those who beheld it.[943]

Unfortunately the apparent increase in stability in the Captaincy over this period, however heartening it may have been to the Griquas and their friends, was superficial only. As is clear from various of the passages quoted above, the land was increasingly passing out of Griqua hands, and after 1854 the Griquas found themselves deprived of British support and placed under increasing pressure by the more powerful Orange Free State.

Concerning the sale of Griqua land, the *Friend* of Bloemfontein had as early as 1851 issued a serious warning in an editorial headed "Griqua farms"; it was probably composed by the magistrate of Bloemfontein, C.U. Stuart, a Scotsman who acted unofficially as editor during the early years, and who was known as a supporter of the missions and well disposed towards the Griquas.[944]

Every man has his own troubles. "There is a ghost in every house", as the story has it. So may Captain Adam Kok exclaim.

Our distant reader may here be reminded that the Griquas, by the treaty between Sir Peregrine Maitland and Adam Kok, have been prevented selling their farms to British subjects. This treaty, so far as the prohibition on this point is concerned, is, we fear, little better than a dead letter. That many Griquas are over head and ears in debt to Boers we have no doubt. These Boers gently lend cash and give sugar, coffee, cattle, &c., taking receipts for the same, carefully wrapping up the documents till the day of reckoning, when they will be forthcoming to the Land Commission three years hence as claims for Griqua places.⁹⁴⁵ We do not say seven years, for as matters are gradually ripening for closing accounts between the traders, Boers and Griquas, we are much inclined to think that Captain Adam Kok will have a party of his own people against him in his laudable endeavours to preserve the integrity of the Griquas as a nation, and that matters must shortly be squared.

Our attention has recently been attracted to this subject by rumours that there are few farms belonging to Griquas that have not been secretly sold to Boers. The Griquas are awkwardly situated. They are exposed to a temptation that seems too great for their self-denial. Their leased farms having been valued, or nearly so, for improvements up to February 1848, they are required to pay large sums to Boers on the termination of leases, otherwise to let these sums be liquidated by a rent to be fixed on the termination of the present leases. The Boers have shrewdly enough offered large cash prices for the farms in perpetuity, and it has now become a question amongst the Griquas whether they will sell their farms at once, thereby pocketing in the year 1851 what their children's children may perhaps receive in 1881. A goodly number of the Griquas are of opinion that a "bird in hand is worth two in the bush"—hence some sharp contentions amongst the politicians of Philippolis, some of whom think that posterity may take care of itself.

Captain Adam Kok has, we fear, a good deal of bother in maintaining his position between the fire of the "old original Griquas", who would finger the cash at once, and "young Griqua Land", who would most laudably "hold its own"—and justify the favorable opinion formed of its virtue, perseverance and lawful ambition by the Revd Dr Philip, Mr Freeman and others. If the Griquas will but resist debt and groceries, the Boers will lose their chance of the farms, but it would seems that pretty gownpieces for the *vrouws* and sundries will finally settle the question. It will not be forgotten, we trust, that we have warned both Boers and Griquas of their danger.⁹⁴⁶

An illustration of the continual squabbling, petty violence and increasing friction between the Griquas and the whites who had settled in their territory is provided by the case of T.J. de Villiers of the farm Cyferfontein in the Fauresmith district, who complained to the Free State authorities of being attacked and assaulted by "armed Griquas", in the words of the State Attorney of the Free State, after a dispute about money he owed them for cutting bulrushes. The following description of what is alleged to have occurred is from the affidavit of J.F. Combrink of the same farm.

> On the 9th September last [1859] I was busy washing corn about 140 paces from the house. I then saw Abraham Bergover [and] Piet Bergover, Basters, and another young Baster whose name I do not know,[947] and Klaas Leeuw or Malitzani, galloping up to the house. Before the door Abraham Bergover jumped from his horse and walked up to the door. He spoke in approaching the door. I could not understand what he said, but coming back from the door he said, "Today I want my money." Then he went back to the horses, walked up to the door for the second time, pushed open the door and went into the house. I then saw that the door was pushed shut. I could not see by whom. Piet Bergover and Klaas Leeuw or Malitzani then pushed open the door and went into the house. I then left my work and ran up to the house. About ten paces from the house I saw Tobias de Villiers standing in the doorway with his gun and the Basters before the door. The Basters had two guns with them. They then stormed up and went into the house again. I went in, took the guns from the Basters and de Villiers, and pushed out the former and spoke to them. Thereupon de Villiers appeared in the doorway with an unsheathed sword.[948] Then the Basters jumped past me again and caught hold of the sword. Then I went in and threw out all three of them. I asked whether they weren't afraid that such behaviour might lead to war. Thereupon Klaas Leeuw said de Villiers might shoot one of them dead, then we [*they*] might shoot him dead and the others could be hanged. I told him it was better for them to go away. They said they had now come to ask for their money. If they didn't get it, they would come in another way. I then told de Villiers it was better to pay them if he still owed them something. He then paid them, and after having cursed and sworn some more, they left.[949]

According to de Villiers, Abraham Bergover on arrival had cried, "Damned Boer, today I want my money, either you dead or me", and Leeuw declared, "De Villiers could kill one of them, then we would have shot him dead, then the others could have been hanged, for we want war and have come to seek blood."

An illustration of attempts by the Griquas, during the same period, to uphold their authority in the Captaincy against the truculent white settlers in the area is provided by the complaint of Peter Ennis, formerly of Vlakplaats in the Fauresmith district, who had become involved in a dispute with a Griqua, Andries Stoffels. According to Ennis, in passing Philippolis, "I was arrested on the highway by 40 to 50 Griquas and forced to go to the Griqua court. When I got there, I was told that as I had struck a Griqua, I was fined £25 *by them*", and he submitted a complaint to the Free State authorities demanding their protection, "as I was not a Griqua subject". Adam Eta Kok of Sterkfontein, who was acting as Provisie Kaptyn at the time, wrote to the Acting President of the Free State on 12 October 1859 about the matter:

> The true state of affairs is as follows.
>
> A certain Griqua subject, Andries Stoffels, owed P.E. a sum of money which he partly repaid by service, accompanying P.E. on a journey to Grahamstown, further promising him to come and live with him for the balance of the money owing, on condition that P.E. would establish himself on a farm partly assigned to P.E. by Captain Adam Kok. In the meantime P.E. hired another farm from a Griqua, so that A.S. refused to live with P.E., promising, however, to pay him.
>
> Having received a message, A.S. betook himself to P.E., upon which P.E. threatened to deal with him in accordance with a warrant he alleged he had received from the magistrate of Philippolis, and on A.S. persisting in his refusal to live with P.E., P.E. had him held down by two Hottentots and hit with a piece of wood about 4 inches thick over his face and head in an inhuman manner, after which he fastened A.S. to the wagon with a brake-chain. The result of this maltreatment was that A.S. was ill for a long time and still has three wounds on his head.
>
> For this I had Peter Ennis summonsed, regarding him as a Griqua

subject, seeing that he hires a Griqua farm. As he paid no attention to this summons, I had him fetched from the commonage when he was passing through Philippolis and brought before me, heard the case of A. Stoffels against him, found him guilty of the crime of assault, and fined him £15 [*sic*].

I wish further to remark that it is not clear to me in how far I have encroached on the authority of the O.F.S. Government in punishing a person who has mistreated another in such a way, especially as I regarded this person as subject to the laws of the Griqua Government, as he occupied a Griqua farm. Should this be the case, then it was done in ignorance, and I shall be most pleased if the Free State Government would come to a clear understanding with us about who are Free State burghers and Griqua burghers, in order to avoid further unpleasantness.[950]

An additional factor in the increasing antagonism between Griqua and Free State subjects was noted by John Mackenzie, who as a missionary and a newcomer to the country was possibly more sensitive to certain nuances of South African society than the seasoned observer. Discussing the reasons which caused the Griqua decision finally to quit Philippolis in 1861, he added:

In the case of the Griquas there was added the strong caste feeling, or prejudice on account of their colour. They might be good, intelligent and wealthy; they were only "bastaards and Hottentots" after all. This had not been so manifest in the early years of their contact with the Dutch in the district of Philippolis. It was then not unusual for a Dutchman to give his hand in greeting to a Griqua and call him "oom" (uncle) or "neef" (nephew)—in short, to treat him as an equal; but as the Colonists increased in number their clannish feeling returned.[951]

Initially the Griqua Captaincy had attempted to assert itself against the Free State by calling on the support of the British Government, in accordance with the treaties concluded successively with Napier, Maitland and Smith, but after the Free State in 1857 made known the secret supplementary terms to the Bloemfontein Convention,[952] it became clear that the Griquas would not be able to maintain their authority in the Transgariep. The High Commissioner and Governor at the time was Sir George Grey, and while Grey was in many ways a high-handed and autocratic man intent on establishing white control over South Africa, and as such does not enjoy much favour with modern historians, it must be admitted that he seems to have done his best to obtain some justice for the Griquas. It was at the instigation of Grey that the Cape Executive Council in 1861 sent an official minute to the British Government in favour of Adam Kok and his people, an expression of friendship and goodwill which, though belated and largely ineffectual, nonetheless deserves to be recorded.

> His Excellency the Governor, fearing that Her Majesty's Government may in some respects have been misinformed as to the real character, disposition and services of Captain Adam Kok, requests the Executive Council to place on record a short minute expressive of their views on these points.
>
> With reference to the matter thus brought by His Excellency the Governor under the consideration of the Council, the members are unanimously of the opinion that no native Chief in South Africa deserves so well of the Colony and of Her Majesty's Government as Captain Adam Kok—no thefts from the Colonists have ever been charged against the Griquas, and it is certain that Adam Kok and his people have at all times, and occasionally under trying circumstances, shown a disposition, or rather a determination, to support British authority against all opposition.
>
> Captain Adam Kok and his people have no doubt raised some questions regarding the construction of a certain treaty entered into with Sir Harry Smith, but they have always done so in a friendly spirit, and neither in this or in any other point, as far as the Council believes, have forfeited their right to be regarded as firm and true allies of the Queen and the Colony.[953]

10. The trek to Nomansland (1861–1863)

In spite of its epic proportions, the trek of the Griquas to Nomansland (later Griqualand East) after the abandonment of the Philippolis Captaincy, is not one of the better-known episodes in South African history. Detailed accounts of it are nonetheless available, and it can best be described in the words of contemporaries.

When Sir George Grey visited the Captaincy in August 1858, Adam Kok discussed with him the increasingly intolerable position in which his people had been placed with regard to the Orange Free State after the British withdrawal: "I have talked much to him about affairs of state [*lands zaken*]," Kok reported to Nicolaas Waterboer afterwards, "and he seems to be a very sensible man."[954] What is more, Grey was also prepared to give active proof of his goodwill towards the Griquas.

To quote the author of the anonymous article "The Griquas and their exodus" which appeared in the *Cape Monthly Magazine* in 1872:[955]

> The best solution of the problem seemed to be that those Griquas who still held farms should sell them, and all should move to some other part. A few suggested Namaqualand, a few more the Campbell Grounds,[956] others suggested the eastern side of the Drakensberg, Nomansland. Sir George Grey warmly supported this proposal. Arrangements were made to visit that part, and if the report were favourable, the majority of the people would "trek" thither; and these were therefore the causes of the exodus of the Griquas from Philippolis to Nomansland.
>
> Early in 1859 the exploring expedition, encouraged by Sir George Grey, left Philippolis with wagons and oxen, horses and guns; more than a hundred able-bodied men, with their wagon-drivers and leaders, started with their Chief Adam Kok.[957] They crossed the Orange River and passed on in a south-east direction near the present site of Dordrecht till they reached Theodore's Rand, and then, travelling in a north-eastern direction, passed the

heads of the Tsomo and Gatberg, onward over the eastern spurs of the Drakensbergen and their intermediate plains and numerous streams, until they reached the country between the Umzimvubu and Umzimcooloo Rivers. They found but very few inhabitants, and slaughtered large quantities of game, and some of its destroyers, the lions. Here the majority remained while a portion visited Faku, the Chief of the Amapondas, and the towns of Natal, with the sugar and coffee plantations.

Pleased with the capabilities of this Nomansland, and promising themselves unlimited supplies of coffee, sugar and rice, which they were to raise for themselves in this land of promise, they determined to return by a direct route across the lofty Drakensbergen. They crossed the Kniga and availed themselves of a footpath, which they widened for the wagons, and after a great deal of labour they reached the summit at a neck called by them Ongeluks Nek, because a man was shot accidentally while pulling a gun out of a wagon. The footpath descended on the western side along a ridge too narrow for a wagon, and they had therefore on the summit of the range to turn southwards for some miles, passing above a magnificent waterfall, and with a sweep towards the west began the descent. So steep was this in many parts that, beside locking three wheels, an oxhide was attached, on which several sat, that by their weight they might check the speed of the descent. The sliding down the highest part of the range took but a very short time in comparison with the making of a track across the spur of the range to the deep kloofs near the Orange River until they passed Moiroos's[958] kraal and the Tele River, and then passed by Hanglip and Smithfield on to Philippolis.

In January 1860 the Chief Adam Kok called together his subjects, to set before them the report of the expedition, and to consult upon the expediency of trekking to Nomansland.[959]

"After I reached home I was not too tired to undertake the journey to the Cape," Kok later recalled, "but before that I reported to my men all I have seen here, and I informed them at the time, as far as I was concerned, I intended to come to this country. I also said there were no white men; there was plenty of water. A good country to live in and for men who will work. I do not depend much upon stock farming. I said to my people if they will agree to it I shall trek. The majority agreed to it, and I went to the Cape."[960]

In enumerating the reasons for the Griquas' decision some years afterwards, John Mackenzie mentioned the growing prejudice against them, as already quoted,[961] and added:

> As some [white] Colonists preferred a country where there would be fine fountains, plenty of game and numerous "volk" in the surrounding villages, with only just enough Europeans to supply them with ammunition, moleskin, prints and a little coffee and sugar, so the Griquas sought a place where they might again become "menschen" and cease to be "volk" and "schepsels" (creatures). They were selling, it was true, some of the finest sheep-runs in South Africa, but they were getting hard cash in return, and there was no sentiment binding them to the country, which was not "the land of their sires" except such of them as happened to be Bushmen.[962]

In spite of Grey's willingness to help, however, certain conditions were set for the move to Nomansland. In the words of Kok, describing his visit to Cape Town at the end of 1860,

> When I came there, I had a conversation with the Executive Council. We discussed about this country [*Nomansland*]. Sir George Grey gave me to understand that if I came to this country I should come as a British subject. I opposed this, for this reason, there is a large extent of our country that has fallen out of Griqua hands through the British Government and given to the Boers, and therefore I consider we ought to have this country given to us as compensation. Sir George Grey opposed this. We argued on this point for two days. At the last I said to Sir George Grey, I had better take this way, as I had a Council and people to consult and I must bring the matter before them. There our agreement stopped.[963]

Given the bleak choice between losing their independence to the Boers or the British, the Griquas finally chose the latter.

"At that time," wrote the author of "The Griquas and their exodus",

> nearly half a million of acres of land were in the possession of the Griquas and their Government. This had to be disposed of, purchasers had to be found for their farms in the country and their cottages in the town, extra wagons and oxen were to be bought up; supplies of clothing and groceries were to be laid up; and many other matters had to be attended to, which demanded time. (...)
>
> Fortunately for them their farms, being good, commanded large prices, and the greater part of the first instalment was taken up in wagons and oxen, mules and sheep; only two or three held a mortgage bond as security, the purchasers being indignant at the want of trustworthiness being implied in it and declining the purchase if the bond were insisted upon. Still, very few of those who sold without a bond received the price agreed upon. Of course, when there was plenty of money it seemed inexhaustible to those who had handled but small sums, and there were not wanting pressing invitations to buy things which it was said they would be sure to need in the desert land they were going to; heavy stocks were laid in of necessary articles, which were not husbanded at first because of their quantity.[964]

One remaining record of the general sale of Griqua property at this time is the advertisement for the church buildings at Philippolis which appeared in the *Friend* in August 1861, tenders being called for the purchase of "the Building which had been used as a Church, capable of containing 600 people", "the School Rooms, consisting of one large room and four smaller rooms", and "the Parsonage, consisting of a Dwelling House with seven rooms besides kitchen and pantry, a pakhuis with two rooms, a coach house, and a double water erf".[965] According to Dower's subsequent account, however, the sale of these buildings would appear to have afforded as little profit to the Griquas as that of their other property.

> The church, parsonage and school at Philippolis were sold for something like £3000, while other landed property belonging to

the Church was sold for £4000. Of these sums, only about £500 was paid in cash and deposited in the bank at Colesberg. The purchase price was secured by mortgage bonds on valuable property, to be paid off after a given time when the people had reached their new home. Meanwhile the interest would be available for the minister's support.[966] He was to accompany them, and after a visit to Cape Town joined them at Hanglip in the south of Basutoland.

During Mr Philip's absence the bond holders, in a way not to their credit, got the Finance Committee of the Church persuaded to consent to a transference of the bonds from valuable to valueless property. On Mr Philip's return he denounced the dishonesty of the transaction on both sides, and pointed out the almost certain loss to the Church in certain contingencies. The result was rupture between the minister and the Chiefs and the men who had been principal actors in the transaction, ending in Mr Philip's resignation and retirement to take up the work he did so well in the rising town of Queenstown.[967] Thus all the carefully laid plans for the erection of new buildings for church and school work in the new country went to the wall. There was bungling and knavery in the whole transaction.

Now they had no minister and could not have supported one if they had had him. They had no buildings and no money to erect them. Just then the Free State-Basuto War broke out.[968] All the civil courts of the Orange Free State were closed for years in consequence, and when civil business was resumed, the agents had so manipulated matters that (culpably or not, it is difficult, perhaps impossible, to say) all that remained of the splendid provision made for Church work was the £500 in the Colesberg bank, and £1340 recovered in 1874, after much litigation.[969]

All this, however, still lay in the future, and John Mackenzie has left a first-hand account of the Griqua community of Philippolis during the brief and final phase of its greatest prosperity.

In 1862 I certainly saw Griquas in Philippolis standing at their doors in the morning attired in showy dressing-gowns and smoking their pipes. Now some might wonder what the world was coming to when they gazed on such a spectacle. The explanation, however, was simple. The people were selling their farms at the time, and had too much money in their pockets. They bought the dressing-gowns, and a good many other things, to please the eloquent shopkeepers.[970]

"Going into a store," a Cape Government report was later to declare concerning this period in Griqua history, "a man would perhaps buy a suit of clothes for himself, with dresses for his family, and a little sugar and coffee for immediate wants; but the balance would go in sardines, silk handkerchiefs, ribbons and articles of even greater absurdity."[971]

"As the winter of 1860 passed away," recalled the author of "The Griquas and their exodus",

> some began to pack up and move from the farms they had sold to the neighbourhood of Hanglip, a mountain near the Orange River, and then just within the Basuto border. On the road passing Smithfield might be met a single bullock wagon with its span of oxen, while before and behind small numbers of different kinds of stock were driven on; further on you would meet one household encamped with tents, a large tent wagon, a good horse wagon, a buck wagon, a tent cart and large quantities of stock, quite a patriarch moving with his children. At a greater distance you would meet two or three families moving onward together with their wagons and stock; vehicles of every description, shape and age were pressed into the service, some forming a ludicrous contrast to the new brightly-painted wagons.[972]

Among the records of the Griqualand West Land Court are preserved a number of lists compiled by the Griqua fieldcornets in January 1861, containing "Names of the subscribers who are trekking with Kapityn A. Kok to the New Land as Griqua subjects:" that drawn up by fieldcornet Samson Marais gives the names of 86 male heads of families.[973]

"After the winter of 1861," continued "The Griquas and their exodus", "the remainder of the people left Philippolis for Hanglip. The Griqua Government purchased wagons and oxen for the conveyance of the people; and as summer closed in 1862, the Griquas settled down within a radius of ten to fifteen miles from Hanglip, near which their temporary church had been erected for a twelvemonth."[974]

"The Captain and other influential Griquas are making great preparations for 'trekking'," a correspondent of the *Friend* reported from Philippolis in October 1861.

> Some of the Captain's wagons have already started for Hanglip, and the Captain and others expect to leave by the end of the present month. It is believed therefore that the Free State will next month assume the government of this place. Good prices are readily given for trek-oxen, which are at present in great demand and fetch from £9 to £12 each. Building is beginning to be the order of the day, bricks are required, and so are all kinds of mechanics;[975] in fact everything tends to show that ere long this place will become a thriving business town.[976]

And a month later:

> The only news I can send you at present is that Captain Adam Kok has left this temporarily, and so I may say have all the influential Griquas. The Captain has paid us a visit twice since he removed to a farm about a couple of hours from this, and I believe he will favor us with his final visit this week.
>
> The business of this town is very dull, and Philippolis, once a lively business place, seems at present to have changed into one of the dullest holes I ever was in. Merchants and others are now feeling the truth that the Griqua nation have left, and where many shops here took a few months ago *cash sales* to the amount of £15 or £20 per diem, they now take about as many shillings. We have six shops, but I firmly believe that unless something stranger in the shape of a miracle speedily turns up, ere long some of them will be closed.
>
> The Dutch have had the church cleaned up in a more respectable style than it has been for many years, and some talk of divine service being held shortly. If this is done it may create a little more stir and energy in our business life, but the period for so doing has not yet been fixed. We have no magistrate and apparently not the vestige of a law. (...)

When shall we be under Free State rule? is a question one may hear almost daily. Some wonder what would be the upshot of such an annexation, and others are cudgelling their brains to find out what will become of us if we are left alone to sink or swim. Other questions also present themselves to the minds of our thinking inhabitants, viz., whether the Free State has the power to take over the government of this district without consulting the people? And granted again that the people are willing to throw in their lot with the Free State, can such be done without the sanction of Captain Adam Kok? (...)

We must have a different state of things than we have at present. Civilization demands it, inasmuch as we cannot continue as we are now without making the startling truth apparent that we are retrograding into a state of moral, social and political degradation.[977]

On 26 December 1861 a deed of sale was signed by which all remaining Government lands in the Captaincy were acquired by the Orange Free State for the sum of £4000.[978] In April 1862 the official proclamation of the Philippolis district was published by the Free State authorities,[979] and in the same month Ds. Colin Fraser Jr was inducted as minister of the local Dutch Reformed congregation: the Griqua capital had become a Free State village.

Some Griquas remained behind in the Philippolis district after the general exodus of their people, and four years later the aged catechist and teacher W.F. Corner could declare in his memorial to the Volksraad:

> That since [the Griquas'] departure, he has remained here, and since that time until now he has taken upon him those offices, by means of which they have been reminded of the fact that they have an immortal soul.
>
> That he has during the past four years daily taught coloured children, and has preached the Gospel on Sundays to adults and children.[980]

For the rest, however, these people seem to have been left to their lot, to survive as best they could, the Captaincy had finally ceased to exist.

"The number of families who are now ready to go over are 1500," wrote Adam Kok from Hanglip in March 1862 to Sir Philip Wodehouse, the new High Commissioner. "The amount of stock is certainly upward of 200 000 sheep, beside a great many horses and cattle (...)."[981]

The winter of 1862 which the large trek party spent here, marked a turning point in the fortunes of the Griquas, and the beginning of a prolonged series of hardships. According to "The Griquas and their exodus":

> Bushuli[982] had often visited and begged from them, but never molested them. But the year 1862 is remembered as one of intense drought, when draught oxen realized £12 tot £14 each, and all supplies beyond the Orange River were at famine prices. This drought proved very disastrous to the Griquas; hundreds of cattle and horses and thousands of sheep and goats died in every direction; the air seemed tainted, and the vultures, numerous as they were, could not devour the carrion. The losses were especially great where a good many were encamped together, and not a blade of grass could be seen for miles round the camp. Many a man lost five hundred sheep, and was left with two or three score; many of them lost 900 out of 1000, others 100, 1200 and 1500 sheep out of their flocks; the poor as well as the rich lost most or all of their milch cows, on which they depended so largely, and numbers of horses died. Added to this, Bushuli and his Basutos now seized all the horses they could steal.[983]

"When I arrived at Hanglip in the month of December 1861," Adam Kok himself stated in this regard,

> the only complaints I heard was [sic] that the Bushmen and Basutos had stolen horses from the Boers and taken them through where we were. (...) Then in 1862 a great number of horses were stolen from us, amongst which were six of my riding horses and one stallion. At the same time there were horses of Jan July and his father stolen.[984] I sent for Jan July to look for his horses as well as mine, of which he brought four horses (well-known ones) back which he removed from Pushuli's people. Of these one was my

stallion, and a brown riding horse and two of his own horses. After these horses were lost, many lots of horses were lost—amongst them five of mine. Then I sent Jan July to report this to Moshesh, because he could explain matters, as he had received the four horses.

After that again four trek oxen of mine were stolen. We traced the spoor of these oxen to the Cornet's Spruit, and there we found the haunch of an ox and some meat hidden in a rock; but we did not find any of the oxen. This was in the country occupied by Morosi's and Pushuli's people. After that there were seven more of my horses stolen and eleven young fatherland cattle. We traced the spoor of the cattle to the Orange River, but could not trace it on the other side. Of the seven horses I recovered five, which were found in the mountain above the Telle, among Morosi's people. I cannot remember every case of theft, but thieving was going on all day long. Upon one occasion, about 5 p.m. one day, I lost one hundred young ewes.[985]

According to the report of a later Cape Government Commission investigating the affairs of Griqualand East, "[Kok's] losses overberg were extremely heavy, what with trickery and other things. The failure of his agent alone left him with an unsatisfactory claim of about £30 000. He further saw his stock melt away here; and, on the whole, found himself in deep pecuniary difficulties."[986]

Towards the end of 1862, however, the final stage of the journey could be commenced, which was also to be the longest, hardest and most dangerous, and there is a singular account of it by a participant, a Griqua identified only as "Kerneels", who accompanied the trek as a boy, and whose recollections of it were taken down verbatim by J.H. Rademeyer in Griqualand East and published in a book which appeared in 1938. Because of its remarkably evocative quality, it is given here in the original as well.

My hêr, toet oens uut die Vrystaat vertrek had hiernatoe was eek sommer nog 'n kêreltjie, maar dat geheuge my nog goed hoe swaar dat gegaan het met die trek sam. Daar was nog nie patte sôs vandag nie, en ôr die berge had dat maar moeitlik gegaan; grôt kleperse moes uut die pad gerol word, en mar baie soutjies moes oens die waense die hôgtes lat afgaan. Mar oense Kaptein was 'n baie goeie man, en hy't mar altyd vir hy se mense moed geïnpraat en gasê, dat mak nie sak hoe oens seukel nie, anderkant die berge sal dit beter gaan mit oens sam. Die mense was baie gehôrsamag vir hulle se grôt Kaptein, en wat hy gesê het, dat was goed.[987]

[Sir, when we left the Free State to come here I was still a little fellow, but I remember well how hard it was on trek. There were no roads yet like today, and it was difficult crossing the mountains: big stones had to be rolled out of the way, and we had to let our wagons down the heights very carefully. But our Captain was a very good man, and he was always encouraging his people and saying that it didn't matter how much trouble we had, on the other side of the mountains it would go better with us. The people were very obedient to their great Captain, and what he said was acceptable to them.]

To continue the account given in "The Griquas and their exodus":

About September and October [1862] they left Hanglip, crossed the Orange River, then the Tele and the kraal of Moiroos, onward over roads which had to be repaired after every shower on account of the steep ascents, to the Witsenberg [*Witteberge*], near the foot of the lofty range of the Drakensbergen. There gradually most of them mustered, and working parties were told off to make the road up the steep face of the great range and along the summit to Ongeluks Nek, where the descent was to commence. The hope expressed that this road would prove a highway into the Colony had soon to be abandoned, the difficulty of making it passable for wagons was very great, and the very uneven nature of the ground approaching the Drakensbergen, with the long and steep ascent and descent of the mountain ranges, rendered it impossible to maintain it in repair without very great expense. The wrecks of wagons were to be seen in different parts of the route, and some wagons were at first left for the want of oxen to draw them.

On the summit of this lofty range so circuitous a route was taken to avoid some deep valleys that it took them two days with the bullock-wagon to reach Ongeluks Nek, whence they looked down on the silver thread of the Kniga; further on, Mount Currie, where the chief village is [now] situated;[988] beyond, the most distant Zuurberg range, while the prospect in that direction was terminated by the territory and mountains of Natal; to the north-east they looked along the tops of the range on which they were standing; to the north and north-west the mountains of Basutoland, looking like angry billows petrified; to the west the Koesbergen and the mountains beyond Smithfield; to the south-west the Kraaibergen near Aliwal [North] and, beyond, the Praambergen and others; while south and east were the lofty spurs and deep valleys and wild-looking country falling away from this mighty range of mountains. The panorama is there very grand, and worth the trouble of ascending the hill to the south of Ongeluks Nek.

The steep descent was not made without some mishaps, but the beginning of February 1863 saw them resting on the banks of the Kniga, whence they soon passed on to Berg Vijftig, which under the name of Mount Currie became the headquarters of the tribe.[989] Very much impoverished as they were, the remnant of their stock had to become accustomed to a new country, an ordeal under which thousands more of their sheep failed, so that many who were the wealthiest at Philippolis are among the poorest now; while in other cases care and time have so far improved the remnants of their flocks that they are slowly but, we believe, steadily rising to a state which, though it never will be as prosperous as when they left Philippolis, will be a great advance upon their late condition.[990]

This optimism, unfortunately, was to prove unfounded, and in the event the new Kokstad Captaincy did not long survive the death of Adam Kok III in 1875, at least not in a readily recognisable form. By 1926 the total Griqua population of the Kokstad area had been reduced to 1472 people, and the position occupied by the Griquas in what had meanwhile become the Union of South Africa is indicated by the negative and disparaging account of their history given by the Rehoboth Commission in the section of its report devoted to them, and the memorandum drawn up by the magistrate at Kokstad in January 1925 which the Commission quotes at some length.

> They are now town dwellers, and although more tenacious of their town erven than they were of their farms, I have no doubt that economic pressure will bring about a steady decrease of such holdings. As a class they are poverty stricken. Many suffer from malnutrition and often starvation owing to unemployment, drink and generally thriftlessness. The mortality amongst children is high—chest complaints and stomach trouble being responsible. The adults are susceptible to pulmonary diseases. The population, if not on the decrease, remains practically stationary. (...)
>
> Their social life is one of bickering and quarrels, and it is impossible to secure a united front with progress and improvement of their conditions as the object in view. Many attempts have been made in the past to compose their differences, but without success, and to-day they are hopelessly divided among themselves. This is seen more especially in church affairs, where they divide themselves into three distinct church bodies. (...)
>
> In conclusion I may say that in my opinion the "Griqua" as a separate class are doomed to extinction. This will be slow but sure. Melting away of race and dispersion set in many years ago. They will gradually become absorbed in the great coloured class which is ever on the increase in this country.[991]

In spite of their unpromising situation at the beginning of the twentieth century, however, the Kokstad Griquas succeeded in retaining their sense of identity under the leadership of A.A.S. le Fleur (1867–1941),[992] who had married the daughter of Adam Muis Kok, heir and successor to Adam Kok III, establishing their own religious body, the Griqua Independent Church, and finally acquiring a viable centre of national life at Kranshoek near Plettenberg Bay.[993] Far from being "doomed to extinction", as stated so confidently in 1925, they survived into the new South Africa, to be officially recognised as a "separate ethnic community" in 1997.[994]

Appendix: Statement by Adam Kok II

In 1834–35, Dr Andrew Smith, while visiting Philippolis, made some notes concerning information on the early history of the Kok family obtained from Adam Kok II. These have been published together with Smith's Journal,[995] *but apart from possible errors of transmission or transcription they are so cursory that it is hard to make any sense of them. The following text, copied from the published Journal, includes comments and tentative emendations (placed between square brackets) which may help to make it more comprehensible, and of greater use to researchers.*

'Griquas'

Cornelius [Kok I] was son of Adam Kok [I]. Adam [Kok I] had a farm at Picket berg which, not being productive, he sold and purchased another. This he afterwards sold and left for Kamiesberg. He was appointed Chief of the party, consisting of several of his relations, by the Dutch Government, and he received a Captain's staff.

In 1795 they removed higher up the country to the banks of the Great River, to the vicinity of what is called Bethesda [*Kokskraal*]. Old Adam, finding himself weakening, transferred his staff to Cornelius [I], the father of Adam [II] and Cornelius [II]. Cornelius [I] was born at Picketberg. When about 84 years old no Boers lived north of Oliphants River [*sic*].[996]

(…)

Some time after living on the [Great] river, he [*Cornelius I*] went back to Kamiesberg and got Silver Fonteyn, sold it again, and went to live at Campbell. He died 74 years of age, in 1820.

[Adam] Kok [II], aged 64 [in 1834], lived when young and was born at Kamiesberg. His grandfather, Jan Pinnear [*Pienaar*], a Dutch bastard, father of his mother, lived there. His father [*Cornelius?*] was born in Zwartland.[997] Adam Kok [I], his grandfather, had a place in Zwartland. By oppression of the Boors he sold his place, and went to Hantam and became a servant of Lispur [*Losper?*], then went to Kamiesberg and got a place about Besonder Muid [*Besondermeid*]. His father [*Cornelius II*] had Zigloer Fonteyn [*Silwerfontein*] after he had lived some time on the Orange River. Olivier Fonteyn [*Oliewenfontein*] his father also bought. Dam Kok [*Adam Kok II*] had to lie with his fee [*cattle*]⁹⁹⁸ on the Orange River.

Old Barend [Barends] used to live in the Kamiesberg with Piet van Iver [*van den Heever?*]. His father, Claus Barend, remained with van Iver. The four brothers Barend: one went off to the river with cattle and met with the Koks. Barend had war with Afrikaner, and the first fled up the river to Hardcastle. After this, Barend, when on a journey, visited Sack River, where Kicherer, Kranomer [*Kramer*] and Anderson were, and, being asked if he would wish a teacher, was told yes [*sic*]. The place on Sac River being so bad, they determined with the Bastards who were with them to go to Hardcastle and build a church.⁹⁹⁹ (…) [Adam] Kok [II] came after this, lived about two years with his father's cattle, and then went off to Kamiesberg again, and there stopped three years. He arrived at the same time as Mr Anderson married [*1806*].

(…)

His [*Adam Kok II*] great-grandfather was a slave.

(…)

Chronology

1804
December: LMS missionaries settle at Leeukuil (afterwards Klaarwater) and establish a mission for the Basters

1813
7 August: Griqua Captaincy established at Klaarwater (Griquatown) with Adam Kok II and Barend Barends as Provisie Kaptyns

1820
8 August: Robert Moffat placed at Griquatown as missionary
Adam Kok II leaves Griquatown
December: Andries Waterboer elected Kaptyn at Griquatown

1822
Bergenaars leave Griquatown
Philippolis established as mission for Bushmen

1825
28 August: Dr Philip meets Bergenaars on the Riet River
October: conference summoned by Dr Philip at Griquatown; Adam Kok II elected Kaptyn of the emigrant Griquas in the Riet River area and the Bergenaars

1826
10 January: election of Adam Kok II approved by British authorities
winter: Griquas settle at Philippolis
22 July: mission station at Philippolis ceded to Griquas
Adam Kok II resigns and is succeeded by Cornelius Kok II

1828
Death of Cornelius Kok II; Adam Kok II resumes office

1834

19 January: meeting of Adam Kok II with Henry Somerset, Commandant of Kaffraria

11 December: treaty concluded between Andries Waterboer of Griquatown and British Government

1835

winter: visit of Adam Kok II and party to Cape Town

12 September: death of Adam Kok II on the Berg River

1836

26 January: Abraham Kok elected Kaptyn

1837

7 January: meeting of Abraham Kok with Andries Stockenstrom, Lieutenant-Governor of the Eastern Province, on the Orange River

25 February: treaty concluded between Abraham Kok and Andries Waterboer

September: Barend Lucas becomes Kaptyn

Adam Kok III elected Kaptyn

1838

winter: Griqua "civil war"; Abraham Kok and Cornelius Kok II attack Philippolis

Abraham Kok deposed

9 November: treaty concluded between Adam Kok III and Andries Waterboer

1842

"Mocke rebellion" in the Transorange

1843

2 January: conference of Adam Kok III with John Hare, Lieutenant-Governor of the Eastern Province, at Colesberg

14 April: death of Peter Wright at Philippolis

5 October/29 November: treaty concluded between Adam Kok III and British Government ("Napier Treaty")

1845

29 April: British forces assisted by Griquas defeat rebel Boers at Swartkoppies

June: conference of Adam Kok III with Sir Peregrine Maitland at Touwfontein

8 October: British Resident appointed in the Transgariep

1846

5/19 February: treaty concluded between Adam Kok III and British Government ("Maitland Treaty")

March: Resident's seat transferred from Philippolis to Bloemfontein

1848

January: interview of Adam Kok III with Sir Harry Smith at Bloemfontein

24 January: treaty concluded between Adam Kok III and British Government at Bloemfontein; the Philippolis Captaincy divided into a leasable and an unleasable portion

3 February: Sir Harry Smith proclaims British sovereignty over the Transgariep

29 August: British forces assisted by Griquas defeat rebel Boers at Boomplaats

1850

12 July: Conrad Windvogel appointed Griqua Government Secretary in succession to Hendrik Hendrickze

1854

23 February: Bloemfontein Convention signed between Boers of the Transgariep and British Government: withdrawal of British sovereignty and establishment of the Republic of the Orange Free State

1859

Exploring expedition (*Kommissietrek*) from Philippolis to Nomansland (Griqualand East)

1860
9 November: memorandum concerning Griqua occupancy of Nomansland drawn up by Sir George Grey

1861
26 December: sale of Griqua lands in the Philippolis Captaincy to the Orange Free State

1862
22 April: Philippolis proclaimed as district of the Orange Free State

1862–63
Griqua trek to Nomansland

Endnotes

Introduction: The Kok dynasty and the Griquas of the Transorange (1713–1825), pp.9–37

1. Christoffel Esterhuys(e) or Esterhuyzen was an immigrant of unknown origin who arrived at the Cape *circa* 1692, married a coloured woman, and died on the farm Weltevreden at Bottelary in the Stellenbosch district in 1724. See De Villiers/Pama, p.207; Heese/Lombard 2, p.223.
2. CA, CJ 783 pp.4–16, Charges against Tromp of Madagascar and others (3.2.1714); the reference to Claas Kok occurs on p.12.—This reference was brought to my attention by Robert Ross, *Cape of Torments* (London: Routledge & Kegan Paul, 1983), p.89; note, however, that in the relevant endnotes (p.142), nos.30 and 31 have been interchanged. I am grateful to Dr Ross for his help in this regard.
3. For further information on this case, see CA, CJ 318 pp.102–110; CJ 5, pp.7–9.—I am much indebted to Loretha du Plessis of the Cape Town Archives Repository for her help in tracing these documents. See further, H.F. Heese, *Reg en onreg*, Bellville: Instituut vir Historiese Navorsing, 1994, p.267. According to the Cape Town Archives Repository this reference (to the Leibbrandt Manuscripts series) is incorrect.
4. Ross, *op. cit.*, p.142 n30[=31], quoting VOC 4073, a file in the VOC Archives, Algemeen Rijksarchief, The Hague. There is no mention of this in the documents in the Cape Town Archives Repository referred to above.
5. For the Guriqua, see Elphick, pp.134–135; Nienaber, pp.242–248, 432–448.
6. Penn:Orange River, p.36; referring to CA, LM 49 Res (13.3.1739).
7. Leonard Guelke & Robert Shell, "Landscape of conquest: frontier water alienation and Khoikhoi strategies of survival, 1652–1780", *Journal of Southern African Studies* 18,4 (Dec.1992); referring to CA, RLR 12 no.201 (30.3.1751).
8. See the statement of Adam Kok II in the Appendix, p.249 above.—Martin Legassick is not correct in calling Adam Kok a "manumitted slave"; Legassick:Northern Frontier, p.370.
9. See Appendix, p.249 above.
10. *The early Cape Hottentots*, ed. I. Schapera (Cape Town: Van Riebeeck Society, 1933), p.135.
11. Elphick, p.191. This seems to be the staff appearing in two portraits (ca 1860) of Kok's great-grandson, Adam Kok III of Philippolis, in the album of the Revd W.B. Philip, University of Cape Town, BC 226.
12. Elphick, p.46.
13. For this development, see Guelke & Shell.
14. Guelke & Shell, p.811.

15. Patrick Cullinan, *Robert Jacob Gordon, 1743–1895* (Cape Town: Struik Winchester, 1992), p.93B.
16. Wikar, p.98.
17. Lichtenstein II, p.316.
18. CA, 1/STB 3/12 p.[1] (14.11.1790). Two distinct "legplaatsen" seem to be referred to in this document, "de Spitskopje en de Valleij", the latter of which was situated "aan de boven zyde der groote rivier" and granted to Kok "nu ruym twintig jaaren [geleden]". However, "en" might also stand for "in", a transposition which was common at the time, and which would make this a reference to a single farm, "the Spitskopje in the valley".
19. Lichtenstein II, p.301.
20. Wikar, p.24.
21. Penn:Orange River, p.60. The Baster family of Pienaars probably derive from the same branch of the family as Petrus Pienaar (baptised 1750), a son of Jacob Pienaar (baptised 1718) who died in the present Tulbagh district in 1787; De Villiers/Pama, p.692.
22. Wikar, p.315.
23. CA, 1/STB 3/12 p.[1] (14.11.1790).
24. For the Korana, see: Engelbrecht *passim*; Nienaber, pp.647–698.
25. For the legal and illegal trade in firearms along the river, see Cornelius Kok in CA, 1/STB 3/12 p.[1] (14.11.1790).
26. Campbell:Travels (1822), p.52.
27. Thompson I, p.116.
28. Campbell:Travels (1815), pp.164, 156.
29. BMB (1835), p.38.
30. *Gedenkschriften van het Nederlandsch Zendelinggenootschap*, 2de deel (Rotterdam: Nicolaas Cornel, 1805), p.252.
31. Campbell:Travels (1822) II, p.190.
32. Campbell:Travels (1815), p.284.
33. Report (1816), p.25.
34. "net suid van die Oranje omtrent by die teenswoordige plaas Eksteenkuil (net suid van Kanoneiland)"; Cornelissen, p.88.
35. Campbell:Travels (1822) II, p.262.
36. Campbell:Travels (1822) II, p.262.
37. Transactions II, 30.
38. P.B. Borcherds, *An auto-biographical memoir*, facs. repr. (Cape Town: Africana Connoisseurs Press, 1963), p.118.
39. Lichtenstein II, p.316.
40. See Appendix, p.249 above (statement of Adam Kok II).
41. CWMA 141–142 (LMS 10/3/D) ("A short account of the most particular and important circumstances attending the government of the Griqua people", 1827).
42. Transactions III, p.215.
43. Campbell:Travels (1822) II, 269. Silwerfontein is situated to the south-east of modern Springbok in Namaqualand.
44. Burchell I, p.363.

45. Ross, p.15.
46. Lichtenstein II, 316.
47. Transactions III, 215.
48. Penn:Orange River, pp.85–86.
49. Quoted in Mission at Griquatown, p.36; as corrected from the original German text.
50. A term used by Burchell, as he explains, in preference to "Bastaards".
51. According to an explanatory note in the original, about 480 kilo.
52. Burchell I, 112.
53. *The Genadendal diaries, vol. I (1792–1794)*; ed. H.C. Bredenkamp & H.E.F. Plüddemann (Bellville: UWC Institute for Historical Research, 1992), 94.
54. J.J. Kicherer, *Berichten van den predikant Kicherer, aangaande zijne zending tot de heidenen* (Amsterdam: Johannes Allart, 1805), p.93.
55. Transactions III, 217–218.—She was the mother of one Jan Kok, who had been among the first of the Basters to be baptized by the missionaries at the end of 1807; in the baptismal register he was described as "Jan Kok Christiaanszoon" and his date of birth given as February 1783, "dus bij de 25 jaar oud"; Doop Boek (22.11.1807).
56. Report (1803), p.165.
57. For further information on the establishment of missionary work in the Transorange, see Mission at Griquatown; Schoeman:Kicherer.
58. Philip:Researches I, 56. See also Anderson's later account (1825) as quoted by Philip, pp.57–60.
59. Doop Boek.
60. J.J. Kicherer, *Berichten van den predikant Kicherer, aangaande zijne zending tot de heidenen* (Amsterdam: Johannes Allart, 1805), p.94.
61. For Barends, see DSAB V.
62. VA, GS 1548 p.16.
63. Report (1820), pp.88–89.
64. Campbell:Journal III, 143. For the early career of Waterboer, see Schoeman:Early mission.
65. Burchell I, 251.
66. Burchell I, 253.
67. Burchell I, 246.
68. Burchell I, Chapters 16 & 17.
69. Burchell I, 261.
70. Burchell I, 333.
71. Burchell I, 253–254.
72. Thompson I, 82.
73. Burchell I, 256.
74. Burchell I, 282–283.
75. Burchell I, 254–255, 339.
76. Campbell:Travels (1815), p.166.
77. Burchell I, 274–276.
78. Burchell I, 189.

79. Burchell II, 161.
80. Burchell I, 362.
81. Campbell:Travels (1815), p.256.
82. Campbell:Travels (1822), II, 264.
83. Burchell I, 249.
84. Burchell I, 189.
85. Campbell:Travels (1815), p.164.
86. Burchell I, 50.
87. Campbell:Travels (1815), pp.252–256.
88. Campbell:Travels (1815), p.253.
89. Apparently the same person as Kort or Dik Adam Kok; see n116 below.
90. Aborigines Committee (1837), pp.150–151.
91. Campbell:Journal III, 153–154.
92. Campbell:Journal III, 157.
93. Campbell:Travels (1822) II, 231, 237.
94. Campbell:Travels (1822), p.59.
95. Campbell:Travels (1822) II, 231.
96. Transactions IV, 184.
97. CWMA 78 (LMS 6/4/B), 4.10.1816.
98. Campbell:Travels (1815), p.324.
99. See Chapter 7 below for further details.
100. CWMA 77 (6/4/B), 17.9.1816; Legassick:Griqua, p.202.
101. Aborigines Committee (1836) p.213.
102. CWMA 77 (LMS 6/4/A), 31.7.1816.
103. Thompson I, 71; cf. CWMA 118 (LMS 9/2/A), 16.2.1824.
104. CWMA 79 (LMS 6/4/C), Nov. 1816.
105. Doop Boek.
106. Campbell:Journal III, 143.
107. Campbell:Travels (1822) II, 249.
108. Campbell:Travels (1822) II, 239.
109. Thompson I, 75.
110. Thompson I, 77.
111. Thompson I, 114.
112. This would seem to refer to 1811–1812.
113. Report (1814), p.504.
114. Campbell:Travels (1822) II, 231–232.
115. Robert Moffat, *Missionary labours and scenes in Southern Africa* (London: John Snow, 1842), p.107.
116. G.21–1871, p.56.—Hendrickze uses the names "Kort Adam" and "Dik Adam" interchangeably, and describes him as a blacksmith. The person he refers to is the same individual as Kort Adam Kok, who was one of the founders of Campbell (Knoffelvallei) (see pp.22–23 above); Aborigines Committee (1837), pp.150–151.
117. Aborigines Committee (1836), p.212.

118. CWMA (LMS 10/3/D), "Short account", 1827.
119. CWMA Journals 1584 (10.4.1820; 6.3.1820).
120. Aborigines Committee (1837), p.150.
121. Thompson I, 71.
122. CWMA 141–142 (LMS 10/3/D), "Short account", 1827.
123. Aborigines Committee (1836), p.212.
124. Aborigines Committee (1836), p.213.
125. Smith:Journal, p.287B.
126. Thompson I, 71.
127. Thompson I, 114.
128. VA, GS 1548 pp.14–21; Eng. transl. in G.21–1871, pp.55–57.
129. Hodgson, p.82.
130. Aborigines Committee (1836), p.214.
131. Though strictly speaking synonymous, the term "Transorange" has been used in this book for the area to the north of the Middle Orange in which the Griquatown Captaincy was situated, and "Transgariep" for the present Free State, where the Philippolis Captaincy was later to be established.
132. Campbell:Travels (1815), pp.247–248. —What was usually referred to as the "Modder River" by Campbell and his contemporaries is now the lower Riet River. Andrew Smith wrote in 1834: "The river [is] called by the Griquas, etc., Black Mudder River, by the Boers Riet River'; Smith:Diary I, 190. Campbell added to the confusion by naming the two rivers he mentioned the Cradock and the Alexander respectively. The "Black River" was more properly the name of the Orange above its confluence with the Vaal.
133. Campbell:Journal III, 167.
134. CWMA 141–142 (LMS 10/3/D), "Short account", 1827.
135. Arnot, p.191.
136. Doop Boek.
137. Smith:Diary I, 199–200.
138. At Griquatown and Campbell.
139. Hodgson, p.76.
140. Smith:Diary I, 200.
141. Smith:Diary I, 200.
142. Aborigines Committee (1836), p.214 *passim*.
143. Arnot, p.191.—Skanse is to the south-west of the modern Fauresmith, while Sannaspoort is Fauresmith itself, and Boomplaats is 60 kilometres to the south-east, near the modern Trompsburg.
144. Philip:Researches II, 90–91; see also II, 332–344.
145. Legassick:Griqua, p.428.
146. See Armstrong, *passim*.
147. i.e., by the representatives of the British Government in Cape Town.
148. Aborigines Committee (1836), p.215.
149. Arnot, p.154.
150. This was, incidentally, the staff which Kok had, according to the same declaration by Waterboer, thrown away on leaving Griquatown, which may serve as a reminder

of the undependable and opportunistic character of all these statements.
151. Aborigines Committee (1837), pp.150–151.
152. Arnot, p.154.
153. Griqua Records, Document 23.— The 108 individuals whose marks appear on this document represented most notably the families Kok (15 men), Isaak(s), Van der Westhuizen and Schorpioen (6 each), and Goeyman (5). Twelve are identified as or known to have been Korana, and five Batswana.
154. See Penn:Orange River, p.42.
155. See Hans Lucas, Chief of the Kora tribe of Katte; Engelbrecht, p.16.
156. Volksraadsnotule IV, 297.
157. Arnot, p.191.
158. The reference is confused and confusing: from his mention of the salt pan and the Bergenaars, and from other indications, it appears that Warren had been travelling from Ramah to the Riet River.
159. The Malmesbury area of the Cape Colony, roughly the area where the Kok group had originated.
160. John Melvill at Griquatown.
161. Quoted in Sir Charles Warren, *On the veldt in the seventies* (London: Isbister, 1902), p.47.
162. Aborigines Committee (1836), p.218.
163. Aborigines Committee (1836), p.218.
164. For Melvill, see DSAB IV.

1. *Dr Philip in the Transorange (1825), pp.39–59*

165. For the history of the LMS mission to the Bushmen, see Schoeman:Boesmanskool.
166. Stockenstrom I, 228.
167. See pp.32–33 above.
168. Piet Sabba, the former assistant at Ramah, who was living in the vicinity of Philippolis.
169. Philip:Researches II, 90–97 *passim*.
170. Presumably for the second time, on his way back from the interior.
171. For Peter Wright, see further p.55 above.
172. CWMA Africa Odds 623 (7.12.1832).—For this development, see pp.55–56 above.
173. Aborigines Committee (1837), p.144.
174. The mission at Toornberg (Torenberg, Tooverberg) was established in 1814.
175. On the Orange River becoming the northern boundary of the Colony in September 1822.
176. Two British Commissioners appointed to inquire into the state of the Cape Colony, who pursued their investigations from 1823 until 1826.
177. The Colonial village of Colesberg was laid out on the Toornberg site in 1830.
178. This seems to be a particularly opportunistic claim on Philips' part; it was not the opinion of the Griquas themselves. Cf. the statement of Adam Kok III in 1845,

"no lands can be hired or sold among my people without my consent, and it is contrary to our laws to sell land to any person not being a Grikwa subject. I should not be able to alienate any portion of my territory without the consent of all my people, as such an act would require the change of one of our fundamental laws"; Griqua Records, p.93.

179. Maj. Gen. Richard Bourke, Acting Governor during the period 1826–28.
180. A letter to Philip dated 31 May 1842; see Griqua Records, Document 42.
181. Griqua Records, Documents 39 and 40.
182. Bethanie was established by the Berlin Missionary Society in Griqua territory in 1834. This statement would seem to imply that Kok's people were settled along the Riet River from the Vaal as far eastward as the present Reddersburg area.
183. CWMA 266 (LMS 18/4/A), "The tenure by which the Griquas hold the lands of Philippolis", August 1842).
184. See p.93 above.
185. Philip:Researches II, 103–104.
186. Kaptyn Cornelius Kok III; see pp.71–72 above.
187. CWMA Africa Odds 623 (7.12.1832).
188. Opposite the Colonial district New Hantam, i.e., in the Philippolis district.
189. Papers relative, I, 225.
190. Words between brackets scored through.
191. Added in the margin: "This is the opinion of all the missionaries in this quarter."
192. CWMA 126 (LMS 9/4/A), 17.10.1825.
193. This refers to a protracted dispute which arose after the Bataung of Moletsane had attacked the settlement of the Rolong Chief Sehunelo at Matlwase (Maquassie) beyond the Vaal in October 1824 and destroyed the property of the Wesleyan missionaries there. The Griquas had decided on somewhat flimsy evidence that Sehunelo himself had been responsible for the attack, and fined him 600 head of cattle.
194. CWMA 141–142 (LMS 10/3/D), "Short account", 1827.
195. John Bartlett, a missionary artisan, had accompanied Philip into the interior, and was placed at Campbell.
196. Waterboer and Cornelius Kok, as would appear from Moffat's subsequent remarks.
197. Jonathan Gleig, who was possibly on leave from India, and Captain Charles Warren were at Griquatown at this time.
198. *Apprenticeship at Kuruman*; ed. I. Schapera (London: Chatto & Windus, 1951), pp.205–206.
199. Quoted in Legassick:Griqua, pp.468–469. See also the remarks of Andries Stockenstrom quoted on p.58 above.
200. Aborigines Committee (1837), p.144.
201. Griqua Records, Documents 21–23.
202. For Wright, see DSAB I; Wilson. For further information on his appointment to Griquatown, see his letters in CWMA 126 (LMS 9/4/A), Cape Town, 15.11.1825, and 129 (LMS 10/1/A), 28.1.1826; and for his ordination, the letter of George Barker, CWMA 129–130 (LMS 10/1/B), Theopolis, 31.3.1826.—His wife Margery was to live to a ripe old age, in spite of ill health, dying in 1886 in her 90th year.

203. This would have been in March 1826; but see n208 below.
204. The Lower Riet River.
205. Note added in the original: "[*word illegible*] this is the document they attempted to show you lately".
206. This refers to the Griquatown Captaincy.
207. CA, 1/GR 10/6 Clark–Stockenstrom (10.9.1827).
208. CWMA 130 (LMS 10/1/C), "Copy of a letter from Mr Wright to Mr Clark"; it is quoted in full in Early mission at Philippolis.—This letter has been filed in the LMS Archives under 1826, but as far as the microfiche version can be deciphered, it seems in fact to be dated "10 May 1827", which would moreover correspond to the sequence of events described by Wright. The earlier dating does not seem feasible.
209. See Clark's account of this in CWMA 134 (LMS 10/1/A), 16.1.1827; and Wright's comment in CWMA 130 (LMS 10/1/C) (see preceding note).
210. CWMA 130 (LMS 10/1/C) (see n206 above).
211. CWMA 141–142 (LMS 10/3/D), "Short account", 1827.
212. John Melvill, who was by that time stationed at Philippolis as missionary.
213. Aborigines Committee (1836), 216–217.
214. See Stockenstrom II, 372–390.
215. For the history of this mission, see Pellissier, *passim*; Schoeman:Boesmanskool.

2. The early years of the Captaincy (1826–1832), pp.61–78

216. CWMA Journals 1592 (20.2.1827).
217. GTJ (16.2.1843).
218. Smith:Diary I, 192.
219. i.e., the area between the Riet and the Orange.
220. Smith:Journal, p.146.
221. Stockenstrom II, 376 and *passim*.
222. See Engelbrecht, pp.50–51.
223. Philip:Researches II, 334.
224. Smith:Diary I, 183.
225. See the references to Adam Kok's letters on the subject listed in Griqua Records, p.232.
226. Skietmekaar, 12 kilometres to the north-west of the present Fauresmith.
227. Probably Vogelstruiskooi, 20 kilometres south-west of the modern Koffiefontein, where the Coloured leader Adam Opperman was to settle in the 1860s.
228. Fytje was Anna Isaac's Bushman attendant (see below). The punctuation in this document is ambiguous, and it is not clear how many individuals are being named.
229. Arnot, pp.174–175.
230. Arnot, p.178.
231. Griqua Records, Document 28.
232. Hodgson, p.382.
233. G.58–1879, p.56. See also *Cape Monthly Magazine* V (1872), p.329; CWMA Journals 1596 (26.5.1832).

234. Griqua Records, Document 27.
235. Kirby, p.165.
236. Volksraadsnotule V (1860–61), 403.
237. Griqua Records, Document 25; see also Document 26 (12.10.1829).
238. An editorial note published with the letter states, "we have (…) ascertained that it is the composition of an actual living Griqua, of pure descent from the original Natives of this part of Africa".
239. A reference to Ordinance 50, which became law in the Cape Colony in July 1828.
240. "*Plaatsen*", in the sense of "farms".
241. Apparently a reference to an earlier official protest by the Griquas than that of 29 January 1829, which is the earliest traced (see p.65 above); however, the same document may possibly be meant.
242. This must have been Gideon Joubert of the division New Hantam just across the Orange River, described by G.A. Kolbe in 1832 as "the nearest Veld Cornet to this boundary"; CWMA Journals 1596 (21.7.1832).
243. Editorial note to the original text: "The word *afvat* is an expression peculiar to South Africa, as the acts which it expresses are."
244. Presumably the Bamboesberg range in the Tarka region of the Cape Colony.
245. Unidentified clipping in the scrapbook of W. Harrison, NLCT MSB 224,1(4); possibly from the *South African Commercial Advertiser* (see n290 below).
246. Griqua Records, p.24.
247. Aborigines Committee (1837), p.147.
248. See p.168 above.
249. Schreiner, p.76.
250. See p.49 above.
251. His grandfather had been Cornelius I; his uncle at Campbell was Cornelius II.
252. i.e., to westernising influences.
253. Cornelius Kok farmed at Kalkfontein to the north-west of Philippolis, where in another letter of Melvill he is described as making a dam.
254. CWMA 148 (LMS 11/3/A), 1.1.1829.
255. BMB (1835), p.29 (translated).
256. Kirby, p.147.
257. On the death of Adam Kok II on 12 September 1835, his age was given as 53, which, if accurate, would mean that he had been born in 1782; see Schoeman:Death. According to Andrew Smith, however, he was "aged 64" in 1834, which would make his year of birth 1770; see Appendix, p.149 above. In DSAB IV his date of birth is given as "c.1760", but this seems unlikely, as the birth date of his father, Cornelius Kok I, is stated to have been 1746, also following Smith, according to whom he died, "74 years of age, in 1820". The eldest son of Adam Kok II, Cornelius Kok III, was born about 1795 and Adam Kok III in 1811, so that circa 1770 would seem to be a likely birth date for him.
258. Smith:Journal, pp.31–32.
259. Kirby, p.146.
260. There are various spellings of his surname, but this is the form in which he himself signed his name; see Griqua Records, p.xiii n.*

261. DSAB V.
262. VA, GS 1548 pp.14–21.
263. Doop Boek (dup), 25.12.1808 et seq.
264. Doop Boek, 26.10.1813 ("door de Gemeente op zijn belijdenis aangenomen").
265. See *Catalogue of pictures in the Africana Museum*, comp. R.F. Kennedy (Johannesburg: Africana Museum, 1966), I, 141 (B613).
266. Aborigines Committee (1836), pp.213, 216.
267. CWMA 212 (LMS 15/3/A), 9.1.1837.
268. Kirby, p.146.
269. BMB (1835), p.29 (translated).
270. Smith:Diary I, 77.
271. Kirby, p.147.
272. Reproduced in Smith:Journal, p.141.
273. Leather trousers.
274. Porter, p.40.
275. BMB (1835), p.29 (translated).
276. G.A. Kolbe, the then missionary.
277. Smith:Diary I, 72.—The Basters at Philippolis formed the core of Kolbe's congregation, which may help to explain his negative opinion of Hendrickze, and Kolbe was in fact driven from the station by the Griqua party some years later.
278. Smith:Journal, p.141.
279. BMB (1835), p.29 (translated).
280. CA, GH 19/4 408–410 (Aug. 1834, extracts).
281. Kirby, pp.146–147.
282. Smith:Diary I, 200–201.
283. CA, AC 11 pp.47–48 (A.B. Armstrong, 28.10.1833).
284. Porter, p.40.
285. See the account by Pieter Davids in Smith:Diary, I, 123–124; comment by G.A. Kolbe, CA 1/GR 10/35 (7.10.1831); ditto by Peter Wright, CWMA 169 (LMS 12/4/D), 3.11.1831; Smith:Journal, p.260; Legassick:Griqua, pp.424–431 (with further references).

3. The development of the Captaincy (1832–1843), pp.79–96

286. The original followers of the Koks, as opposed to the Basters of Philippolis, whom Kolbe referred to as "New Griquas"; these terms are not common.—The individual mentioned was presumably Hendrik Hendrickze; see Philip's own account below.
287. It might also show their wish to be left to settle their own affairs free from undesired interference, however well intentioned.
288. CWMA Journals 1597.
289. One-and-a-half lines in the note left blank for the names omitted in transcription.
290. Philip's son-in-law, John Fairbairn, editor of the *South African Commercial Advertiser* in Cape Town.
291. Rhodes House, Oxford: Macmillan Papers, no.622.

292. That is, as far as the logic of this involved sentence can be followed, the Old Inhabitants or Baster section of the community, who formed the core of the LMS congregation at Philippolis, believed that the "Bergenaar" section of the Griqua population supported the raiders.
293. A coloured settlement established on the Eastern Frontier in 1829.
294. Aborigines Committee (1837), pp.144–145.
295. Aborigines Committee (1837), pp.145–146.
296. The text gives "Adam" here, indicating the later Kaptyn, Adam Kok III, but from the context it is clear that Abraham Kok is meant.
297. Smith:Diary I, 78.
298. CA, 1/GR 10/6 (27.1.1827).
299. CA, GH 19/4 pp.408–410 (extract).
300. BMB (1835), p.36 (translated).
301. For these various developments, see Schoeman:Death.
302. See Griqua Records, Documents 33 and 34.
303. Smith:Diary, I, 77.
304. CA, GH 19/4 pp.408–410 (extract).
305. Oberholster, p.30, quoting CA, CO 791 8 (4.2.1836).
306. Aborigines Committee (1836), p.620.
307. G.58–1879, p.99.
308. CWMA 213 (LMS 15/3/A), 27.1.1837.
309. CWMA 213 (LMS 15/3/A), 27.1.1837. For Stockenstrom's account of the meeting see Griqua Records, Document 36.
310. CWMA 213 (LMS 15/3/A), 1.2.1837.
311. See Griqua Records, Document 37.
312. CA, LG 495,36 pp.120–125 (Peter Wright to Andries Stockenstrom, 1.3.1837).
313. CWMA 213 (LMS 15/3/A), 1.2.1837.
314. CWMA 219 (LMS 16/1/A), 5.3.1838.
315. See: Legassick:Griqua, pp.551–554; Ross, pp.38–40.
316. The reference is to Philippolis, where Atkinson had arrived on 12 August 1836.
317. Fleetwood Rawstorne, who was to be much involved in the subsequent affairs of Philippolis.
318. CWMA 217 (LMS 15/4/B), 25.12.1837.
319. The election had already taken place by the time Atkinson wrote to the LMS in London on 25 December 1837.
320. Pellissier, p. 290 (translated from the Afrikaans translation).
321. The Philippolis Captaincy is meant; for the use of this term, see p.162 above.
322. CWMA 219 (LMS 16/1/A), 5.3.1838.
323. CWMA 217 (LMS 15/4/B), 25.12.1837.
324. Peter Wright, Journal for 1838; MS in the possession of Chris Roux, Ramah, Hopetown district.
325. See p.82 above.
326. Arnot, p.155; see also Legassick:Griqua, pp.552–553 (with references).—For Cornelius Kok, see further p.171 above.
327. Smith:Diary, I, 77.

328. Kirby, p.147.
329. Smith:Diary, I, 77.
330. Aborigines Committee (1836), p.620.
331. Backhouse:Narrative, p.352.
332. Dower, p.78.
333. Griqua Records, Document 38. For the supplement (1850), see Document 102.
334. For Oberholster, see DSAB V.
335. Griqua Records, Documents 39 and 40.
336. For these developments, see Schreiner, pp.83–91.
337. Schreiner, p.99.
338. Schreiner, p.103.
339. See CA, GH 8/10 pp.193–196.
340. See p.44 above.
341. See Griqua Records, Document 56.
342. See Griqua Records, Documents 51–55.
343. For the number of deacons at Philippolis, see p.158 above.
344. *Missionary Magazine* (1843), p.528.
345. CWMA 275 (LMS 19/1/D), 24.4.1843.

4. *The people of the Captaincy, pp.97–116*

346. "Families" are obviously meant throughout.
347. CWMA 135 (LMS 10/2/B), 2.4.1827.
348. CWMA 164 (LMS 12/2/A), "Report".
349. Armstrong, p.45.
350. Basotho and Batswana, both speakers of Sotho languages, were not always clearly distinguished by outsiders at this stage.
351. The Regshande (Right Hand Korana) at Bethanie; see p.100 above.
352. Griqua Records, Document 70.
353. Former slaves. See further pp.106–107 above.
354. G.58–1879, p.5.
355. Arnot, p.191.
356. GTJ (16.2.1843).
357. GTJ (16.2.1843).
358. Probably the battle of Swartkoppies on 2 May 1845, which had been followed by negotiations at Touwfontein; see p.176 above.
359. *Cape of Good Hope Observer* (6.2.1849), pp.85–86.
360. Eugène Casalis, *My life in Basuto Land*; tr. J. Brierly (London: Religious Tract Society, 1889), p.140.
361. Griqua Records, Document 11.
362. BMB (1835), pp.38–39 (translated).
363. For "Class" see n370 below.
364. Armstrong, p.45.
365. Philip:Researches II, 345n.

366. Smith:Diary I, 160–161.
367. *Cape of Good Hope Literary Gazette* V, 2 (Feb.1835), p.20.
368. Methuen, p.287.
369. Huis van die Armes, p.50.
370. Engelbrecht, p.16.—He may have been the same person as Armstrong's "Class" referred to above (p.100).
371. Engelbrecht, p.45n.
372. The "Matabeele" were the amaNdebele of Mzilikazi; the "Tambookies" were amaThembu from the Eastern Cape.
373. As migrant labourers often known as "Mantatees".
374. Schreiner, p.41.
375. BMB (1849), pp.5–6 (translated).
376. BMB (1848), p.81 (translated).
377. See, *inter alia*: Huis van die Armes, *passim*; Pellissier, *passim*; Volksraadsnotule I–V *passim*.
378. See, *inter alia*: Ross:Griqua government, p.29; G.37–1876, pp.46 (nos. 63, 64), 196–197.
379. Arbousset, p.10.
380. See p.24 above.
381. CWMA 135 (LMS 10/2/B), 2.4.1827.
382. CA, 1/GR 10/6 (6.2.1827).
383. Burchell, pagination not recorded.
384. Smith:Diary I, 81. This was between Philippolis and Bethulie; "Bosch Spruit" in the original.
385. James Cameron, "Journal" (entry for 20.6.1842, and elsewhere), Cory Library, Grahamstown, MS.15,006.
386. Arbousset, p.10.
387. For this subject, see Douglas Varley, "The Bethelsdorp catechism of 1804", *Africana Notes & News* IV,1 (Dec. 1946).
388. Arbousset, p.11.
389. Quoted in Schreiner, p.38. See further p.113 above.
390. CA, 1/GR 10/4 (1.8.1831).
391. Smith:Diary I, 184.–For this office, see p.157 above.
392. CA, CO 362 pp.12–13; CA, CO 1 (9.9.1869); CA, SGLC 22 no.385; Griqua Records, p.145 and elsewhere.—For contemporary references to Heemro at Bethelsdorp, see Kitchingman papers, pp.116, 117. Also the diary of F. Drège (21.10.1836), NLCT MSC 64,8(1).
393. Doop Boek (dup); Schoeman:Krotz.
394. Dower, p.164n. According to the genealogies, Carolus la [*sic*] Fleur was married in the Independent Church at Langkloof in 1860 to Annatjie Cloete of Matjiesdrif; Heese/Lombard 2, 320. This is the only other record of the family traced.—For A.A.S. le Fleur, see DSAB V; Rainer.
395. Basutoland Records II, 5.
396. Volksraadsnotule III, 338.
397. JME (1837), pp.197–200; (1838), p.240 (translated).

398. JME (1837), pp.200–202.
399. CA, GH 19/4 pp.686–689.
400. Backhouse:Extracts, p.35.
401. Huis van die Armes, pp.115, 123–124.
402. JME (1852), 326 (translated).
403. JME (1852), p.326; (1856), p.403.
404. BMB (1852), p.211 (translated).
405. Solomon:Two lectures, p.19.
406. JME (1855), p.172.
407. Dower, p.45.
408. G.58–1879, p.5.
409. Possibly a reference to the language studies then being undertaken by C.F. Wuras of Bethanie.
410. Schreiner, p.27 (translated from the original).
411. CWMA 213–214 (LMS 15/3/B), 30.6.1837.
412. Methuen, p.65.
413. Dower, p.57.
414. George T. Nurse, *The origins of the Northern Cape Griqua* (Johannesburg: Institute for the Study of Man in Africa, 1975), p.10.
415. Van Zyl, pp.22, 244–245.—In standard Afrikaans: "Ons vra sitplek [=*staanplek*] vir ons en ons kinders; nou is ons soos vlieënde voëls, en selfs die Kaffers bevuil ons." "Ons is maar van dieselfde bloedintrek [=*familie*], want hy wat Dam Kok was, is ons almal se grootvader. Lê sy spore dan nie oral van Piketberg tot hier by Silwerfontein en doer by Griekwastad nie?"
416. Lindley, p.35.
417. Arnot, p.174.
418. Arnot, p.190.
419. *Cape of Good Hope Literary Gazette* V, 2 (Feb.1835), p.20.
420. Arnot, pp.195–196.
421. Arbousset, p.12.
422. Malherbe; also (*inter alia*) Campbell (1815) I, 89; Transactions IV, 185–191 *passim*; CWMA *passim*; Stockenstrom II, 375; Legassick:Griqua, p.347 n40.
423. Griqua Records, pp.62, 207–208; CWMA 349 (LMS 25/1/B), 30.4.1850; Dower, pp.60–62.
424. "way of life".
425. Schreiner, p.93.
426. English in the German original.
427. Schreiner, p.62 (translated from the original).
428. Dower, p.169; Ross, pp.105, 192 and *passim*.
429. Ross:Griqua government, p.33, giving references to Dower pp.45, 82; CA, GO 1 (8–9.3.1871).
430. CWMA 423 (LMS 29/3/A), 9.3.1855; ditto 436 (LMS 30/3/A), 29.1.1857; CWMA Odds 570 (8.8.1849); Midgley, p.259; Griqua Records, p.142.
431. Griqua Records, p.126 n2.
432. Volksraadsnotule I, 365.

433. Armstrong, p.43.
434. CA, CO 362 p.216 (12.10.1829).
435. CA, 1/GR 10/35 (statement by Abraham Kok).
436. JME (1837), p.201.
437. CA, SGLC 28 no.97.
438. G.58–1879, p.47.
439. Dower, pp.57–58.
440. See pp.63–64 above.
441. See p.105 above.
442. Heese/Lombard I, 475; Schreiner, p.71; Freeman, p.227; Auxiliary (1853) p.69, (1854) p.43.
443. CWMA 221 (LMS 16/1/C), 18.6.1838.
444. Schreiner, p.38.
445. G.37–1876, p.45.
446. G.58–1879, p.46; Dower, p.57.
447. For sealing letters.
448. Printed calico.
449. These three men were probably drivers or servants.
450. This amount was a little over £1 in British currency.
451. CA, GH 19/4 pp.388–391.
452. BMB (1835), p.29 (translated).
453. Smith:Journal, p.145.
454. Probably with ochre.
455. Smith:Diary I, 80.
456. Smith:Journal, p.35.
457. Backhouse:Extracts, p.59.
458. Smith:Journal, p.144.
459. Backhouse:Extracts, p.54.
460. i.e., some kind of western dress.
461. CWMA 144 (LMS 11/1/C), 1.7.1828.
462. See Smith:Journal, pp.33–35.
463. Doop Boek (general notes).

5. Life in the Captaincy (1836–1843), pp.117–139

464. Griqua Records, p.93.
465. Smith:Journal, p.137.
466. Smith:Journal, p.137.—To these remarks, Smith added a note concerning the "capriciousness of springs in South Africa": "The inhabitants of Europe can form but little idea of the obstacles to improvement in countries so circumstanced, and ought, therefore, to be cautious in too often ascribing want of success to the character of the people."
467. Quoted in Schreiner, pp.35–36.
468. Backhouse:Extracts, p.54.

469. Backhouse:Extracts, p.58.
470. He is known to have been in possession of the farm Schietfontein, on the road between Philippolis and Ramah, which he sold in 1854; VA, GS 1548 p.106. The *werf* described in the following quotations seems, however, to have been to the north-east of Philippolis.
471. CWMA Journals 1592 (22.6.1827).
472. CWMA Journals 1592 (10.8.1827).
473. BMB (1836), p.29 (translated).
474. Smith:Journal, p.136.
475. Smith:Diary I, 176.
476. See Schoeman:Early mission.
477. Goeyman was strictly speaking a Baster from the Colony. Sabba was referred to as a "Griqua-Hottentot" by the Germans, for what these designations may be worth; BMB (1836) [p.29].
478. BMB (1836), p.29 (translated).
479. Arnot, p.178.
480. Cumming I, 136–137.
481. Griqua Records, p.165.
482. Hamelberg, p.142.
483. J. Beijer, *Journal, gehouden van Port Elisabeth (Algoabaai) naar Reddersburg (O.V.S.)* (Kaapstad: Saul Solomon, 1871), p.131.
484. CWMA 164 (LMS 12/2/A), "Report".
485. Methuen, p.282.
486. Methuen, p.78.
487. CWMA Journals 1592 (20.1.1827).
488. CWMA Journals 1592 (13.4.1827).
489. CWMA 164 (LMS 12/2/A), "Report".
490. Backhouse:Extracts, pp.4, 54.
491. CWMA 135 (LMS 10/2/B), 2.4.1827.
492. Smith:Journal, p.31.
493. BMB (1835), p.29 (translated).
494. Backhouse:Extracts, p.54.
495. The Moravian mission station of Shiloh, near the modern Queenstown.
496. Schreiner, p.35.
497. Quoted in Schreiner, p.38.
498. Backhouse:Extracts, p.4.
499. CWMA 209 (LMS 13/1/E), "Report".
500. CWMA 217 (LMS 15/4/B), "Report"; where there is also a sketch and plan of the projected house.
501. CWMA 213–214 (LMS 15/3/B), 30.6.1837.
502. CWMA 221 (LMS 16/1/C), 18.6.1838.
503. Backhouse:Extracts, p.4.
504. Griqua Records, Document 3.
505. Smith:Diary, pp.177–178.
506. Reproduced in Smith:Journal, p.31.

507. CWMA Journals 1592 (21.3.1827).
508. CWMA Journals 1596 (1.4.1832).
509. See Bell's views of the exterior and interior (1834–35) reproduced in Smith:Journal, pp.32, 32.
510. CWMA Journals 1592 (15.7.1827).
511. CWMA 170 (LMS 12/4/E), "Report".
512. CWMA Journals 1596 (14.1.1832).
513. CWMA Journals 1596 (5.8.1832).—The reference is to the Wesleyan mission station Buchuaap (Boetsap) beyond the Vaal, where Barend Barends and his followers were living.
514. CWMA Journals 1596 (7.11.1831).
515. JME (1836), pp.136–137 (translated).
516. CWMA Journals 1596 (6.5.1832).
517. CWMA Journals 1596 (1.4.1832).
518. Henry Martyn, an English missionary in India, who had attracted much attention by his early death in 1812.
519. BMB (1835), pp.38–39 (translated).
520. Smith:Diary I, 71.
521. Smith:Diary I, 78.
522. Smith:Diary II, 180.
523. CWMA Journals 1596 (8.7.1827).
524. Schreiner, p.65.
525. CWMA Journals 1592 (5.4.1827).
526. BMB (1835), p.29 (translated).
527. Griqua Records, Document 4.
528. Report (1835), pp.94–95.
529. Schreiner, p.64.
530. Griqua Records, Document 8.
531. Figures from Report, *passim*.
532. Report (1844), p.104.
533. Schreiner, p.33.
534. Schreiner, p.49.
535. Schreiner, p.58.
536. Schreiner, p.63.
537. Schreiner, p.72.
538. Schreiner, p.93.
539. Schreiner, p.71.
540. See p.113 above.
541. Schreiner, p.75.
542. CWMA Journals 1592 (13.4.1827).
543. CWMA Journals 1596 (2.4.1832).
544. CWMA 213–214 (LMS 15/3/B), 30.6.1837.
545. CWMA Journals 1596 (28.11.1832).
546. Cf. Schreiner, p.45.
547. Schreiner, p.65.

548. Schreiner, p.33.
549. Schreiner, p.39.
550. Schreiner, p.75.
551. Schreiner, p.72.
552. CWMA Journals 1592 (23.6.1827).
553. See pp.118–120 above.
554. CWMA 213 (31.7.1837; entries for 10 & 15 May).
555. Schreiner, p.81.
556. Schreiner, p.64.
557. Schreiner, p.39.
558. Report (1835), pp.94–95.
559. See for example Schreiner, p.33.
560. Hodgson, p.389.
561. CWMA Journals 1596 (23.4.1832).
562. CWMA Journals 1596 (3.9.1832).
563. Report (1835), pp.94–95.
564. Schreiner, p.37.
565. Schreiner, p.41.
566. Schreiner, p.41.
567. Schreiner, p.59.
568. Schreiner, p.104.
569. Schreiner, p.106.
570. Griqua Records, Document 19.
571. Report (1835), p.94–95.
572. Report (1836), p.98.
573. Schreiner, p.64.
574. Schreiner, p.78.—This was probably the new Tswana translation of the Bible by Robert Moffat (1840).
575. CWMA Journals 1596 (18.1.1832).
576. CWMA 213–214 (LMS 15/3/B), 30.6.1837.
577. CWMA 217 (LMS 15/4/B), "Report".
578. CWMA 221 (LMS 16/1/C), 18.6.1838.
579. Schreiner, p.37.
580. CWMA 153 (LMS 11/4/A), 29.10.1829.
581. Schreiner, p.37.
582. BMB (1836), p.28 (translated).
583. CWMA 212 (LMS 15/3/A), 9.1.1837.
584. Philip:British residents, p.89.
585. CWMA Journals 1596 (5.9.1832).
586. CA, GH 1/10 (13.1.1846).
587. *Gouvernements Courant van de O.V.S.* (10.11.1857).—In the old cemetery in Bloemfontein there is or was a headstone recording the death of Alexander Davidson, a Scot, who had died in 1853 at the age of 82, and his wife Isabella, died 26.12.1849.
588. CA, MOOC 124/1859; CA, Death notice 6/9/88 no.6540. See also [Joseph Orpen], *History of the Basutus of South Africa* (Cape Town: Saul Solomon, 1857), p.8.

589. CWMA 212 (LMS 15/3/A), 9.1.1837.
590. Schreiner, p.66.
591. Quoted in Schreiner, p.127 n39, from GTJ (8.2.1844).
592. Adams, pp.66–67.
593. CWMA 341 (LMS 24/1/A), 12.3.1848.
594. Backhouse:Extracts, p.56.
595. Schreiner, p.70.
596. Schreiner, p.38; Backhouse:Extracts, pp.6–10.
597. Schreiner, p.70.
598. "are prepared to take cattle …".
599. Schreiner, p.69.
600. BMB (1841), p.159 (translated).
601. BMB (1835), p.36.
602. Backhouse:Extracts, p.55.

6. The Government of the Captaincy: Officials, pp.141–159

603. See Griqua Records, Documents 1–19.
604. For the government of the Kokstad Captaincy, see: CA, GO 2; G.58–1879, pp.60–61; Dower, pp.17–19.
605. Elphick, pp.46–47.
606. Burchell I, 253.
607. Lichtenstein II, 319.
608. Elphick, p.47.
609. Engelbrecht, pp.89–90.
610. Engelbrecht, p.39.
611. Lichtenstein II, 302–303.
612. "*Untermagistratspersonen*" in the original German; *Reise* II, 396. He is more likely to have meant this in the sense of "municipal officials", similar in status to the Cape field-cornets.
613. Lichtenstein II, 305–306.
614. Lichtenstein II, 301.
615. Burchell I, 357.
616. Campbell:Travels (1815), p.252.
617. Campbell:Travels (1815), pp.253–255.
618. CWMA 62 (LMS 5/3/A), 3.1.1814.
619. Arnot, p.335.
620. Papers relative, p.213.
621. Papers relative, p.211.
622. See his statement in this regard on p.28 above.
623. The Governor, at that time Lord Charles Somerset.
624. Papers relative, p.211.
625. Papers relative, p.212.
626. Aborigines Committee (1837), p.146.

627. See p.82 above.
628. Smith:Journal, p.141.
629. Elphick, p.47.
630. See pp.141–143 above.
631. Aborigines Committee (1836), p.218.
632. See pp.14–15 above.
633. See pp.33–34 above.
634. Andries Stockenstrom, in *Cape of Good Hope Observer* (28.8.1849), p.552.
635. Volksraadsnotule I, 365.
636. Ross:Griqua government, p.34.
637. See p.111 above.
638. Elphick, p.47.
639. Presumably the area in the Transgariep where the Bergenaars had settled.
640. CWMA 141–142 (LMS 10/3/D), "Short account" 1827.
641. Campbell:Travels (1815), p.252.
642. Smith:Journal, p.287.
643. Transactions (1829), 124.
644. Griqua Records, Document 25.
645. Griqua Records, Document 26.
646. Armstrong, p.47.
647. Smith:Journal, p.138.
648. Griqua Records, Document 15 (par.7).
649. Smith:Diary I, 190; Legassick:Griqua, p.430.
650. Transactions (1829), p.124; CWMA 149 (LMS 11/3/A), 23.1.1829.
651. Doop Boek; CWMA 149 (LMS 11/3/A), 23.1.1829.
652. CWMA 141–142 (LMS 10/3/D), "Short account" 1827.
653. Campbell:Journal, 22.8.1820.
654. CWMA 89 (LMS 7/3/C), 31.12.1817; CA, 1/GR 12/10 (15.1.1825).
655. CWMA 125 (LMS 9/3/C), 29.9.1825; CA, 1/GR 10/35 (Jan.1836).
656. Ross, pp.33–34, 37.
657. Source not noted.
658. Griqua Records, Documents 37 (par.12) & 38 (par.12).
659. CA, GH 19/4 pp.408–410.
660. Smith:Diary I, 77.
661. See p.74 above.
662. See caption to portrait reproduced in Smith:Diary I, Plate 5.
663. Griqua Records, Document 30 (27.6.1834).
664. Griqua Records, Document 32.
665. Griqua Records, Document 100.
666. Griqua Records, Document 2.
667. Griqua Records, Document 4.—In the same way the Natal Volksraad in the 1840s was responsible for making municipal regulations for Pietermaritzburg.
668. Smith:Journal, p.73.
669. Smith:Journal, pp.138–139.
670. Smith:Journal, p.141.

671. See pp.155–156 above.
672. Smith:Journal, p.139.
673. Griqua Records, Document 15 (par.3) (translated).
674. Smith:Diary I, 180.
675. Schreiner, p.86.
676. CWMA Odds 570 (LMS 1/5/A), 8.8.1849; Volksraadsnotule V, 150.
677. Smith:Journal, p.137.
678. Smith:Journal, p.138.
679. CWMA 141–142 (LMS 10/3/D), "Short account" 1827.
680. CWMA Journals 1595 (20.2.1828).
681. Friend (5.8.1859).
682. Griqua Records, Document 5.
683. Griqua Records, Document 6.
684. Griqua Records, Document 2.
685. CA, GH 19/4 p.408.
686. Midgley, p.259.
687. Note in Griqua law code, CA GO2.
688. Smith:Diary I, 184.
689. See p.105 above.
690. Griqua Records, Document 13 (par.5).
691. Smith:Journal, p.147.
692. Smith:Journal, p.50.
693. Griqua Records, Documents 12 & 13.
694. CWMA Journals 1596.
695. JME (1855), p.173.
696. CWMA 423 (LMS 29/3/A), 9.3.1855.
697. Arnot, p.256.
698. Griqua Records, Document 102.
699. Griqua Records, Document 38 par.10.
700. Griqua Records, Document 102.
701. Arnot, p.188.
702. See p.98 above.
703. *Cape of Good Hope Observer* (6.2.1849), p.86.
704. Date not noted.

7. *The Government of the Captaincy: Laws and customs, pp.161–172*

705. Griqua Records, Document 29.
706. Griqua Records, Document 37 par.3.
707. Backhouse:Extracts, p.59.—This could possibly be a misreading of "Hankey River", for W.A. Hankey was treasurer of the LMS from 1816–32, and the name might well have been given by Campbell during his visit in the winter of 1820 in the arbitrary way customary with missionaries.
708. The modern Ladybrand area.

709. Griqua Records, Document 39 par.1.
710. Griqua Records, Document 73 par.5.
711. Campbell:Travels (1815), pp.160, 258.
712. Kirby, pp.146–147.
713. Griqua Records, Document 38 par.3 (translated).
714. F. Lion Cachet, *De worstelstrijd der Transvalers* (Amsterdam: J.H. Kruyt, 1881), p.124.
715. Griqua Records, Document 2 par. 2 (translated).
716. CWMA 219 (LMS 16/1/A), 5.3.1838.
717. Schreiner, pp.57, 61.
718. Volksraadsnotule II, 500.
719. Griqua Records, Document 97 (translated).
720. Volksraadsnotule V, 370; VI, 41
721. Grant made to "*Coenraad Windvogel de jonge*" of the farm Tafel Kop "*gelegen in het Distrikt Ibisa onder Zuurberg*" (16.2.1867); original in private ownership. Reproduced as frontispiece to Griqua Records.
722. Griqua Records, pp.58–59.
723. Griqua Records, Document 106.
724. Griqua Records, Document 144 par.1 (translated).
725. Griqua Records, Document 4 par.6.
726. Griqua Records, Document 11 (translated).
727. Griqua Records, Document 70 par.2.
728. Text given in Griqua Records, Document 35.
729. Griqua Records, Document 36.
730. CA, 1/CBG 4/1/1 p.7.
731. Griqua Records, Document 39 p.41.
732. Griqua Records, Document 40 par.5.
733. Griqua Records, Document 107 (translated).
734. CWMA 141–142 (LMS 10/3/D), "Short account" 1827.
735. Arnot, pp.335–336.
736. Griqua Records, Document 42.
737. Griqua Records, Document 1 (translated).
738. Griqua Records, Document 70 par.3.
739. *Report from the select committee on the Kafir tribes…* (Imperial Blue Books, 1851), p.38.
740. Incorrectly transcribed "Kraalskoek" in the source quoted. The Kraalshoek Korana were a small group under Kraalshoek or Khameb which broke away from the Regshande at Bethanie; Engelbrecht, p.55.
741. "*dat zulk plaatz zal verhuurt wezen*"—not clear in the original.
742. Volksraadsnotule III (1858), 306.
743. Griqua Records, Document 29. See also Volksraadsnotule V and VI, *passim*.
744. Griqua Records, various documents *passim*.
745. Griqua Records, Document 32.
746. Smith:Journal, p.141.
747. Smith:Diary I, 183.
748. Goliat Yzerbek, for whom Witvoet had acted as regent.

749. Griqua Records, Document 73 par.7.
750. Volksraadsnotule I, 150–151.
751. BMB (1836), p.22.
752. CA, SGLC C 4/76.
753. Huis van die Armes, pp.85–88; Volksraadsnotule III, 180.
754. Schreiner, p.47.
755. Aborigines Committee (1836), p.214.
756. Griqua Records, Document 37 par.11.
757. CA, GO 2; the Philippolis section is reproduced in its entirety in Griqua Records, Documents 1–19.
758. Griqua Records, Document 42.
759. CWMA Journals 1596 (23.5.1832).
760. CA, SGLC sequence (file number of note not recorded).
761. In the GO series ("Griekwaland-Oos").
762. Smith:Diary I, 178.
763. Smith:Journal, p.139.
764. Smith:Diary I, 182.
765. Schreiner, p.107.
766. CA, 1/GR 10/6 (undated).
767. See also Griqua Records, Documents 106 & 129.
768. See Griqua Records, Documents 107 & 118.
769. Armstrong, p.46.
770. Kirby, p.149.
771. Smith:Journal, pp.145–149 *passim*.
772. Smith:Journa*l*, p.150.
773. Legassick:Griqua, pp.569–570.
774. See Arnot, pp.254–255 for the text of this.
775. See Legassick:Griqua, p.623.
776. The mother of John Bartlett Jr was Johanna Margaretha Goeyman, and he was therefore the nephew of Jan Goeyman, the original catechist at Philippolis.
777. Lindley, p.88; Griqualand West, pp.70, 73; Bloemhof Blue Book, pp.247, 138.
778. Griqua Records, Document 159.
779. Griqua Records, Document 135.
780. "Letsea" was Moshweshwe's son Letsie.
781. Griqua Records, Document 160.
782. See Griqua Records, Documents 56, 73 and 75.
783. Griqua Records, Documents 128, 132, 161 & 162.
784. Griqua Records, Document 156.

8. The Captaincy in the 1840s (1843-1851). pp.173–200

785. The surname Fortuin was well known in missionary circles in the Griqua Captaincy, and so much interesting information about this family has been recorded that it is worth summarising it here. W.P. Fortuin accompanied the earliest

missionaries from Roodezand (Tulbagh) to the Sak River in 1799 and was baptised there two years later; see Schoeman:Kicherer *passim*. "Fortuyn, a member of the church" was a schoolmaster at Hardcastle at the time of Burchell's visit in 1811, Willem Fortuyn (probably the same person) was chosen as one of the first magistrates at Griquatown in 1813, and the "profession of faith" by Maria Fortuin, as "edited and recorded in Dutch by a Griqua, deacon of the Church at Griquatown", was translated into French by the missionary Prosper Lemue in 1831; see respectively: Burchell I, 235 & II, 154; CWMA 62 (LMS 5/2/A), 3.1.1814; JME (1833), pp.318–320. Robert Moffat mentioned in 1841 that "the Infant School [at Griquatown] under the care of Troy Vortuin, a native female of a respectable family, reflects great honour on her abilities and perseverance"; Robert Moffat, *Missionary labours and scenes in Southern Africa* (London: John Snow, 1842), p.206. In 1860 and 1863, Geertruida Fortuin was still listed as a member of the congregation at Griquatown; Doop Boek (*"Lijst der gemeentê"*).

786. CWMA 279 (LMS 19/2/D), enclosure to 17.10.1843.
787. Kitchingman papers, p.232.
788. Wilson, p.227.
789. Porter, pp.42, 49, 51.
790. Short skirts; a reference, as appears immediately afterwards, to the poem "Tam o' Shanter".
791. Possibly the Governor is here meant.
792. Porter, pp.47–49.
793. Obviously in the sense of "the Griqua capital".
794. Adam, pp.65–66. The "stubble weed" was presumably red grass (*rooigras*).
795. Griqua Records, p.95.
796. Auxiliary (1845), pp.29–30.
797. Communion service.
798. John Wright, his brother-in-law.
799. Auxiliary (1845), pp.30–31.
800. Approximately 150cm, 90cm and 90 metres respectively. CWMA 320 (LMS 18/3/A), 25.10.1842.
801. Auxiliary (1844), p.32.
802. Griqua Records, p.93.
803. Cumming I, 138–140.
804. Methuen, p.283.
805. Auxiliary (1843), pp.38–39.
806. Griqua Records, p.93.
807. Backhouse & Taylor, pp.439–440.
808. Methuen, p.64.
809. Schreiner, p.50.
810. Methuen, p.287.
811. Auxiliary (1844), p.31.
812. CWMA 320 (LMS 23/1/A), 30.6.1847.
813. Freeman, p.232.
814. CWMA 320 (LMS 23/1/A), 30.6.1847.

815. A derogatory diminutive of "Hottentots", here seemingly meant to indicate Griquas.
816. Cheap readymade clothing.
817. Dolman, pp.152–154.
818. Backhouse & Taylor, pp.440–441.
819. See Freeman, pp.232–233.
820. Auxiliary (1844), p.31.
821. Report (1848), p.112.
822. Griqua Records, Document 96.
823. Griqua Records, p.98 (par.8).
824. Basutoland Records I, 112. For Sutton, see DSAB III, p.776.
825. CWMA 213 (LMS 15/3/A), 27.1.1837 (Kolbe).
826. Kitchingman papers, pp.261, 265, 267.
827. For Warden, see DSAB I; Midgely, *passim*.
828. Basutoland Records I, 113.
829. British Presence, p.20.
830. The normal stages on the route from Colesberg were: Orange River, De Vries's, Philippolis, Vissershoek, Touwfontein, Boomplaats, Kalwerfontein, Wildebeesfontein, Bethanie, Kulfontein, Wildebeesvlakte, Bloemfontein, and this was calculated as being a journey of some 25 hours on horseback (*Cape Almanac* for 1850, unpaginated).
831. Wilmot, p.47.
832. Moshweshwe of the Basotho, Moroka II of the Barolong, Moletsane of the Bataung, Sekonyela of the Batlokwa, and Gert Taaibosch of the Kei Korana.
833. Griqua Records, Document 76.
834. Richard Southey, his secretary.
835. CWMA Odds 542 ("About the year 1826…").
836. Philip:Memorials (27.11.1848). No further information on this source has been noted; it is presumably among the Macmillan papers at Rhodes House, Oxford.
837. *Report from the select committee on the Kafir tribes…* (Imperial Blue Books, 1851), pp.34–35.
838. Smith:Autobiography II, 233.
839. Theal follows this version in volume III of his *History of South Africa since 1795*, which appeared in 1904 (p.272). For further texts giving the Griqua view, see Griqua Records, pp.104–105, 120, 126–129, 137–138, 147–148.
840. BMB (1848), pp.132–133 (translated).
841. Dower, p.8.
842. Griqua Records, Document 105.
843. See Griqua Records, Document 77; also pp.110–173 *passim*.
844. Griqua Records, Document 132.
845. Thomson had quit Philippolis shortly before; see below.
846. British Presence, pp.33–34.
847. Auxiliary (1848), p.26.
848. Report (1850), p.89.
849. CWMA 350 (LMS 21/1/B), 7.5.1850.

850. CWMA Odds 575 (LMS 1/6/C), 6.11.1849.
851. CWMA 349 (LMS 25/1/B), 30.4.1850.
852. CWMA 350 (LMS 21/1/C), 27.5.1850.
853. CWMA Odds 572 (LMS 1/5/C), 1.9.1849.
854. Auxiliary (1848), p.26.
855. CWMA 349 (LMS 25/1/B), 9.4.1850.
856. CWMA 348 (LMS 25/1/A), 29.1.1850.
857. CWMA 349 (LMS 25/1/B), 30.4.1850.
858. CWMA 349 (LMS 25/1/B), 26.3.1851.
859. CWMA 350 (LMS 25/1/C), 27.5.1850.
860. "I am almost as near the 50 years as Mr Th[omson] is near the 30," he wrote to J.J. Freeman; CWMA 350 (LMS 25/1/B), 7.5.1850.
861. CWMA 345 (LMS 24/1/B), 9.7.1849. The biographical information which follows comes from the same source.
862. CWMA 350 (LMS 25/1/B), 7.5.1850.
863. CWMA Odds 572 (LMS 1/5/C), 1.9.1849.
864. CWMA Odds 572 (LMS 1/5/C), 1.9.1849.
865. CWMA 350 (LMS 25/1/C), 25.6.1850. Obviously the women had their own chairs in the church; see also Hamelberg's account, p.208 above.
866. Griqua Records, Document 99.
867. CWMA 395 (LMS 27/3/B), 29.9.1852.

9. The Captaincy in the 1850s (1851–1861), pp.201–233

868. CWMA Odds 572 (1/5/C), 1.9.1849.—As regards the problems experienced with irrigation, see further the remarks by Prosper Lemue on p.218 above.
869. CWMA 332–333 (LMS 23/4/B), 14.9.1848.
870. Reference not identified.
871. It would seem that the building had become oblong on being enlarged, and now presented its narrow side to the street.
872. CWMA Odds 572 (LMS 1/5/C), 1.9.1849.
873. CWMA Odds 572 (LMS 1/5/C), 1.9.1849.
874. CWMA Odds 572 (LMS 1/5/C), 1.9.1849.
875. J.J. Freeman was due to visit Philippolis at the end of the year as deputation of the LMS in England.
876. CWMA Odds 572 (LMS 1/5/C), 1.9.1849.
877. CWMA Odds 572 (LMS 1/5/C), 1.9.1849.
878. CWMA 349 (LMS 25/1/B), 14.5.1850.
879. CWMA 350 (LMS 25/1/C), 18.6.1850.
880. CWMA 351 (LMS 25/1/C), 9.7.1850.
881. Friend (20.8.1850).
882. CWMA 351 (LMS 25/1/D), 16.7.1850.
883. Basutoland Records I, 416, 419, 415.
884. VA, GS 1548 pp.14–21 (5.2.1863).

885. The former slaves; see pp.106–107 above.
886. CWMA 400 (LMS 28/1/A), 1.7.1853.
887. This had been common practice in South African churches until very recently, and pews were still a novelty. Hamelberg could write of Bloemfontein in 1856, "I went to church, where everyone has to provide his own chair. (…) There are as yet no pews, but these are to be installed"; Hamelberg, p.146.
888. Freeman, pp.228–230.
889. i.e., those in the Philippolis Captaincy.
890. Gray, pp.16–17.
891. As opposed to the traditional Afrikander or fat-tail sheep.
892. This would seem to reflect difficulties on the part of the Griquas in adapting their traditional social patterns to the more competitive style of nineteenth-century Northern Europe in the manner expected of them by outsiders.
893. The estimates of visitors to Philippolis in this regard varied dramatically, depending as they did on the season of the year and the rainfall at the time of the visit.
894. Merriman, pp.133–134.
895. Edward Solomon; see pp.214–215 above.
896. Hamelberg and his Dutch travelling companion, L.F. van Foreest.
897. An early British resident at Philippolis; possibly a shopkeeper.
898. There was, in other words, no entrance hall or passage as in European houses.
899. This was also a former Dutch custom, much commented on by British visitors to the Cape at the beginning of the century.
900. An unidentified acquaintance at Beaufort West, through which Hamelberg had passed on his journey inland.
901. Kok was referring to the Captaincy as a whole, not merely the unleasable portion of his territory.
902. Hamelberg, pp.140–141 (translated).
903. Griqua Records, Document 109.
904. Cecil Northcott, *Robert Moffat* (London: Lutterworth Press, 1961), p.265.
905. Dower, pp.21, 79.
906. 'klippenhuisjes'.
907. i.e. wearing western clothes.
908. Hamelberg, pp.141–142 (translated).
909. The so-called "apprentices"; see pp.106–107 above.
910. Probably Slammert Marais, whose name occurs in collection lists for the mission in 1853 and 1854, and who is mentioned as a deacon in this period. It is typical of the situation existing at the time that the white missionary should refer to him by his first name only.
911. In 1830, when Lemue as a young missionary newly arrived in South Africa had been on his way to the interior.
912. This refers to the Church at Philippolis having become independent; see p.215 above.
913. At this time still Edward Solomon.
914. JME (1855), pp.172–175 (translated).
915. The present Transkei.
916. This was W.J. Crossley, later to become Griqua Government Secretary.

917. Solomon, pp.19–21.
918. Mackenzie, pp.59-60.
919. Friend (12.9.1857).
920. CWMA 429 (LMS 30/1/A), March 1857.
921. CWMA 436 (LMS 30/3/A), March 1857.
922. Auxiliary (1856), p.39.
923. G.58–1879, p.51.
924. Auxiliary (1853), pp.68–69; (1854), pp.42–43.
925. "Bella Wiesie" was probably Betta (Elizabeth) Wiese (see pp.112–113 above).
926. Auxiliary (1856), p.38.
927. Auxiliary (1856), p.38.
928. Auxiliary (1853), p.68.
929. VA, VR 184 pp.107–108 (translated).
930. For W.F. Corner, see Schoeman:Early mission.
931. See n956 below.
932. Griquas and their Exodus, pp.334–335.
933. See Schoeman:Dagster.
934. It is in the Grey Collection of the National Library, Cape Town.
935. Friend (3.8.1860).
936. Friend (6.12.1861), "Griqualand".
937. Friend (1.11.1859).
938. Friend (14.12.1860).
939. Friend (30.8.1861).
940. Part of a horse's harness.
941. CA, SGLC 28 no.68.
942. CA, SGLC sequence.
943. Friend (11.11.1852).
944. For Stuart see DSAB V. He was married in 1850 to a sister of the LMS missionary Holloway Helmore.
945. In the sense of "farms".
946. Friend (20.2.1851).
947. Marthinus Bergover, according to De Villiers's account.
948. The white population of the Cape had commonly been armed with swords as well as guns in the eighteenth century, and swords are still mentioned occasionally in the interior during the nineteenth.
949. Volksraadsnotule V (1860–61), 147–149 (translated).
950. Volksraadsnotule V (1860–61), 150–153 (translated).
951. Mackenzie, p.64.
952. See p.215 above
953. A.118–1861, p.25 (18.2.1861).

10. The trek to Nomansland (1861–1863), pp.235–247

954. CA, SGLC 22 pp.137–138.

955. The article may have been the work of W.B. Philip, the last minister of the Griqua congregation at Philippolis, although he did not accompany them on the final trek over the Drakensberg described here, and the style seems also more lyrical than that of his known writings. The author appears at any rate to have written from close personal knowledge of the events described.
956. The territory of the Campbell Captaincy to the west of the Vaal, which had been ceded by Cornelius Kok II in 1857 to his nephew Adam Kok III; see SESA 3, 14a.
957. This was the so-called "*Kommissietrek*".
958. The settlement of the Phuthi Chief Moorosi in the Quthing area of what is now the extreme south of Lesotho.
959. Griquas and their exodus, pp.333–334. See further Friend (8.7.1859, 16.12.1859); also *Fort Beaufort Advocate* (13.8.1869).
960. G.37–1876, p.196.—From Kok's reference to the visit of Prince Alfred to South Africa, his journey to the Cape must have taken place at the end of September 1860.
961. See p.232 above.
962. Mackenzie, p.65.
963. G.37–1876, p.194.
964. Griquas and their exodus, pp.334–335.
965. Friend (30.8.1861).
966. This was W.B. Philip.
967. For Philip's own account of these developments, see CWMA 476 (LMS 32/4/A), 7.5.1863.
968. This was in June 1865, after the Griquas had left.
969. Dower, pp.21–22.
970. Mackenzie, p.61.
971. G.58–1879, p.51.
972. Griquas and their exodus, pp.335–336.
973. CA, SGLC 28 nos. 8, 28, 59.
974. Griquas and their exodus, p.336.
975. Labourers.
976. Friend (8.11.1861), report dated 23.10.1861.
977. Friend (6.12.1861), report dated 20.11.1861.
978. Griqua Records, Document 156.
979. Griqua Records, Document 157.
980. VA, VR 184 p.107 (translated).
981. G.53–1862 (28.3.1862).
982. The Chief Posholi or Poshodi, a brother of Moshweshwe, who lived in the vicinity with his people.
983. Griquas and their exodus, p.336.
984. For Jan Julie, see p.102 above.
985. G.37–1876. pp.196–197.
986. G.58–1879, pp.51–52.
987. Rademeyer, pp.69–71.

988. This refers to Kokstad.
989. Here they established Kokstad as their capital.
990. Griquas and their exodus, pp.336–337.
991. U.G.41–1926, p.24.
992. For Le Fleur and his family, see p.105 above.
993. For the later development of the Griqua people, see the article "Griquas" by J.J. Oberholster in SESA 5 (1972), 353–358.
994. See "Griqua race is recognised", *Eastern Province Herald* (3.7.1997), p.10.

Appendix: Statement by Adam Kok II, pp.251–252

995. *Andrew Smith's journal of his expedition into the interior of South Africa, 1834–36*; ed. William F. Lye (Cape Town: A.A. Balkema, 1975). The text here transcribed occurs on pp.183–184.
996. Possibly: "Old Adam (...) transferred his staff to Cornelius (...) when about 84 years old"?
997. Swartland was the present Malmesbury region, but this may also be a reference to Piketberg.
998. Possibly the Dutch "*vee*", but this is also Scots usage, and Smith was a Scot by birth.
999. Actually at Rietfontein, in 1801.

Sources

Aborigines Committee (1836)—*Report from the select committee on aborigines (British settlements)* (Imperial Blue Books, 1836).
Aborigines Committee (1837)—*Report from the select committee on aborigines (British settlements)* (Imperial Blue Books, 1837).
Adams, Buck: *The narrative of Private Buck Adams*, ed. A. Gordon-Browne (Cape Town: Van Riebeeck Society, 1941).
Arbousset, T.: *Narrative of an exploratory tour...*; tr. John Croumbie Brown (Cape Town: A.S. Robertson, 1846).
Armstrong, A.B.: Report of a journey to the "Griqua and Coranna countries" (Kat River Post, 1833) (MS), CA AC 11 pp.26–60.
Arnot, David, and Francis H.S. Orpen: *The land question of Griqualand West* (Cape Town: Saul Solomon, 1875).
Auxiliary—Report of the Cape Town Auxiliary [to the London] Missionary Society.
Backhouse: Extracts—James Backhouse, *Extracts from the letters of James Backhouse* (Lindfield: W. Eade printer, 1837–41).
Backhouse: Narrative—James Backhouse, *A narrative of a visit to the Mauritius and South Africa* (London: Hamilton, Adams & Co., 1844).
Backhouse, James, & Charles Taylor: *The life and labours of George Washington Walker* (London: A.W. Bennett, 1862).
Basutoland Records, collected and arranged by Geo. M. Theal (Cape Town: W.A. Richards, 1883).
BMB—*Berliner Missionsberichte* (journal of the Berlin Missionary Society).
British presence (The) in the Transorange, 1845–1854; ed. Karel Schoeman (Cape Town: Human & Rousseau, 1992).
Burchell, W.J.: *Travels in the interior of Southern Africa*, repr. (London: Batchworth Press, 1953).
CA—Cape Town Archives Repository.
Campbell: Journal—John Campbell, "Journal" (1819–21) (MS), NLCT MSC 77.
Campbell: Travels (1815)—John Campbell, *Travels in South Africa*, 3rd ed., corrected (London: Black, Parry & Co., 1815).
Campbell: Travels (1822)—John Campbell, *Travels in South Africa, undertaken at the request of the London Missionary Society; being a narrative of a second journey into the interior of that country* (London: LMS, 1822).
Cornelissen, A.K.: Langs Grootrivier (ca 1995) (duplicated TS).
Cumming, Roualeyn Gordon: *Five years in a hunter's life in the far interior of South Africa* (London: John Murray, 1850).
CWMA: Council of World Mission Archives; microfiche ed. (Zug: IDC, 1987). Unless otherwise specified, the sequence "Incoming Letters (South Africa)" is meant.

De Villiers/Pama—C.G. de Villiers, *Genealogies old South African families*, ed. C. Pama (Cape Town: A.A. Balkema, 1981).

Dolman, Alfred: *In the footsteps of Livingstone*, ed. John Irving (London: John Lane, 1924).

Doop Boek—"Doop boek voor de bejaarde[n] en kinderen, 1807–1870" (microfiche), NLCT MSB 924. Official Griquatown baptismal register; original now at Kuruman.

—: Karel Schoeman, "Die Griekwastadse doopboek, 1807–1824: 'n alfabetiese naamregister" (Kaapstad: S.A. Biblioteek, 1997).

Doop Boek (dup)—"Doop boek voor de bejaarde[n] en kinderen, 1807–1869" (microfiche), NLCT MSB 924. Duplicate copy of official Griquatown baptismal register; original now at Kuruman.

Dower, William: *The early annals of Kokstad and Griqualand East*, facs. reprod. with introd., notes and index by Christopher Saunders (Pietermaritzburg; Univ. of Natal Press, 1978).

DSAB—*Dictionary of South African biography*.

Early (The) mission at Philippolis, 1823–1837; ed. Karel Schoeman (*in the press*).

Elphick, Richard: *Khoikhoi and the founding of white South Africa* (Johannesburg: Ravan, 1985).

Engelbrecht, J.A.: *The Korana* (Cape Town: Maskew Miller, 1936).

Freeman, J.J.: *A tour in South Africa* (London: John Snow, 1851).

Friend—*The Friend* (Bloemfontein newspaper).

G.11—1857: *Correspondence between H. E. Sir G. Grey and H.M.'s Secretary of State for the Colonies, on the affairs of the Cape Colony, Natal, and adjacent territories, 1855–1857.*

G.21—1871: *Correspondence between H.M. High Commissioner and the President of the O.F.S. relative to (…) the country in which diamonds have been discovered.*

G.37—1876: *Report of a Commission to inquire into the affairs of the territory of Griqualand East.*

G.58—1879: *Report of a Commission appointed to inquire into the causes of the recent outbreak in Griqualand East.*

Gray, Robert: *A journal of the Bishop's visitation tour through the Cape Colony, in 1850* (London: SPG, 1851).

Griqua Records: the Philippolis Captaincy, 1825–1861; ed. Karel Schoeman (Cape Town: Van Riebeeck Society, 1996).

"Griquas (The) and their exodus", *Cape Monthly Magazine* V (July–Dec. 1872).

GTJ—*Graham's Town Journal* (newspaper).

Hamelberg—*Die dagboek van H.A.L. Hamelberg, 1855–1871*; red. F.J. du Toit Spies (Kaapstad: Van Riebeeckvereniging, 1952).

Harington, A.L.: *Sir Harry Smith—bungling hero* (Cape Town: Tafelberg, 1980).

Heese/Lombard—J.A. Heese, *South African genealogies, 1–4*; ed. R.T.J. Lombard (Pretoria: HSRC, 1986–92).

—: *South African genealogies, 5*; ed. and augm. by GISA (Stellenbosch: Genealogical Institute of South Africa, 1999).

Hodgson, T.L.: *The journals of the Rev. T.L. Hodgson, 1821–1831*; ed. R.L. Cope (Johannesburg: Witwatersrand Univ. Pr., 1977).

Huis (Die) van die Armes: die Berlynse Sendinggenootskap in die O.V.S., 1834–1869; red. Karel Schoeman (Kaapstad: Human & Rousseau, 1985).

JME—*Journal des Missions Evangéliques* (journal of the Paris Missionary Society).
Kirby, P.R.: *Sir Andrew Smith* (Cape Town: A.A. Balkema, 1965).
Kitchingman papers (The): missionary letters and journals, 1817 to 1848; ed. Basil le Cordeur & Christopher Saunders (Johannesburg: Brenthurst Press, 1976).
Legassick, M.C.: *The Griqua, the Sotho-Tswana, and the missionaries, 1780–1840* (Ann Arbor, Mich.: University Microfilms, 1970).
Legassick, Martin: "The Northern Frontier to c.1840: the rise and decline of the Griqua People", in *The shaping of South African society, 1652–1840*; ed. Richard Elphick & Hermann Giliomee; 2nd ed. (Cape Town: Maskew Miller Longman, 1989).
Lichtenstein, Henry: *Travels in Southern Africa* (Cape Town: Van Riebeeck Society, 1928–30).
Lindley, Augustus F.: *Adamantia: the truth about the South African Diamond Fields* (London: W.H. & L. Collingridge, 1873).
Mackenzie, John: *Ten years north of the Orange River* (Edinburgh: Edmonston & Douglas, 1871).
Macmillan, W.M.: *Bantu, Boer and Briton; the making of the South African native problem* (London: Faber & Gwyer, 1929).
Merriman, N.J.: *The Cape journals of Archdeacon N.J. Merriman*; ed. D.H. Varley & H.M. Matthew (Cape Town: Van Riebeeck Society, 1957).
Methuen, Henry H.: *Life in the wilderness* (London: Richard Bentley, 1846).
Midgley, J.F.: *The Orange River Sovereignty (1848–1854)* (Archives Yearbooks 12, II; 1949).
Mission (The) at Griquatown: an anthology; ed. Karel Schoeman (Griquatown: Griekwastad Toerisme Vereniging, 1997).
Nienaber, G.S.: *Khoekhoense stamname; 'n voorlopige verkenning* (Pretoria: Academica, 1989).
NLCT—National Library (formerly South African Library), Cape Town.
Oberholster, J.J.: *Die anneksasie van Griekwaland-Wes* (Archives Yearbooks, 1945).
Papers relative to the condition and treatment of the native inhabitants of South Africa (Imperial Blue Books, 1835).
Pellissier, S.H.: *Jean Pierre Pellissier van Bethulie* (Pretoria: Van Schaik, 1956).
Penn, Nigel, "The Northern Cape frontier zone, 1700–c.1815". Thesis—D.Ph., UCT (1995).
Penn: Orange River—Nigel Penn. "The Orange River frontier zone, c.1700–1805", in *Einiqualand: studies of the Orange River frontier*; ed. Andrew B. Smith (Cape Town: UCT Press, 1995).
Philip, John: *Researches in South Africa* (London: James Duncan, 1828).
Philip, Peter: *British residents at the Cape, 1795–1819* (Cape Town: David Philip, 1981).
Porter, William: *The Touwfontein letters of William Porter (May–July 1845)*; ed. Karel Schoeman (Cape Town: S.A. Library, 1992).
Rademeyer, J.J.: *Kleurling-Afrikaans: die taal van die Griekwas en die Rehoboth-Basters* (Amsterdam: Swets & Zeitlinger, 1938).
Rainer, Margaret, "Andries Abraham Stockenstrom Le Fleur and the Griquas of Kranshoek", *Quarterly Bulletin S.A. Library* 52,2 (1997).
Report of the [London] Missionary Society. Annual report.
Ross—Robert Ross, *Adam Kok's Griquas* (Cambridge: Cambridge Univ. Press, 1976).
Ross: Griqua government—Robert Ross: "Griqua government", *African Studies* 33,1 (1974).

Schoeman: Boesmanskool— Karel Schoeman, "Die Londense Sendinggenootskap en die San: die stasie Boesmanskool en die einde van die sending, 1828–1833", *S.A. Historical Journal* 30 (May 1994).

Schoeman: Dagster—Karel Schoeman, *"De Dagster van Philippolis*—'n vergete koerant", *Quarterly Bulletin S.A. Library* 46,3 (March 1992), 100–105.

Schoeman: Death—Karel Schoeman, "The death of a Kaptyn: Adam Kok II at the Berg River, 1835", *Quarterly Bulletin S.A. Library* 51,2 (Dec. 1996).

Schoeman: Early mission—Karel Schoeman, *The early mission in South Africa, 1799–1819* (in the press).

Schoeman: Kicherer—Karel Schoeman, *J.J. Kicherer en die vroeë sending, 1799–1806* (Kaapstad: S.A. Biblioteek, 1996).

Schoeman: Krotz—Karel Schoeman, "Die herkoms van Abraham le Fleur: 'n paar aantekeninge oor die familie Krotz van die Transgariep", *Quarterly Bulletin S.A. Library* 52,3 (1998).

Schreiner, Gottlob: *The missionary letters of Gottlob Schreiner, 1837–1847*; ed. Karel Schoeman (Cape Town: Human & Rousseau, 1991).

Smith: Diary—Andrew Smith. *The diary of Dr Andrew Smith, 1834–1836*; ed. Percival R. Kirby (Cape Town: Van Riebeeck Society, 1939–40).

Smith: Journal—*Andrew Smith's journal of his expedition into the interior of South Africa*, 1834–36; ed. William F. Lye (Cape Town: A.A. Balkema, 1975).

Smith, Harry: *The autobiography of Lieutenant-General Sir Harry Smith* (London: John Murray, 1901).

Solomon, Edward: *Two lectures on the native tribes of the interior* (Cape Town: Saul Solomon, 1855).

Stockenstrom, Andries: *The autobiography of Sir Andries Stockenstrom* (Cape Town: Juta, 1887).

Thompson, George: *Travels and adventures in Southern Africa*, I; ed. V.S. Forbes (Cape Town: Van Riebeeck Society, 1967).

Transactions of the Missionary Society (Mission journal of the LMS).

U.G.41—1926: *Report of the Rehoboth Commission* (1926).

VA—Free State Archives Repository, Bloemfontein.

Van Aswegen, H.J., *Die verhouding tussen Blank en Nie-Blank in die O.V.S., 1854–1902* (Archives Year Books 34; 1971).

Van Zyl, D.H.: *'n Griekwa-"ietsigheid" (iets oor die Griekwas)* (Kaapstad: Nasionale Pers, 1947).

Volksraadsnotule—*Notule van die Volksraad van die O.V.S.*, I–VII (1854–1863).

Wikar, H.J.: *The journal of Hendrik Jacob Wikar (1779)*; ed. E.E. Mossop (Cape Town: Van Riebeeck Society, 1935).

Wilmot, Alex.: *The life and times of Sir Richard Southey* (London: Sampson Low, Marston & Co., 1904).

Wilson, K.J.: "Godfather to the Griquas: an outline of the early history of the Griqua people and the life of their missionary Peter Wright" (pref. 1976) (TS), NLCT MSB 805.

Sources of illustrations

W.J. Burchell, *Travels in the interior of Southern Africa* (1822–24): no.1
MuseumMAfricA, Johannesburg: nos.2–8, 10–12
Cape Town Archives Repository: no.9 (A1415(73), no.2); no.19 (AG 7539)
James Backhouse, *A narrative of a visit to the Mauritius and South Africa* (1844): no.13
Morija Museum & Archives, Morija, Lesotho: nos.14, 17
Mrs Freda Louw, Colesberg: no.15
National Library, Cape Town: nos.16, 18, 27 (PHA)
National English Literary Museum, Grahamstown: no.20
University of Cape Town: nos.21–24, 26
S.J. Halford, *The Griquas of Griqualand* (1949?): no.25
Free State Archives Repository, Bloemfontein: no.28 (VA)

Index

abduction, *see* slave trade:trade in abducted children
Aborigines Committee (Great Britain), 43, 57–58, 148
Abrahams, Hendrik, 143
Adams, Buck, 135–136, 178
adultery, 87, 112–113
Afrikaans language, *see* Griqua Afrikaans
Afrikaner, Klaas, 13, 18, 259
Agent, *see* Colonial Agent; Government Agent (Griquatown)
agriculture, *see* farming
Ainsworth, James, 213
alcohol consumption, *see* drunkenness; liquor trade
"Alexander River", 41, 43, 47
Alfred, *Prince*, 283 n960
alienable territory (1846), *see* leasable territory
alienation of land, *see* inalienability of land; leasing of farms to whites
Aliwal North, 246
Allemansdrif, 70
ammunition, *see* guns and ammunition
"anarchic" faction (Philippolis) 57, 207. *See also* Bergenaars:as political faction.
Anderson, William, 18, 71, 119, 143, 144, 250
"apprentices" (ex-slaves), *see* ex-slaves
April, Hendrik, 114
Archbell, James, 54
armed forces, *see* military organisation
arms, *see* guns and ammunition; swords
Armstrong, A.B., 77, 97, 100, 170
Atkinson, Eliza, 113, 129
Atkinson, Theophilus, 85, 87(2x), 90, 123–124, 138, 162, 167–168

Auxiliary Mission Society (LMS), 23, 102, 113, 131, 211, 223–224

Baatje, Carolus, 105
Backhouse (mission), 188
Bain, A.G., 108
Balie, Adam, 23
Bamboesberg, 69
Barends (family), 10
Barends, Barend, 19, 20, 250; in Cape Town, 20, 21; as interpreter, 13; as native agent, 23; as Provisie Kaptyn, 15, 22, 27, 29, 144, 164; leaves Griquatown, 28; at Griquatown conference (1825), 49, 51; raid on Mzilikazi (1831), 33, 77–78, 83. *See also* Daniëlskuil.
Barends, Klaas, 10, 12, 12–13, 14–15, 19, 145, 250
Barends, Piet, 14
Barker, George, 261 n261
barter, *see* trade and barter (general)
Bartlett, Johanna Margaretha (Goeyman), 277 n776
Bartlett, John, 53, 171
"Baster" (name), 102
Baster, Klaas, *see* Barends, Klaas
Baster people: origin, 10; incomers from Bethelsdorp, 24, 103, 105, 106; from elsewhere in Cape Colony, 103, 105–107 *passim*;
  in Transorange, 24, 39, 103, 105; at Philippolis (1822–26), 39, 55, 152; in Philippolis Captaincy, 103–105, 109, 109–110; as political faction, 57, 80, 82, 104, 109, 111, 128, 134, 151, 158; independent groups, 105–106.
  See also Griqua people:early history

290

(before 1813); "Old Inhabitants" (Philippolis).
"Baster-Hottentot" (name), 102
"Basterland" (name), 162
Batenhuisen, Hendrik, 68
"Bati's" (Caledon River valley), 105
Batlhaping, *see* Tlhaping tribe
Beaufort West, 27, 109, 214
Beersheba (mission), 105, 112, 157
Beijer, J., 121
Bell, Charles, 74, 113, 116, 124, 152
Bell, John, 85
Berends, *see* Barends
Berg River, 9, 84, 107
Berg Vijftig (Kokstad), 246
Bergenaars (raiders), 32, 34, 35–37, 39, 41–54 *passim*, 74, 101, 168; area of occupancy, 32(*2x*); as political faction, 57, 77–78, 81, 82–83, 85, 89, 128, 148, 151, 207
Bergover, Abraham, 230, 231
Bergover, Marthinus, 282 n947
Bergover, Piet, 230
Berlin Missionary Society, 100, 166–167. *See also* Bethanie (mission).
Besondermeid, 250
Bethanie (mission), 47, 97 (266 n351), 99, 101, 102, 106, 137, 193, 194, 214, 279 n830; status, 100, 152, 166–167
Bethelsdorp (mission), 24, 39, 103, 104, 105, 106, 110, 113
Bethesda (mission), 14, 25, 249
Bethulie (mission), 59, 88, 98, 101, 102, 106, 188; status, 161, 166
Bezuidenhout, Hans, 223
Bibles, *see* books
"Binnelanders" (Basters), 102
Bitterbos Korana, 63
"Black Mudder River", 259 n132
"Black River", 30, 61, 73; use of name, 259 n132
blacksmiths, 20, 135, 258 n116
Bloem, Jan, Jr., 32, 35, 87, 102, 171(*2x*)
Bloemfontein, 162, 189–190, 191, 193–194, 281 n887
Bloemfontein Convention (1854), 215; secret addenda, 215, 232–233
Bloemfontein Treaty (1848), 193–194, 195, 206, 233
Boer (family), 23
Boer, Dirk, 23
Boer, Jager, 23, 151
Boers, *see* emigrant farmers (1825–48); Republican Boers; Riet River Boers (1840–49)
Boesmansfontein, 56, 134; massacre (1826), 56
Boetsap, 28, 125 (271 n513)
Bokkeveld, 12
books, 114, 133–134, 188
Boomplaats, 32, 112, 176, 196, 214, 217, 279 n830; battle (1848), 156, 195
Boshof, J.N., *Pres.*, 221–222
Bossiespruit, 104, 161, 188
Bottelary, 255 n1
Bourke, Richard, 46, 54
Bowden, W.H.A., 226–227
brandy trade, *see* liquor trade
Breësand, 12–13
Breipaal, 188
"Briquas", *see* Tlhaping tribe
British Government, *see* Aborigines Committee (Great Britain); British Resident; Cape authorities; Select Committee on the Kafir Tribes (1851)
British Resident, 98, 171–172, 189–190, 207; proposed, 70; appointed, 189
Bronkhorst, Sybrand, 110
buchu (cosmetic), 21
Buchuaap (mission), 28, 125
Buffelboud (family), 99, 167
Burgers, Willem, 108
Bushman languages, 107
Bushman School (mission), 59, 98
Bushmen, 13, 32, 66, 144; as clients and dependents, 13, 14, 23, 61, 64, 99, 118, 120(*2x*); and Kok family, 13, 61; at Toornberg (Colesberg), 44, 45; in

Philippolis area, 39, 45, 58, 61–62, 98; as original owners of area, 61, 66, 97, 237; in Philippolis Captaincy, 97, 98–99, 185–186;

    conflicts, 32, 36, 61–62, 69, 98–99; trade in abducted Bushman children, 62; "Law on Bushmen" (1846), 99; missions, 17, 30, 39, 185–196; Bushman origins of Andries Waterboer, 19. *See also* Philippolis (mission) :as Bushman mission (1822–28).

"Caffers", *see* Xhosa people
Caledon, 147
Caledon Institute (mission), *see* Bethulie
Caledon River valley, 28, 32, 99, 101, 105, 109, 190
Cameron, James, (LMS), 198
Cameron, James, (WMS), 104
campaigns: against Korana, 63–64; against "Mantatees", 26, 29. *See also* raiding expeditions.
Campbell, 28, 90, 108, 184; established, 23; description, 26; Cornelius Kok I settles here, 25; mission, 261 n195
Campbell, John, 22, 110, 143–144
Campbell Captaincy: status, 29, 29–30, 33–34, 91–92, 149, 170, 171; Adam Kok II as Kaptyn, 28, 29–30, 33–35; resigns, 33, 34; Cornelius Kok II as Kaptyn, 33–34, 91–92, 149; Adam Kok III as Kaptyn, 171, 283 n956
Campbell Grounds, 235
Cape authorities: and Griqua settlement in Transorange, 46, 54, 86, 95, 163–164; official relations, 16, 67, 93, 146(2x), 147, 171–172, 176, 212; and appointment of Kaptyns, 29, 29–30, 33, 49, 56, 72, 85, 147–148, 171; and Bergenaars, 33, 36–37, 39–40; and emigrant Boers, 48, 65, 163–164; support for Captaincy abandoned, 164; testimonial to Adam Kok III (1862), 233. *See also* British Resident; conferences…;

Government Agent (Griquatown); treaties…
Cape Colony: boundaries, 54, 65, 260 n175; newspapers, 65, 70 (263 n245), 76, 77, 176; following of Cape precedents (Philippolis Captaincy), 76, 148, 157; trading with Colony, 16(2x), 20, 26–27, 32. *See also* Colesberg.
"Cape Corps" (45th Regiment), 189
Cape Monthly Magazine, The: anonymous article (1872), 225–226, 235–241 *passim*, 245–245; possible author, 283 n955
Cape Mounted Riflemen, 70, 77
Cape of Good Hope Punishment Act (1836), 163
"Cape smoke" (brandy), 131. *See further* liquor trade.
Cape Town: visits by Basters and Griquas, 16, 17, 20, 21, 84, 114–115, 237
capital punishment, 144, 156, 158–159, 227
Captain (office), *see* Kaptyn
Carmel (mission), 217
Casalis, Eugène, 106
Cathcart, George, *Sir*, 194
cattle farming, 12, 13, 23, 26
cattle raiding, *see* raiding expeditions
cattle theft, 61, 98–99, 158, 159
cattle trade, 15, 16, 20, 136, 137
Cedarberg, 12
Cedras (Motswana), 13
Christianity (general), 17, 18, 126, 127, 128, 183, 212; criticised by "An Oppressed Griqua" (1830), 66–70 *passim*. *See also* London Missionary Society; Philippolis (mission); religious instruction (general).
Christie, George, 197
church affairs, *see* Congregational Church (Philippolis); Philippolis (mission)
civil war (1838), 90–91
"civilisation", *see* westernisation
Clark, James, 39, 55–57, 59, 122, 170
"Class" (Korana), *see* Klaas
Clerk, George, *Sir*, 194, 215

Cloete (family), 12
Cloete, Annatjie, 267 n394
Cloete, Cotje, 228
clothing, *see* dress
code of law, 141, 168
Coetsé, Jacobus, 12
Coetzee, Frans, 106
Coetzee, Karel, 98–99
Coetzee, Piet, 106
Coetzee, Sophia (Fytjie), 106
coinage, 21
Cole, Lowry, *Sir*, 150
Colesberg, 44, 45, 70, 72, 75, 77, 80, 93, 95, 136, 137, 194, 199, 239; established, 45, 138; Civil Commissioner, 88 (265 n317), 189; route to Bloemfontein, 113, 216–217, 179 n830
Colonial Agent: suggested, 89
colour consciousness, *see* discrimination (racial)
Combined Council (Philippolis & Griquatown), *see* Joint Council
Combined Court (Philippolis & Griquatown), *see* Joint Council: as court of appeal
Combrink, J.F., 230
commandant (office), 22, 85, 156
commandoes: against Bushmen, 62, 69. *See also* campaigns; military organisation; raiding expeditions.
Commissioners of Inquiry (1823–26), 44
conferences 1813 (Griquatown), 22
conferences 1821 (same), 28–29
conferences 1823 (same), 146, 168
conferences 1824 (same), 33–34
conferences 1825 (same), 42, 48–54
conferences 1837 (Orange River), 85–86, 163–164; (Griquatown), 87
conferences 1838 (Philippolis), 90–92
conferences 1840 (same), 171
conferences 1842–43 (Colesberg), 95
conferences 1845 (Touwfontein), 99 (279 n830), 176, 177
conferences 1854 (Fauresmith), 111

Congregational Church (Philippolis), 158, 215, 221, 224–225; sale of church buildings (1861) 238–239
Constabel, Arnoldus, 151
Corner, W.F., 225, 242
Corner, W.O., 225
Cornet Spruit, *see* Kornetspruit
corporal punishment, 159, 228
costume, *see* dress
Council (Philippolis), *see* Joint Council (Philippolis & Griquatown); Raad (body)
courts of law, *see* Joint Council (Philippolis & Griquatown); magistrates
"Cradock River", 36, 47, 51
Crossley, W.J., 169, 222 (282 n916), 224
Cumming, R. Gordon, 182–183
currency, 21
Cyferfontein, 230

Dagster (De), (newspaper), 226
Damara people, 13, 107
dancing, 116, 185
Daniëlskuil, 23, 26, 28, 35, 42–43, 54, 121
Danster (Xhosa raider), 112
David, Jan, 156–158 *passim*
David's Graf, 64, 161
Davids, Petrus, 145
Davids, Pieter, 23, 164 n285
Davidson, Alexander, 135
Davidson, Isabella, 272 n587
de Bruin, Joseph, 82, 132, 152
de Bruin, Lodewyk, 81, 152
de Kock, S.N., 199–200
de Villiers, T.J. (Tobias), 230–231
de Vries (family), 113
de Vries, Jan, 113
de Vries, Mietje, *see* Vries, Mietje
"de Vries's", 279 n830
de Wit, — (Beaufort West), 214
Demerara (West Indies), 225
Diamond Fields dispute, 64, 112, 171, 227
Dickson, W.A., & Co., 227
Difaqane, *see* Dithakong (battle); "Mantatees"; refugees

Dirks, Cupido, 151–152
discrimination (racial), 10, 17, 232, 237
"district" (term), 162
Dithakong (battle), 26, 29
Dolman, Alfred, 186
Doortje (Klaarwater), 17
Dordrecht, 235
Douglas, 157, 188
Draai, Piet, 86, 112, 223
Dragoon Guards, 177, 178
Drakensberg, 191, 210, 235–236, 244–246
Drège, F., 267 n392
dress (traditional), 20–21, 22, 31, 62, 100, 115–116, 203, 213; painting of face and body, 115 (2x), 213. *See also* buchu (cosmetic); ochre (cosmetic).
dress (western), 21, 75, 93, 100, 104, 114, 115 *passim*, 183, 186, 187, 213, 214; leather clothing, 72 (264 n273), 115, 178, 183, 184, 186
drunkenness, 18, 131–133, 185, 219, 227, 245. *See also* temperance societies.
D'Urban, Benjamin, *Sir*, 84
Dutch East India Company, 10, 12, 13
Dutch language, 14, 15, 18, 21–22, 24, 104, 183; in Philippolis Captaincy, 107, 108, 134, 176, 215, 226; in schools, 130–131; profession of faith mentioned (Griquatown), 278 n785.
dwellings (traditional), 36, 117–118, 177, 178, 234
dwellings (western), 36, 104, 122–124, 182, 203–204, 222–223

economic progress, 181–183, 207, 208–209, 217–218, 221–226
education (general), 130, 131, 220, 221, 222. *See also* literacy; school teachers; schools.
Eksteenkuil, 256 n34
Elphick, Richard, 141, 142, 148, 149, 150
emancipation of slaves (1834), 106. *See also* ex-slaves ("apprentices").
emigrant farmers (1825–48): permitted to cross Orange (1825), 64; in Transgariep, 39, 43, 45–46, 46, 62, 64–65; figures, 46; first white settler, 64–65; status of settlers, 163–164, 210; ordered back to Cape Colony, 65; and liquor trade, 131–132, 133, 137, 220; as slave owners, 106;

conflicts, 36, 37, 45–46, 64, 65, 68, 157, 168, 169, 178, 179–180 *passim*, 183; protests by Griqua Raad, 65, 68; protest by "An Oppressed Griqua" (1830), 65–70; statement by Cornelius Kok and Jan Bloem (1840), 171; "treaty" (1840), 48, 93, 94, 140.

See also leasing of farms to whites; Republican Boers; Riet River Boers (1840–49); sale of land to whites; Trekkers.
emigration of Griquas: projected, 68, 235. *See also* Griqualand East; Kommissietrek (1859)
Engelbrecht (family), 12
Engelbrecht, J.A., 142–143
English language, 130–131
Ennis, Peter, 231–232
epidemics, 17, 130, 134
Esterhuijs, Christoffel, 9, 255 n1
ex-slaves ("apprentices"), 106–107, 217
Excelsior, 28
executions, *see* capital punishment

Fairbairn, John, 81, 176, 192
Faku (Mpondo Chief), 236
farming, 14, 23 *passim*, 67, 101, 182, 182–183, 209, 217–218, 225; statistics, 121. *See also* cattle farming; fountains; gardens; horse breeding; irrigation; mills; Philippolis (Griqua capital): gardens; sheep farming; tobacco cultivation; wheat farming.
Faure, Abraham, 39, 44–45
Fauresmith, 32, 111, 121, 207, 221, 226, 227, 230, 259 n143
fieldcornets (emigrant farmers), 164

fieldcornets (Griquas), 142, 156–157, 163, 185, 240
firearms, *see* guns and ammunition
Fish River, 110
Flooks, J.G., 226
food, 20, 26, 114
Fortuin (family), 277–278 n785
Fortuin, Geertruida, 175, 278 n785
Fortuyn, Willem, 145
Fossey, James, 135
fountains, 33, 64, 70–71, 90, 101, 117, 118, 122, 166, 182, 269, 269 n466. *See also* Philippolis (Griqua capital):fountain.
Fraser, Colin, Jr., 242
Fraserburg, 17
Free State, *see* Orange Free State (Republic); Orange River Sovereignty; Transgariep
Free State-Sotho War (1865–66), 239
Freeman, J.J., 111, 165, 192, 195, 204, 208–209, 229
The Friend (newspaper): editorial (1851), 221–222
Frontier Wars, 84, 110, 189
fugitives, 106, 145
Fytje (Bushwoman), 64, 120

game, 120–121, 217, 236. *See also* hunting expeditions.
Ganganup (Gangenaup), 188
gardens, 18–19, 67, 101, 144. *See also* Philippolis (Griqua capital):gardens.
Gatberg, 236
Genadendal (mission), 17
Glegg, Jonathan, 197
Goeyman (family), 260 n153
Goeyman, Elizabetha Johanna Jacoba, *see* Wiese, Elizabetha Johanna (Betta)
Goeyman, Gert, 24, 30–33 *passim*, 35, 28
Goeyman, Hans, 32
Goeyman, Jan, 24, 31, 105, 119–120, 277 n776; at Philippolis, 39, 103, 122, 151, 200; family, 112–113, 223, 225
Goeyman, Johanna Margaretha, *see* Bartlett, Johanna Margaretha
Goeymansberg, 32
Gordon, R.J., 12 *passim*
government (Philippolis Captaincy), *see* government records; Kaptyn (office); law book; laws (general); Raad (body). *See also references under* judicial system; officials.
Government Agent (Griquatown), 32, 36, 147
government records, 141, 168, 168–169
Government Secretary, *see* Raad (Philippolis Captaincy):secretary
Graaff-Reinet, 23, 37, 39, 85, 103, 105, 113, 157
Grahamstown, 71, 195
Gray, Robert, *Bishop*, 210–211
Great Britain, *see* Aborigines Committee; Cape authorities; Select Committee on the Kafir Tribes (1851)
Great Trek, 87. *See further* Republican Boers; Trekkers.
Grey, George, *Sir*, 194, 195, 235, 237; testimonial to Adam Kok III, 233
Griqua Afrikaans (language), 107, 108, 244–245
Griqua languages, *see* Griqua Afrikaans; Xiri
Griqua Independent Church, 247
Griqua people: early history (before 1813), 9–22, 36, 107, 108–109, 143, 249–250; names, 102, 163; name "Griquas" adopted (1813), 22; definition of term, 109; definitions of Griqua nationality, 98, 102, 109;

as Colonial subjects, 147; development of national identity, 83, 108, 109, 110–111, 163, 170; distinctive life style, 23, 107, 117–118, 165–166, 182, 204, 209; main Christian and surnames, 25; numbers, 219;

later history, 216–217, 246–247; acknowledged as a community (1997), 247.

See also dress; dwellings; education

(general); Philippolis Captaincy; westernisation.
"Griqualand" (Philippolis Captaincy): use of name, 162–163
Griqualand East (Nomansland): trek from Philippolis (1861–63), 102, 113, 235–236; list of names, 240; numbers, 243; status of settlers, 237; population (1926), 246; disparaging report (1925), 247. *See also* Kokstad; Kommissietrek (1859).
Griqualand West Land Court, 227, 240
Griquatown: early history (Klaarwater mission), 14, 17, 18–22; "Hottentot republic", 143; name Griquatown adopted (1813), 19, 22; population, 20; descriptions, 20–22, 26; baptismal register, 19; baptisms, 19, 25; church services, 19, 22; profession of faith mentioned, 278 n785; letter from women of congregation (1843), 173–175; school, 19
Griquatown Captaincy: Captaincy established (1813), 22, 143–144; A. Waterboer on source of authority, 28; government, 144–146, 149–150; laws, 22, 24, 29, 144–146; schools, 26; boundaries, 23, 47, 147, 161; population, 26; missionary influence, 27–28, 146, 149; internal divisions (1821–25), 29–59 *passim*, 146; relations with other Captaincies (general), 82; and Riet River Boers, 93.
See also Campbell Captaincy.
Groen River (Koussie), 12
guns and ammunition, 13, 16, 26, 32, 33, 36, 83, 87, 120–121, 121, 171. *See also* swords.
Guriqua tribe, 9–10, 12, 22

Hamelberg, H.J., 212–214, 216–217
Hanglip, 236, 239, 240, 240–241, 245
Hankey (mission), 197
Hankey, W.A., 275 n707
Hankey River, 161 (275 n707)

Hans, Lucas, 14
Hantam, 13, 249
Hardcastle (mission), 23, 250, 278 n785
Hare, John, 95
Harris, W.C., 189
Hartenaars, 24, 30, 32
Harts River, 24, 28, 97
health, 134, 247
heemraden, 147, 148, 150(2x). *See also* Raad (body).
Heemro, Wenzel, 105
Helmore, Holloway, 282 n944
Hendrickze, Griet (Kok), 74, 84, 112, 114, 163
Hendrickze, Hendrik, 87, 104, 134, 148; spelling of name, 263 n260; origins, 73–74, 108; as Government Secretary, 151, 152, 207; as representative of Captaincy, 84, 111; in Cape Town (1835), 84, 114;
  influence, 74–75, 76, 81–82, 83–84, 89, 92, 128, 195–196; as source of unrest, 57, 78, 80 (264 n286), 207, 216; dismissed (1850), 152, 196, 206–207, 217; last mentioned (1863), 207;
  and Bergenaars, 32, 35, 74, 75, 82; and Bushmen, 61, 62, 74; as interpreter, 13, 99–100; as churchman, 76, 126–127; possible author of published complaint (1830), 65–66; descriptions, 75–77, 151
Hendrik, Jan, 14–15, 23
Hendriks (family), 35
Hendriks, Andries, (uncle of H. Hendrickze), 24, 32, 74
Hendriks, Andries, (brother of H. Hendrickze), 74
Hendriks, David, 74
Hendriks, Hendrik (born ca 1770), 74
Hendriks, Hendrik (Government Secretary), *see* Hendrickze, Hendrik
Hendriks, Jan, 32, 145
Hodgson, T.L., 30, 31, 65, 131
Hogge, W.S., 193, 194

horse breeding, 183
horse theft, 243–244
"Hottentot" (name), 102; "Baster-Hottentot", 102; "Totties", 186
"Hottentot Republic" (Transorange), 143
houses, *see* dwellings (western)
Hughes, Isaac, 196, 201–203
Hughes, Mary, *see* Wright, Mary
hunting expeditions, 12, 20, 99, 120–121, 121, 209
huts, *see* dwellings (traditional)

Ibisa, 276 n721
immigration, *see* emigrant farmers (1825–48); refugees; Trekkers
inalienability of land, 46(2x), 70, 165–166, 260–261 n178. *See also* leasable territory (1846); leasing of farm to whites; sale of land to whites; unleasable territory (1846)
inalienable territory (1846), *see* unleasable territory
irrigation, 67, 101
Isaac(s)/Isaak(s) (family), 260 n153
Isaac, Anna, 63, 129
Isaac, Cobus, 63
Isaac, David, 63–64, 108, 120
Isaac, Fytje, 64, 120
Isaac, Hans, 63
Isaac, Jan, 63
Isaac, Paul, 63
Isaac, Piet, 63
Isaac, Tryn, 63–64, 108, 112
ivory trade, 13, 15–16, 16, 20, 121, 136

Jacob (Bushman), 159
Jacobus (Baster), 106
Jagers (family), 23
Jagers, Abraham, 115
Jagers, Goliat, 151
Jammerberg, 105
Jansen, David, 106, 111–112, 151–152
Jansz, Lammert, 144
"Jochen" (Boer?), 99

Joint Council (Philippolis & Griquatown), 91, 92; instituted, 93, 158; as court of appeal, 98–99, 158–159, 227
Jood (family), 113
Jood, Jan, 113
Jood, Mietje, 113
Joubert, Gideon, 68 (263 n242)
judicial system, *see* capital punishment; corporal punishment; magistrates; Joint Council:as court of appeal
Julie (family), 102
Julie, Jan, 102, 243–244

Kaffer, Elsie, 74
Kaffir River, 137, 161
Kakeis, 12–13
Kakkerlak, Cupido, 24
Kalkfontein, 130, 185, 263 n253
Kalkgat, 216
Kalwerfontein, 279 n830
Kamiesberg, 12, 15, 73, 108, 249
Kanoneiland, 256 n34
Kaptyn (office), 28, 141–143; first Griqua Kaptyn, 10/12; succession, 105, 142–143, 148–149, 247; weakness of authority, 72, 73, 169; as title of Richard Miles, 102. *See also* Cape authorities:and appointment of Kaptyns; Provisie Kaptyn (office); staff of office.
Karoshebbers (Korana), 35(2x)
Kars, Jan (Goesa), 23, 26–27
Kat River, 82, 84, 85, 92, 96, 103, 104, 110, 176, 212
Katte (Korana), 101, 260 n158
Kausobson, Kausob, 102
Kei Korana, 279 n832
Keimoes, 14
Kerneels (Griqua), 244–245
Kgalagadi tribe, 20
Kgora (Tlhaping Chief), 106
Khameb (Kora Chief), 278 n74
Khoi languages (unspecified), 20, 21–22, 104, 107. *See also* Kora language; Xiri (language).

Khoikhoi, 10/12, 141–143, 149, 150; as original inhabitants of Cape, 66. *See also* Griqua people; Guriqua tribe; "Hottentot" (name); Korana people

kidnapping, *see* slave trade:trade in abducted children

Klaarwater (mission), *see* Griquatown

Klaas (Korana), 100, 267 n370

Klaas, Hendrik, 108

Klipplaat (mission), 123

Kniga (river), 236, 246

Knoffelvallei, *see* Campbell

Koesberg, 246

Koffiefontein, 105, 262 n227

Kok (family), 23, 25, 35, 61, 105, 260 n153; origins, 9–10; statement by Adam Kok II (1834–1835), 249–250

Kok, Abraham: proposed Kaptyn of Campbell, 82; appointed commandant, 156; unpopularity, 83–84; in Cape Town (1835), 84, 114; Kaptyn of Philippolis, 85–91, 127–128; raid on Mzilikazi (1837), 87–89 *passim*; deposed, 89–91 *passim*, 149;

descriptions, 85; wife, 108, 112, 115; daughters, 113; farm, 115

Kok, Abraham, (son of Adam Kok I), 22

Kok, Abraham, (son of Cornelius Kok I), 26, 29, 34, 91–92

Kok, Adam, I, 10–13, 249, 249–250

Kok, Adam, II: date of birth, 263 n257; early life, 13, 21, 23, 249–250; werf in Transorange, 13, 26;

Provisie Kaptyn (Griquatown), 15, 22, 27, 29, 29–30, 164; leaves Griquatown, 27, 28; at Campbell, 28, 29–30, 33–34; in Transgariep, 33–36, 41–54 *passim*, 250; followers, 34–35, 54, 56, 167; area of occupation, 47;

negotiations with Dr Philip (1825), 41–42, 43, 46; elected Kaptyn (1825), 50, 52, 54–55, 56; resigns, 49, 71; resumes office, 72; proposed deposition (1832), 82; at Kat River, 84, 85, 92; in Cape Town (1835), 84, 114–115; death, 84; succession, 84–85;

as churchman, 126; as interpreter, 13; weakness of authority, 72, 73, 169; descriptions, 72–73; statement to A. Smith (1834–35), 249–250; wife, 21, 151; father-in-law, 249; mother-in-law, 134; brother-in-law, 141, 145; dependents, 13, 19; residence, 23, 153, 181; property, 115, 134

Kok, Adam, III: date of birth, 263 n257; as acting Kaptyn (1834), 84, 92; at Griquatown (1837), 87;

elected Kaptyn, 89–90, 91, 162; as Kaptyn of Campbell, 171, 283 n956; in Cape Town (1860), 237; and trek to Griqualand East, 235–238, 241, 243–244; recollections of trek, 244–245; death, 246; succession, 247;

address at Ramah, 159; as churchman, 126, 218–219; descriptions, 92–93, 201, 210, 211, 213–214, 221; testimonial by Cape Executive Council (1861), 233;

wife, 108, 112; daughters, 129, 247; (Griet Hendrickze), 72, 74, 84, 112, 114, 163; residence, 134, 211, 213–214; property, 110, 212–213, 220; business affairs, 223, 244

Kok, Adam (Dik/Kort Adam), 22–23; as Provisie Kaptyn (Griquatown), 27, 151

Kok, Adam (Eta), 111, 149, 231–232

Kok, Adam (Muis), 247

Kok, Claas, (progenitor), 9–10, 250

Kok, Cornelius, I: birth, 249; date of birth, 263 n257; in Transorange, 12, 13, 14, 144, 256 n18 ; deputies, 14–15, 149; retires to Campbell, 24–25, 249; death, 25, 249;

statement (1790), 12, 13; descriptions, 14, 15; wife, 10, 249; property, 14, 15, 256 n18

Kok, Cornelius, II: date of birth, 263 n257; in Transorange, 13–15; at Camp-

bell, 26; as Kaptyn of Campbell, 29, 33–34, 49–50; status of Captaincy, 29, 29–30, 91, 91–92, 149, 170–171;
    proposed deposition (1832), 82; deposed (1838), 91–92, 171; formally recognised (1848), 171; resignation and succession, 171, 283 n956;
    and Griquatown Conference (1825), 49–50, 51–52; and raid on Mzilikazi (1837), 87; and Griqua civil war (1838), 90–92; at Philippolis, 170

Kok, Cornelius, III, 49 (261 n186), 71–72; date of birth, 263 n257; widow, 134; farm, 263 n253

Kok, Cornelius, (hanged 1852), 227

Kok, Dirk, 171, 187

Kok, Gert, 84(2x), 114, 151

Kok, Griet, *see* Hendrickze, Griet

Kok, Jan, 63, 257 n55

Kok, Klaas, (progenitor), *see* Kok, Claas

Kok, Klaas, (grandson of Adam Kok III), 198

Kok, Margaretha, 108, 112, 115

Kok, Salomon, 15

Kok, Willem, 23, 151

Kokskraal, 14, 25, 249

Kokstad, 102, 108, 112(2x), 193, 246 (284 n988), 284 n989

Kokstad Captaincy, 98, 105, 107, 163, 168, 169, 246–247

Kolbe, G.A., 77–78, 87–88, 100, 124–125, 135; removal from Philippolis, 87–89 *passim*, 127–128, 128, 138; alleged adultery, 87, 112–113

Kommissietrek (1859), 105, 111, 235–236

Kora language, 13, 100, 107

Korana people, 13, 32, 141–143; as clients and dependents, 13, 14, 35, 144, 147; in Philippolis Captaincy, 62–64, 83, 91, 97–101 *passim*, 137, 186; numbers, 100; conflicts, 64–64; mission work, 17, 100, 166.

    See also Bitterbos Korana; Karoshebbers; Katte; Kei Korana; Kraalshoek Korana; Linkshande; Regshande; Skerpioen Korana; Springbok Korana.

Kornetspruit, 161, 244

Kotze, Karel, 98–99

Koussie (river), *see* Groen River

Kraaiberge, 246

"kraals" (settlements), *see* werfs

Kraalshoek, Jan, 166

Kraalshoek Korana, 276 n740

Kraankuil, Piet, 61, 98

Kramer, C.A., 18, 143, 250

Kramersfontein, 23, 26–27

Kranshoek, 247

Kromelmboogspruit, 188

Krotz (family), 105

Krotz, Adam, 99

Krotz, Frederik, 156, 159, 186

Kruger, Abraham, 32, 62(2x), 78, 100

Krynauw incident (1845), *see* Swartkoppies (battle)

Kulfontein, 179 n830

Kuruman (mission), 13, 23–24, 52, 87, 88, 124

Ladybrand, 105, 276 n708

Land Commission, 229

land grants, 163 (276 n721)

land ownership, 165–166. *See also* inalienability of land; leasable territory (1846); leasing of farm to whites; sale of land to whites; unleasable territory (1846).

Langkloof, 267 n394

Lattakoo (mission), 23–24, 110, 151. *See also* Kuruman.

law book, 141, 168

laws (general), 168

le Fleur (family), 267 n394

le Fleur, A.A.S., 105, 247

le Fleur, Abraham, 105

le Fleur, Marthinus, 105

leasable territory (1846), 165–166, 193; compensation, 193

leasing of farms to whites, 46–47, 70–71,

94, 103, 207, 210, 229, 231–232. *See also* leasable territory (1846); sale of land to whites; unleasable territory (1846).
Leeukuil, 18
Leeuw, Klaas, 230–231
Left Hand Korana, *see* Linkshande
legal code, 141, 168
Legislative Council (Philippolis Captaincy), *see* Raad
Lemue, Prosper, 217–219, 278 n785
Lephoi (Tlhaping Captain), 35, 102, 166
Letsie (Sotho Chief), 171
Links, Gert, 101
Linkshande (Korana), 101
liquor trade, 21, 65, 131–132, 133, 137, 181, 186, 219, 220; legislation, 131–132, 133, 137, 168, 226. *See also* drunkenness.
Lishuani (mission), 28
"Lispur" (Hantam), 250
literacy, 17, 85, 92, 203. *See also* books; education (general).
Livingstone, David, 216
Loding, Charles, 226
Logenberg, Hans, 70
London Missionary Society, 17–18, 22, 104, 125; in Transorange, 14, 17–19, 25, 37, 39, 211; attempts to control Philippolis Captaincy, 46, 48, 94–95, 148; internal dissensions, 87, 88, 162, 167–168. *See also* Auxiliary Mission Society; Campbell, John; Freeman, J.J.; Griquatown; native agents; Philip, John; Philippolis (mission).
Losper (Hantam), 250
loyalists (Transgariep), *see* Riet River Boers
Lucas (family), 35, 100–101
Lucas, Barend, 89, 149
Lucas, Hans, 260 n155
Lucas, Klaas, 101
Lückhoff, 32

Maatschappij (Trekker polity), 93–94. *See also* Republican Boers.
Mackenzie, John, 221, 232, 237, 239–240
magistrates (Griquatown), 24, 143, 145–146, 149–150; as title for *heemraad*, 150
magistrates (Philippolis), 150–151, 154, 155–156, 231
Maitland, Peregrine, *Sir*, 177, 177 (278 n791)
Mahura (Tlhaping Chief), 35
Maitland Treaty (1846), 161, 167, 176, 188–189, 191, 192, 228
"Malitzani" (Klaas Leeuw), 230–231
Malmesbury, 260 n159, 284 n997
"Mankey River", 161
"Mantatees" (Difaqane), 26, 29, 35; as name for migrant labourers, 267 n373
Maquassie, 261 n193
Marais, Samson, 240
Marais, Slammert, 217–218
marriage, 127
Martyn, Henry, 125
mat huts, *see* dwellings (traditional)
"Matabele" (tribe), 101. *See also* Ndebele people.
Matjiesdrif, 267 n394
Matlwase, 261 n193
measles, 17, 129, 134
medical services, 134, 138
meetings (public), *see* conferences…; public meetings
Melvill, John, 32, 37, 53, 124, 146, 147
Merriman, N.J., 211–212
Methuen, Henry, 184
Meyerskraal, 110
midwives, 17, 138
Mieta (Griqua), 108
Miles, Richard (Motswana), 102
military organisation, 22, 26, 85, 90, 97, 141, 153, 163. *See also* commandant (office).
military service (as allies), 156, 190, 195
mills, 217–218, 220, 221
Mills, George, 135
miscegenation, 10, 12, 65
"mission party" (Philippolis), *see* Baster

300

people: as political faction; "Old Inhabitants"
mission schools, *see* Philippolis (mission): school; schools
missionaries, *see* London Missionary Society; Philippolis (mission); Philippolis Captaincy:opposition to missionary control.
"missionary road", 94
"mixed" marriages, 10, 12
Mocambique, 9
Modder River, 63, 100, 119; incorrect use of name, 31, 259 n132
Modderpoort, 28
Moffat, Robert, 27, 52–54, 88, 272 n574, 278 n785
Moletsane (Taung Chief), 191, 261 n193
money, 21
Moodie's Settlers (1817), 135
Moorosi (Phuthi Chief), 236, 244, 245
Moravian Brethren, 17, 170 n495
Moroka II (Rolong Chief), 191
Moshweshwe (Sotho Chief), 97, 101, 136, 171, 190, 191, 215; relations with Griquas, 245, 283 n982
Mount Currie, 163, 246
Mpondo tribe, 236
"Mud River", 20, 26. *See also* Modder River.
Muller, J., 226
municipal government, *see* Philippolis (Griqua capital):municipal government
murder, 98–99, 144, 147, 159, 227, 228
Murray, James, & Co., 156, 226
Mzilikazi (Ndebele Chief), 42, 189; Griqua raid (1831), 33, 77–78, 83; (1837), 87–89 *passim*
Mzimkulu (river), 236
Mzimvubu (river), 236

Namaqua people, 13, 18, 107, 131
Namaqualand, 9, 12, 14, 116, 235, 249
names (personal), 25
Namibia, 13
Napier, George, *Sir*, 86, 95

Napier Treaty (1843), 95
Natal, 93–94, 190, 236, 246, 274 n667
native agents (LMS), 19(*2x*), 23, 24
Ndebele people, 33, 35, 77–78, 87. *See also* Mzilikazi (Ndebele Chief).
"New Griquas" (name), 80, 264 n286. *See further* "Old Inhabitants" (Philippolis)
New Hantam, 50, 70, 263 n242
New Lattakoo (mission), 23–24. *See also* Kuruman.
newspapers, *see* Cape Colony:newspapers; *Dagster (De)*; *The Friend*; *South African Commercial Advertiser*
Niekerkshoop, 18, 23
Niels, Cornelius, 81, 155
Niemand, Piet, 70
Niemand, Valentyn, 114
Nieuwland, 105, 161
Nomansland, *see* Griqualand East
Northern Frontier, *see* Bergenaars; Orange River; Philip, John:Griqua policy; treaties...
Nuweveld, 20
Nzwane (Xhosa raider), 112

Oberholster, M.A., 93, 94, 95, 161. *See also* Riet River Boers (1840–49).
ochre (cosmetic), 115 (269 n454), 184, 187
Oerson (family), 101
official records, *see* government records
officials, *see* commandant (office); field-cornets; Kaptyn (office); magistrates; Provisie Kaptyn (office); Raad (body); salt pans:*opziener, wykmeester*
"Old Captains" (Griquatown), 28
"Old Griquas" (Philippolis), 80
"Old Inhabitants" (Philippolis), 57, 80, 103, 110, 134, 170. *See also* Basters:as political faction.
Old Jacob (Bushman), 98–99
Oliewenfontein, 15, 250
Olifants River, 9–10, 12, 107, 249
Ongeluksnek, 236, 245, 246
"Oorlams" (name), 14, 102

301

Oorlamskraal, 14
Opperman, Adam, 63, 262 n227
Opperman, Frederik, 106
"Oppressed Griqua (An)" (pseudonym), 70
Orange Free State (Republic): established (1854), 215; acquires Bethulie, 166; undermining of Philippolis Captaincy, 169, 215, 228–229; conflicts, 161, 229–232, 235; acquires Captaincy (1861), 171, 172, 241–242. *See also* Volksraad (Free State).
Orange River, 110; names, 259 n132; fords, 33, 39, 186; ponts, 86, 137; early Baster settlement, 12–15 *passim*, 18–19, 249, 250; as Colonial boundary, 64, 67, 260 n175; location of conference (1837), 85–86, 163–164. *See also* Transorange.
Orange River Sovereignty, 162, 210; proclaimed, 190–191; abandoned, 215. *See also* British Resident.
Ordinance 50 (Cape Colony), 263 n239
out-stations (Philippolis), 188. *See also* Ramah: as mission post.
Owen, C.M., 193, 194
ownership of land, *see* land ownership

Paarl, 84, 124
pack oxen, 26, 118
Paris Missionary Society, 98, 99
Pella (mission), 13, 14
Pellissier, J.P., 88, 89, 161, 166
Philip, John, 83, 85, 214–215, 229; Griqua policy, 18, 40, 42, 70, 81–82, 91, 94–95, 147–148, 170; in Transorange (1825), 33–55, 62, 146; at Philippolis (1832), 79–82, 170; (1842), 94; connections with mission at Philippolis, 216; death, 215; praised, 80; criticised, 52, 53–54; relations and protegés, 55, 178, 197, 214–215, 216
Philip, W.B., 216, 221, 226, 239; presumed author of article, 283 n955; photograph album, 255 n11
Philipp, Barend, 167

Philippolis (Griqua Capital): settlement of Griquas (1826), 56–57, 90; transfer of station, 58, 170; attempted move to Boesmansfontein, 134; seat of British Resident, 189, 189–190; taken over by Orange Free State, 241–242;
descriptions, 122–123, 124, 134, 138–139, 177–182 *passim*, 201–206 *passim*, 210, 211(2x), 212–214, 218, 222; population, 122, 213;
Kaptyn's residence, 134, 153, 181, 211, 213–214; gaol, 211, 227, 228; fountain, 55, 139, 177–178, 182, 201, 218; gardens, 177, 180, 181, 182;
church affairs (1855–61), 224–225, 226; sale of church buildings (1861), 238–239, 241, 242; school affairs (1855–61), 213, 221, 222, 224–225; sale of school buildings (1861), 238–239;
municipal government, 124, 169; commerce and trade, 135–136, 156, 226–227, 240, 241; building operations, 123–124, 182, 222, 222–223;
See also "Old Inhabitants" (Philippolis).
Philippolis (mission): established, 39, 44–45; as Bushman mission (1822–28), 33, 39–40, 45–46, 151; abandoned, 59; church building, 122, 124, 177, 181, 202, 208, 218; church services, 99–100, 107–108, 124–126, 184, 196–197, 208–209, 218–219; church attendance, 124–126 *passim*, 127–128, 181, 197, 204, 205, 209, 218, 220; church membership, 127, 128, 184, 204; church council, 158, 218, 219;
mission school, 129–131, 205–206; school building, 129, 203; school attendance, 129–130, 182, 184, 205, 209; infant school, 126, 129(2x), 184; mission house, 123–124, 198–199 *passim*, 203, 218; out-stations, 188; social and cultural role, 129–134, 184,

205; internal dissensions, 139(*2x*), 196, 198–199, 200; suggested division, 162, 167–168; independence from LMS (1855), 158, 215, 224.

See also Auxiliary Mission Society (LMS); Congregational Church (Philippolis); London Missionary Society.

Philippolis Captaincy: settlement of Griquas (1825), 43(*2x*), 47, 54, 55–56, 57–58, 98; original area of occupancy, 47;

name, 161–162; area, 121, 238; boundaries, 47, 121, 161, 214; population, 97–98, 204; citizenship defined, 98, 109, 163, 192; origins of people, 97–98; descriptions, 216–218, 219–221; route Colesberg-Bloemfontein, 216–217, 279 n830;

government, 147–159; origins, 148; Cape precedents, 76, 148, 157; opposition to missionary control, 79–83, 155, 169–170, 195–196, 197, 204, 216; opposition to individual missionaries, 87, 94, 128, 138, 196, 198–199; desire for "political missionary", 204;

weakness of authority, 72, 73, 169; internal dissensions, 79–83, 87, 89–91, 128; "anarchic" elements, 57, 207; military strength, 97; profession of Christianity, 126, 127, 163; relations with Griquatown Captaincy, 86, 170, 171; with Campbell Captaincy, 170–171; with other polities in the Transgariep, 171; projected abandonment; 68, 212, 235;

under British Sovereignty (1858–64), 191, 210; abandoned by British Government, 191–193, 215, 220, 232–233, 235; relations with Orange Free State, 215, 220–221; taken over by Free State (1861), 171, 242.

See also Bergenaars; Bethanie (mission); Bethulie (mission); Cape authorities; Congregational Church; economic progress; education (general); farming; fountains; land ownership; *werfs* (settlements). See further references under government; judicial system; officials.

Phuthi tribe, 283 n958
Pienaar (family), 10, 74, 151, 256 n21
Pienaar, Arnoldus, 70
Pienaar, Cobus, 150, 151
Pienaar, Jan, (Bergenaar), 30, 32, 35, 98, 108
Pienaar, Jan, (father-in-law of Cornelius Kok I), 10
Pienaar, Jan, (father-in-law of Adam Kok II), 249
Pienaar, Jan, (Griqua official), 149, 155, 158–159, 227
Pienaar, Jan Gamja, 223
Pienaar, Klaas, 151
Pienaar, Petrus (Griquatown), 111
Pienaar, Petrus (Hantam), 13
Pienaar, Piet, 111, 145
Pietermaritzburg, 274 n667
Piketberg, 9, 10, 12(*2x*), 108(*2x*), 249, 284 n997
Platberg (Caledon River valley), 105, 109
Plettenberg Bay, 247
political factions (Philippolis Captaincy), see Baster people; Bergenaars; Griqua people:development of national identity; Hendrickze, Hendrik; "Old Inhabitants" (Philippolis); Philippolis Captaincy:opposition to missionary control
polygamy, 22, 127
Port Elizabeth, 113, 129, 195
Porter, William, 75, 77, 177–178
Poshodi (Sotho Chief), 243, 243–244
postal service, 138, 226
Potchefstroom, 93
Potgieter, Antonie, 136
Pramberge (Free State), 188
Pramberge (New England area), 246
Pretorius, Andries, (Boer), 194
Pretorius, Andries, Sr., (Griqua), 110
Pretorius, Andries, Jr., (Griqua), 110

Pretorius, Maurits, 110
Pretorius Rebellion (1848), 194–195, 202
prosperity, *see* economic progress
Provisie Kaptyn (office), 149; (Griquatown), 14–15, 22, 27, 143, 151; (Campbell), 34; (Philippolis), 111, 149, 231
public meetings, 79, 86, 87, 143–144, 164. *See also* conferences...
punishments, 159. *See also* capital punishment.
punitive expeditions, *see* campaigns; commandoes

Quatlhamba Mountains (Drakensberg), 191
Queenstown, 33, 239, 470 n495
Quthing, 283 n958

Raad (body), 65, 80, 81, 84, 89(2x), 149–154, 164; sessions, 148, 153–154, 169; secretary, 105, 152, 168, 169, 207; weakness of authority, 72, 73, 169; and Christianity, 126, 127; and temperance, 133; and Pretorius Rebellion (1848), 194; as town council, 124
Rabie, — (Boomplaats), 217
Rachel (Baster), 106
racial discrimination, *see* discrimination (racial)
Rademeyer, G.H., 244
raiding expeditions, 13, 18, 56, 69, 74, 90, 112, 144. *See also* Bergenaars; "Mantatees"; Mzilikazi (Ndebele Chief): Griqua raids.
Ramah, 41, 118, 157; *werf* (settlement), 105, 108, 115, 187; fieldcornet, 185; as mission post, 30, 39, 118, 185; mission revived, 185–186, 188, 209, 225; sessions of Joint Council, 98, 158–159; as boundary mark, 47, 161
Rawstorne, Fleetwood, 88 (265 n317), 189
Read, James, Sr., 189; in the Transorange, 23–24, 103, 110, 144, 141; and Philippolis, 96, 104, 176; death, 215
Read, James, Jr., 105, 176

reading matter, *see* books
Reddersburg, 121
refugees, 13, 18, 32, 25, 97(2x), 101, 128
Regshande (Korana), 35, 99, 100, 266 n351, 276 n740
religious instruction (general), 119, 185, 187–188. *See also* Philippolis (mission).
Renoster, Moses Adam, 145
Renosterspruit, 161
Republican Boers, 93–94, 95, 176, 190. *See also* Orange Free State (Republic); Pretorius Rebellion (1848); Swartkoppies (battle).
Resident (official), *see* British Resident
riding oxen, 116, 187
Riet River, 30, 31, 33, 35, 41, 47, 63, 99; incorrectly named, 259 n132; as boundary, 161, 188; Riet River ward, 156
Riet River Boers (1840–49), 93–95 *passim*, 190
Rietfontein, 15, 284 n999
Right Hand Korana, *see* Regshande
Roggeveld, 12, 16, 103–104
Rolland, Samuel, 105
Rolong tribe, 261 n193, 279 n832
Roodezand, 277–278 n785

Sabba, Piet, 30, 39, 101, 105, 118–119, 151, 260 n168
Saint Helena Bay, 9
Sak River, 16, 278 n786. *See also* Zak River (mission).
sale of land to whites, 219, 229, 238. *See also* leasing of farms to whites.
Salmon (attendant), 114
salt pans, 36, 157–158; *opziener*, 157, 158
Sannaspoort, 32
Sarel, Piet, *see* Zaarel, Piet
Schalkwyk, Jan, 70
Schalkwyk, Ockert, 64–65
Schalkwyk, Piet, 70
Schietfontein, *see* Skietfontein
Schietmekaar, *see* Skietmekaar
school materials, 129, 203

school teachers, 24, 39, 41, 105, 113, 119–120, 130, 187, 213, 220, 221, 225, 242; women, 26, 113, 130, 131, 278 n785

schools, 19, 26, 130, 185–186, 188, 209, 225. *See also* Philippolis (Griqua Captaincy):school affairs; Philippolis (mission):mission school.

Schorpioen Korana, *see* Skerpioen Korana

Schreiner, Gottlob, 94, 129, 133, 155, 163, 167–169, 169

Schreiner, Rebecca, 129(*2x*)

Schultheiss, C.F.J., 101, 193

Sehunelo (Rolong Chief), 51

Sekonyela (Tlokwa Chief), 190, 191

Select Committee on the Kafir Tribes (1851), 165, 192

Setebe (Korana), 63

settlements, *see* fountains; Philippolis (Griqua capital); Ramah; *werfs*

sheep farming, 211, 218, 219–220, 225, 243, 246. *See also* wool trade.

Shiloh (mission), 270 n495

shops, *see* Philippolis (Griqua capital): commerce and trade; trade and barter (general); westernisation:western commodities

Silwerfontein, 15, 24, 108, 249, 250

Skanse, 32

Skerpioen Korana, 35, 260 n153

Skietfontein, 136, 270 n470

Skietmekaar, 63

Slammert (Griqua), *see* Marais, Slammert

slave trade:trade in abducted children, 32–33, 40–41, 46, 62

slaves, 9, 65, 106, 250. *See also* ex-slaves ("apprentices").

Sleutelspoort, 32

Slypsteen, 27

Smith, Andrew, 153, 157–158; statement by Adam Kok II, 249–250

Smith, Harry, *Sir*, 164, 190–191, 195; meeting with Adam Kok III (1848), 191–193, 193; on H.D. Warden, 190. *See also* Bloemfontein Treaty (1848).

Smithfield, 236, 246

smoking, *see* tobacco consumption

snuff-taking, 133

Solomon, Edward, 196, 199, 207–208, 213, 214–216, 219 (281 n913)

Solomon, Jessie, 214–215, 215–216

Somerset, Charles, *Lord*, 147 (273 n623)

Somerset, Henry, 70, 171

sorcery, 116

Sotho people, 32, 74, 97, 101, 102, 163, 190

Sotho War (1865), 239

Sotho-Tswana, 266 n250. *See further* Sotho people; Tswana people.

South African Commercial Advertiser (newspaper), 176, 264 n290

Southey, Richard, 192

Soutpansdrif, 186, 187

Sovereignty, *see* Orange River Sovereignty

Spitskopje, 256 n18

Springbok (Namaqualand) 256 n43

Springbok Korana, 35, 171

springs, *see* fountains

St Helena Bay, 9

staff of office, 10, 14, 28, 30, 34, 249

Stein, Dou, 70

Stellenbosch, 157, 255 n2

Sterkfontein, 111, 188, 225, 231

Steyn, Douw, *see* Stein, Dou

Stinkfontein, 10

Stockenstrom, Andries, 44, 64, 83, 111; in the Transorange, 37, 39–40, 85–86, 147, 163; statement on Philippolis, 57–58, 148

Stoffels, Andries, 231–232

Stuart, C.U., 228

Stuurman (attendant), 114

surnames, 25

Sutton, William, 189

Suurberg range, 246, 276 n721

Swart, *see* Zwaart

Swartbooi (Bushman), 98, 159

Swartkoppies (battle), 156, 176, 177–180 *passim*, 188, 189, 266 n358

305

Swartland, 36, 249
swords, 23, 282 n948

Taaibosch, Gert (Kora Chief)
Tafelkop, 276 n721
"Tambookies" (tribe), 101
Tarka, 263 n244
Taung tribe, 261 n193, 279 n832
teachers, *see* school teachers
Telle (river), 236, 244, 245
temperance societies, 131–133
Thaba Bosiu, 135, 190
Thaba Nchu, 104, 119
Thembu tribe, 101 (267 n372)
Theodore's Rand, 235
Theopolis (mission), 55
Thomas van Bengalen (slave), 9
Thomson, Agnes (Wright), 176, 177–178, 184
Thomson, W.Y., 176, 181, 195–196, 199; presumed author of report, 179
Tierpoort River, 137, 161
Tlhaping tribe, 13, 18, 20, 23–24, 35, 98
Tlokwa tribe ("Briquas"), 190, 279 n832
tobacco consumption, 210, 213, 216–217; anti-tobacco movement, 133
tobacco cultivation, 14, 20
Toomfontein, 130
Toornberg (mission), 44–45, 151
Touwfontein, 99, 176, 177, 217, 279 n830
trade and barter (general), 13, 31, 136–137, 138, 187. *See also* cattle trade; ivory trade; liquor trade; trading expeditions; wool trade.
trade in abducted children, 32–33, 40–41, 46, 62
trading expeditions, 12, 15–16, 20, 26–27, 116
Transgariep (Free State): definition of term, 259 n131; early settlement by Basters, 30–31, 32, 33–37 *passim*. *See also* Philippolis (Griqua capital); Philippolis (mission); Philippolis Captaincy.
Transorange: definition of term 259 n131.

See also Campbell; Campbell Captaincy; Griquatown; Griquatown Captaincy.
treaties 1834 (Griquatown & British Government), 83
treaties 1837 (Philippolis & Griquatown), 87, 152, 158, 161, 168
treaties 1838 (same), 93, 152, 158, 162
treaties 1840 (Philippolis & Riet River Boers), 48, 93, 94, 140
treaties 1843 (Napier treaty: Philippolis & British Government), 95
treaties 1845 (Maitland Treaty: same), 161, 167, 176, 188–189, 191, 192, 228
treaties 1848 (Bloemfontein Treaty: same), 193–194, 195, 206, 233
treaties 1854 (Bloemfontein Convention: OFS & British Government), 215; secret addenda, 232–233
trek to Nomansland (1861–63), *see* Griqualand East; Kommissietrek (1859)
trekboers, *see* emigrant farmers (1825–48); Riet River Boers (1840–49)
Trekker Republics, 93–94
Trekkers, 93. *See also* Republican Boers.
Tromp van Madagascar (slave), 9
Trompsburg, 130, 259 n143
Tsomo, 236
Tswana language, 13, 134, 209
Tswana people: as refugees, 35, 101; as clients and dependents, 13, 24–25, 35, 147; in Philippolis Captaincy, 97(2x), 101, 102, 122; as church members, 101, 128, 204; at Bethanie, 101
Tulbagh, 16, 124, 256 n21
typhus, 95

Uitenhage, 105
Uithaalder (Bushman), 44
Uitkomst, 130
unleasable territory (1846), 164, 207; boundaries, 188
Ursob (Korana), 101

V.O.C., 10, 12, 13

Vaal River, 20, 70
van den Heever, Piet, 250
van der Kemp, J.T., 104, 106, 113
van der Schalk, C.J., 138, 195, 197, 200, 205, 208, 210; reactions to Philippolis, 201–206 *passim*
van der Schalk, M.A. (Soley), 196, 197, 198–199
van der Westhuizen (family), 160 n153
van der Westhuizen, Antje, 114
van der Westhuizen, Lukas, 111
van Foreest, L.F., 213–214 *passim*, 217
van Heerden, Hendrik, 70
van Iver, Piet, 250
van Loggerenberg, Hans, *see* Logenberg, Hans
van Reenen, Willem, 13
van Ryneveld, W.C., 85
van Schalkwyk (family), *see also* Schalkwyk
van Schalkwyk, Ockert, 65
van Schalkwyk, Ockert Johannes, *see* Schalkwyk, Ockert
van Schalkwyk, Tobias, 65
van Wyk, Andries, 115, 118
van Wyk, Jacobus, 108–109
Vanzylspruit, 188
Vaughan, J., 226
'*veertig jaars geld*' (compensation), 193
Velmink (family), 25(*2x*)
Velmink, Martinus, 35
Vereenigde Raad (Philippolis & Griquatown), *see* Joint Council
Vet River, 93, 190
Viervoet, 207
Vigilant (Bushman), 98–99, 159
villages, *see* fountains; Philippolis (Griqua capital); Ramah; *werfs*
Viret, M.C., 226
Visagie, Andreas, 70
Visagie, Karel, 114
Visser, Floris, 16, 17
Vissershoek, 217, 279 n830
Vlakplaats, 231
Vogelfontein, 217

Vogelstruiskooi, 262 n227
Volksraad (Natal), 274 n667
Volksraad (OFS), 225, 242
Vries, Mietje, 113

Wade, T.F., 81, 147
Warden, H.D., 70, 156, 189–190, 192
Warren, Charles, 35–36, 261 n197
wars, *see* campaigns; civil war (1838); raiding expeditions
water mills, 220, 221
Waterboer, Andries: origins, 19; as native agent (LMS), 23; elected Kaptyn, 27–28, 29, 34, 146, 148, 150; criticism, 32; and Griquatown conference (1825), 49–59, 51–52; and Griqua civil war (1838), 90–91; as mediator, 91; at Philippolis, 91, 125; address at Ramah, 159; statements quoted, 14–15, 27, 28, 30, 34, 51–52, 164
Waterboer, Nicolaas, 149, 235
Watts, James, 202
weapons, *see* guns and ammunition; swords
Webster, Charles, 136
Wepener, 105
werfs (settlements), 23, 117–120, 165, 187–188; chief *werfs* in the Philippolis Captaincy, 185. *See also* fountains; Ramah.
Wesleyan Missionary Society, 28, 42–43, 54, 105, 190, 261 n193, 271 n513
West Indies, 225
westernisation, 22, 36, 71, 108, 109–110, 115, 211, 219–220, 225, 240–241; use of western commodities, 16, 20, 21, 31, 113–114, 205, 210, 237; disparaging accounts, 18, 31, 177–178, 204–205, 208, 212, 216–217; ditto (1925), 247; self-criticism of Griquas (1830), 69.

    See also Christianity (general); dress (western); dwellings (western); education (general); literacy.
wheat farming, 20, 26, 55, 121, 179, 181, 182(*2x*), 185, 222

white settlers, 135–136; undermining of Philippolis Captaincy, 169, 215, 228–229; and liquor trade, 131–132, 133, 137, 220. *See also* emigrant farmers (1825–48); Riet River Boers (1840–49); Republican Boers.
whooping cough, 134
Wiese, Andries, 105, 106, 113, 135, 157
Wiese, Elizabetha Johanna Jacoba (Betta) (Goeyman), 112–113, 223
Wikar, H.J., 12
Wildebeesvlakte, 270 n830
Willem (Korana), 62
Winburg, 93
Windvogel (attendant), 114
Windvogel (Bushman), 99
Windvogel, Conrad, Sr., 168, 207
Windvogel, Conrad, Jr., 276 n721
Witbooi (Baster), 106
Witteberge, 245
Witvoet, Piet, 35(*2x*), 62, 97, 100(*2x*), 166
Wodehouse, P.G., *Sir*, 143
women, 17, 63–64, 112–113, 223; as school teachers, 26, 113, 130, 131, 278 n785; first names, 25; and church societies, 131, 184; letter from Griquatown women (1843), 173–175; profession of faith mentioned, 278 n786; described by W. Porter, 177–178;
by R. Gordon Cumming, 183; by H. Methuen, 184; by A. Dolman, 186–187
wool trade, 136, 222, 223, 225
Wright, Agnes, *see* Thomson, Agnes
Wright, Elizabeth, 199
Wright, John, 173, 176, 181, 196–197, 202, 203, 205
Wright, Margery, 55, 176, 184, 196, 198–199, 203, 261 n202; on death of husband, 95–96
Wright, Mary (Hughes), 202
Wright, Peter, 43, 55–56, 83, 85–91 *passim*, 146; at Philippolis, 57, 94, 95, 181–182; death, 95–96, 173–175
Wuras, C.F., 100, 101, 194, 269 n409
"wyk" (term), 152
wykmeester (office), 105, 157

Xhosa people ("Caffers"), 32, 69
Xiri (language), 107–108, 112

Ysterbek, Goliat, 100, 102, 167

Zaarel, Piet, 186
Zak River (mission), 17, 39, 103, 250
Zevenfontein, 157
Zuurberg range, *see* Suurberg range
Zwaart, Hendrik, 223